ORIGINS AND DESTINY

A SCIENTIST EXAMINES GOD'S HANDIWORK

ORIGINS
AND
DESTINY

DR. ROBERT GANGE

WORD PUBLISHING
Dallas · London · Sydney · Singapore

ORIGINS AND DESTINY
Copyright © 1986 by Robert A. Gange.

Library of Congress Cataloging-in-Publication Data

Gange, Robert, 1936–
  Origins and destiny.

  Bibliography: p.
  Includes index.
  1. Creation.   2. Evolution—Religious aspects—
Christianity.   3. Religion and science—1946–
I. Title.
BS651.G25   1986   231.7′65   86–13334
ISBN 0–8499–0447–1

Printed in the United States of America

  0 1 2 3 9 AGF 9 8 7 6 5 4 3

To Judy,
for patience during lonely hours.

Acknowledgments

Many people helped to make this book possible—some with time, others with support, and a few by doing tasks that freed me to write. Each knows how grateful I am for the help he or she provided while preparing this book. With respect to the manuscript, special thanks go to Nancy Rendina for assistance, John DeVilbiss for review, Vincent DeMarco, Jr., for inspection, and Lynn Pinnow for preparation. I am particularly indebted to Doris Davis for incalculable succor, and Carey Moore who helped to make the book readable.

CONTENTS

GLOSSARY

Adenine molecule   A chemical unit containing equal parts of carbon hydrogen and nitrogen.

Algorithm   A set of rules that instruct how a group of calculations are to be performed.

Amino acid residues   The essential building blocks for protein construction.

Amino acid sequence   The sequence of chemical units used to construct protein.

Amoeba   A single-cell animal.

Anisotropy   A quality in which physical properties change with the direction chosen in a material or a system.

Anthropologist   A person committed to the study of man.

Anthropology   The study of man.

Antioxidant   A chemical that prevents oils and fats from going rancid.

Archeology   The study of ancient times based on digging up buried artifacts.

Argon   A comparatively heavy inert gas.

Astigmatism   An optical imperfection that produces blurred images due to defects in lens curvature.

Astrophysical data   Measurements of planetary behavior and properties, or light, radio and x-ray energy from stars.

Astrophysicist   A scientist who studies laws that describe the behavior of stars and planets.

Atom   Commonly pictured as an ultra-miniature solar system, it is the basic building block from which all materials are made.

Atomic particles   Tiny specks of matter that can be organized to form atoms.

Australo-pithecus   A classification of life called "genus" assigned to ape-like fossils found in eastern Africa.

Background radiation   Recently measured energy that has filled the universe almost from the time of the origin of the universe.

Bacteria   Single-celled organisms that can only be seen through a microscope.

Bacterium   A single-cell life form that resembles a plant cell.

Big Bang   Recent knowledge that the universe exploded into existence.

Biochemical evolution   The belief that nonliving chemicals spontaneously sprang to life.

Biochemists   Chemists who work with chemicals found in living systems.

Bipedal locomotion   Walking upright using two legs.

Black holes   Theoretically predicted pockets of space from which neither matter nor light can escape.

Boson   A class of subatomic particles that statistically behave in a way called "Bose-Einstein."

Carbon dioxide   A chemical compound of carbon and oxygen exhaled by animal life and needed by plant life.

Causality   The notion that each event is the result of a prior cause.

Chromosome   A rod-shaped container of genes.

Classical laws   Older rules describing objects whose existence was assumed to be independent of observations.

Classical object   Anything not subject to quantum laws.

Codon degeneracy   A condition in which different DNA chemical units instruct attachment of the same amino acid.

Cone nebula   A cone-shaped cloud of gas or dust between stars.

Cosmic rays   High-energy particles from outer space.

Cosmological   Of or pertaining to the heavens.

Cosmological data   Measurements of planets and stars.

Cranial index   The ratio of the greatest breadth of a skull to its longest front-to-back length.

Creationism   The belief that existing things were called into being by God's command.

Creationist   As commonly used, a person who believes that the world and all of life came into existence over a time period of six ordinary days.

Criminologist   A person committed to the study of criminals.

Crystallization   The abrupt change of a substance into a well- ordered structured state.

Cystic fibrosis   A disease of the lungs.

Cytochrome-C   A relatively short protein associated with the respiration of living organisms.

Deuterium   A rare, heavy form of hydrogen found in nature.

Diabetes   A disease-producing abnormal sugar metabolism.

Diaphragm muscle   The muscle below the lung that controls breathing.

Disequilibrium processes   Natural motions that continue in a state of change.

DNA   Long chemical strands in living cells which contain information that specifies, procreates and controls all of life.

DNA nucleotide   One of four kinds of chemical units found in DNA as an informational sequence in groups of three.

DNA-DNA hybridization   The overlap or mixing of two DNA segments.

Eccentricity   The degree of a planet's departure from a circular orbit around the sun.

Eddies   Swirls of a gas or liquid.

Electrical charge   A condition of two particles that causes their mutual repulsion, or two opposite conditions that cause their mutual attraction.

Electrical current   The motion of electrical charge.

Electromagnetic radiation   Light and other similar energy traveling through space.

Electron   A very small, stable atomic particle with negative electrical charge that is located away from an atom's center and in its outer fringe.

Electron microscope   A microscope that uses electrons instead of light for the purpose of enlarging tiny objects to very high magnification.

Electron microscopy   The investigation of tiny objects by means of an electron microscope.

Emissivity   The fraction of thermal energy emitted by a hot surface.

Energy positivity   A condition that characterizes useful energy.

Enigma   A perplexing riddle.

Entropy   The name of a mathematical expression that permits scientists to measure the degree to which physical matter disarranges itself with the passage of time.

Enzyme   A chemical structure used by cells to assemble chains of amino acids.

Epistemology   The root or foundational source of something.

Equilibrium state   The state of a system at rest.

Esterase   A set of enzymes that promotes a reaction between water and a group of chemicals formed by mixing acid with alcohol.

Eunuch   A castrated man—usually in charge of a harem.

Evolution   As commonly used, the belief that every biological system on earth was produced by changes in a preceding one.

Evolutionist   As commonly used, a person who believes that all life on earth came from slowly changing natural processes operating over billions of years.

Fermion   A class of subatomic particles that statistically behave in a way called "Fermi-Dirac."

Flatness problem   The present condition of the universe which indicates that it was miraculously tuned at inception to better than fifty decimal places.

Free radical   An active chemical form that reacts with any tissue it contacts.

Galactic magnetism   Magnetic forces within groups of stars.

Gene   A chemical structure that contains genetic information.

Genome   A family of integrated genes packed with information that totally controls the organism.

Grand unification theory   An attempt to mathematically unify the strong binding energies in an atom's nucleus with nature's electrical forces and weak interactions.

Gravitational constant   A fixed number that reoccurs in calculations on gravity.

Heavy particle   A particle with abnormally large mass compared to those found in the nucleus of an atom.

Helium   The lightest of several inert gases.

Hemoglobin   A very special blood molecule that transports oxygen from the lungs to body tissues on 4 iron atoms, each centered in a ring of carbon, hydrogen and nitrogen atoms that is surrounded by a protein chain; there are 270 million of these four entwined chains in each of 30 trillion red blood cells.

Hemophilia   A genetic disease that allows blood to flow from the smallest wound without clotting.

Hieroglyphics   An ancient form of picture writing.

Hominid family   A category used to classify early fossils alleged to lie in man's lineage.

Homogeneous mixing   A mixing of things which assures that they are the same everywhere.

Homogeneity   A condition in which everything throughout the volume of something is the same.

Homologous protein lineage   A family of functionally equivalent proteins.

Homonid fossil   A fossil alleged to lie in man's biological lineage.

Hormone   A class of chemical substances produced in body organs that affect how we feel.

Huge entropy   An expression that describes the large "mixed-upness" of our present universe.

Huntington's disease   A rare nervous disorder that gradually impairs body movements, speech, and mental ability.

Hydrogen   A deadly poison used as a fumigant in cyanide horticulture, flour mills, and the holds of ships.

Hydrogen peroxide   An oxidized state of water.

Hydroquinone   The acid form of a chemical compound used in making dyes.

Hypersphere   A multidimensional space analogous to an ordinary sphere in three dimensions.

Information theory   Modern insights of interchange that allow for the maximizing of information, minimizing of errors, and quantifying of the role of redundancy.

Inorganic molecule   A kind of chemical unit found in nonliving systems.

Inverse square law of gravity   A law that describes how gravity weakens with distance.

Isotope   An atom whose nucleus contains an abnormal number of neutrons.

Isovaleric acid   An acid composed of a chemical compound originally found in the root of the valerian plant which in appearance has the consistency of a thin oil.

Laminar flow   Gas or liquid motion along straight lines.

Lepton   A class of subatomic particles resembling packets of matter-energy which cannot be made smaller, and which do not interact by the strong forces found in the nuclei of atoms.

Macrostate   The state of a system taken as a whole.

Magnetic field   A condition of space produced by the presence of an electrical current.

Magnetic monopole   A comparatively large atomic particle that was theoretically predicted to have one magnetic pole.

Melon   A hemispherical mass of fat near the top of the head of whales, porpoises, and dolphins.

Metaphysical residue   The remains of a thought process that involves much speculation.

Metastable state   A state of temporary stability.

Meteorites   Objects falling from outer space that reach earth's surface.

Molecular anthropology   The attempt to reconstruct man's lineage through study of amino acid sequences in fossils.

Molecular phylogeny   The attempt to reconstruct the lineage of species through study of amino-acid sequences in fossils.

Molecules   The smallest unit of a substance into which atoms combine in a stable way.

Muon   A subnuclear particle belonging to the "lepton" family.

Muscular sclerosis   A disease destroying nerve transmissions to and from the brain.

Muscular dystrophy   A name used to describe any one of several muscle diseases.

Myopic   Near- or short-sighted.

Natural selection   An assumption by Darwin that the fittest survive—a belief which later proved circular in logic when its practical application forced the "survivors" to be effectively defined as the "fittest."

Negative charge   A name given to one of two opposite electrical conditions of a particle.

Neutrino   An extremely tiny particle produced in abundance soon after the universe was created.

Neutron   An electrically neutral stable particle found in the nuclei of atoms approximately equal in size and weight to a Proton.

New Inflationary Theory   An improved version of the Big Bang in which the universe first expands rapidly but then later slows down.

Nitrogen molecules   The smallest structural unit of nitrogen gas that preserves its identity.

Nucleation   A process where something comes into being by growing outward from a disturbance at its center.

Nucleotide base   Any of four kinds of chemical units that cluster into groups of three in an informational sequence along DNA that instructs all life's processes.

Organic molecule   A name given to the chemical units found in living systems.

Paleoanthropologist   A person committed to the study of human and related fossils.

Paleontology   The fossil study of prehistoric life forms.

Parabolic path   A curve traced by objects when falling to earth.

Paradigm   An expression that emphasizes different relations among nouns, adjectives, and pronouns through changed endings.

Particle physics   The study of the smallest units of matter.

Percolate   The passage of bubble-like entities through small spaces.

Pheromones   Chemicals transmitted between organisms of the same species that trigger changes including mating.

Phosphor   A class of materials which produce light when bombarded with electrons at high voltage.

Photon   The basic unit of light energy.

Planck time   An extremely small time period over which the universe would have destroyed itself had it not been supernaturally tuned to a precision of better than fifty decimal places prior to its birth.

Plasma   Commonly used to describe the fluid in which blood cells are suspended, but employed in physics to denote a gas so hot that the heat energy separates the plus and minus charges of the atoms into equal parts.

Polar ice   The ice at the north and south poles of the earth.

Polymer chemistry   The branch of chemistry concerned with long chemical chains.

Polypeptide gene product   Large organic molecules created by linking up many amino acids.

Pongid family   A category used to classify early ape fossils.

Positive charge   A name given to one of two opposite electrical conditions of a particle.

Progeria   A disease that causes premature aging.

Progestin   A crystallized hormone that prepares the uterus for conception.

Protein molecule   Generally regarded as the basic chemical unit of life capable of self-replication when immersed in a nutrient bath composed of its chemical parts.

Proton   A relatively large stable particle with positive charge found in the nuclei of atoms.

Quantum fluctuation   A label describing an unpredictable disturbance made possible by temporarily borrowing energy from the vacuum of space.

Quantum laws   Modern scientific rules that statistically describe the numerical data produced by human observations.

Quantum object   Anything subject to quantum laws.

Quantum physics   The science that applies quantum laws at the atomic level.

Quantum relativistic foundations   The combined resources of two branches of science: Einstein's relativity, and quantum physics.

Quarks   A class of basic particles that come together in different arrangements to build larger particles.

Radiation   Used in physics to describe energy transmission through space, but employed in evolution to denote the alleged appearance of two or more life forms from a common ancestor.

Reflectivity   The fraction of incident energy not absorbed by a surface.

Renaissance   A fourteenth-century European revival of the arts, literature, and learning.

Rest state   A system condition in which no change occurs.

Rhesus monkey   A small, short-tailed monkey common throughout India.

RNA   The chemical template used by a cell to transfer information from DNA for assembling protein.

Self-assembly   The belief that physical matter can self-organize into more complex forms under natural laws.

Serological   Pertaining to the preparation, use, and properties of watery animal fluids including blood.

Sickle-cell anemia   An inherited disease producing abnormal hemoglobin in the blood.

Silica   A chemical compound composed of silicon and oxygen commonly found in the earth's crust.

Singularity theorem   A mathematical proposition concerned with calculations that involve division by zero.

Spherical aberration   An optical imperfection that causes a blurred image due to light along the outer part of a lens being focused at a different point than the light through its center.

Statistical mechanics   A science that describes the behavior of a very large collection of objects using either classical or quantum laws.

Steady state   The belief that the universe has always existed.

Subnuclear particles   Smallest known particles of the universe.

Synonymous amino-acid residue   One of a group of chemical units whose location at a given chemical site is equally likely.

Synthetic theory   The belief that natural selection explains the progression of the increasing biological complexity of fossils with the passage of time.

Szilard   A twentieth-century scientist first to realize that the energy spent by an observer to acquire information will always exceed the energy that the observer can store using that information.

Tau   A subnuclear particle belonging to the "lepton" family.

Temperature excusions   The high and the low of temperature movement.

Theologian   A person who studies Bible truths using concepts created from its teachings.

Theory of relativity   A set of mathematical relations showing that mass and energy come from equivalent space curvatures that can appear differently in different observational situations.

Thermo-chemistry   Chemical changes involving heat.

Thermodynamic   Pertaining to motion connected with heat.

Thermodynamics   The study of the combined effects of heat and motion.

Thermodynamic variable   A mathematical parameter needed to describe a system's total intrinsic condition.

Troposphere   The upper fringe of the atmosphere.

U(1) group   A theoretical symbol denoting the advent of electrical symmetry when the universe cooled sufficiently to separate out weak interactions.

Ultra-violet light   Nonvisible light energy that lies just above "blue" in the color spectrum.

Uncertainty principle   The discovery that we cannot precisely know both the location and the speed of an atomic particle at the same time.

von Neumann   A twentieth-century scientist first to calculate the minimum information needed by a machine to reproduce itself.

Y-chromosome   A chemical structure in a male person's genes that is shaped like the letter "Y."

Zero gravitational entropy   An initial state from which the universe was born that is free of any mixing.

PREFACE

THIS BOOK EMBRACES several areas of scientific inquiry that pertain to human origins and destiny. There is an "A–B–C" to its theme, except in reverse order. The opening chapters take the reader into cosmology, the middle chapters focus on biology, and the latter chapters address anthropology. Each chapter adds pieces to the jigsaw puzzle of how the cosmos and life and man originated, and I attempt to join the pieces without benefit of having seen the picture on the box cover.

Each of us has a world view that we believe corresponds to the true image on the box cover. But since no one has ever seen the box cover, all of us are ignorant of not only the true picture, but its unifying fabric. The relationship between the two is called philosophy, an intuitively held ground rule that cannot be logically falsified. One philosophy, materialism, postulates that the image comes from properties of the fabric. Another, theism, teaches that Intelligence designed the picture, using fabric it created. Thus, the starting point of materialism is fabric while that of theism is Intelligence. Since each world view makes different choices about where to join the pieces, each creates a different world. This means that the final picture we create really comes from the creation that we picture.

Early in my scientific career I became impressed with the way differing world views influence how data is interpreted. I soon realized that all conclusions require assumptions that are colored by philosophy. For example, the earth was once believed to be at the center of the world and the planets were thought to be God's domain. These ideas originated in Greece about 500 B.C. and found their way into the tradition of the church and became accepted by a thirteenth-century theologian, Thomas Aquinas. His imaginings of God's activity were so unified with the ecclesiastical view of physical matter that when confronted with the fact of planetary motion, he concluded that angels must be pushing the planets around in their orbits.

Aquinas's need to interpret events led him to assign a cause to things within his experience. He understood planetary motion in terms of angels—not because the fact of such motion demanded it, but because angels pushing planets made sense within his world view. Today, people believe that chemical slime came to life of its own accord and that in time it became man. As was true of Aquinas, this belief makes sense to their world view. But just like with planetary motion, the fact of biological change is not at issue. Instead, the question is Who or what is doing the pushing?

There is something within man that prompts him to explain what he sees. It is a universal experience common to every generation. But true explanations come from factual observations, and confidence in them grows as we see more. Let me illustrate this with a simple example. In the colder climes, a modern housewife with a broken refrigerator might place a glass bottle on an outside window ledge to keep milk cold during winter. The next morning she awakes to find the bottle cracked and the milk gone, and ponders why it happened. She decides to put out another bottle only to find milk missing and the new bottle broken the next morning. She then recalls reading in the local newspaper about neighborhood thefts and suspects hungry vandals may be stealing her milk. But her husband remembers an article about orphans going door to door asking for food, and wonders whether they may be taking the milk. But a neighbor later suggests looking for the cause in the expansion of water as it freezes.* Taking his advice she changes over to plastic bottles and the problem disappears.

Since no one had actually seen the bottles break, no one really knew *why* they broke. Each person explained the event by assuming something familiar. The housewife presumed vandals, the husband orphans, and the neighbor the expansion of freezing water. Moreover, the fact that the milk bottles were no longer broken may have been a coincidence; perhaps vandals had been responsible but found another food source the day the change was made to plastic bottles. We can believe that expanding water broke the glass bottles only with a certain level of confidence. If we want greater assurance we must repeat the experiment by putting out large numbers of plastic and glass containers on randomly chosen cold nights and record what happens. If bottles are never broken when plastic is used and are always broken with glass, then we know that vandals or orphans are not our problem. Confidence in our conclusion improves when the number of observations increases.

About twenty-five years ago I was invited to address an international conference held at the University of Pennsylvania. Over a thousand scientists and

---

* Most things shrink as they cool, but water mysteriously reverses direction near the freezing point allowing ice to float and fish to survive winter seasons.

engineers were in attendance from countries all over the world. I recall walking to the podium, looking across the huge auditorium and thinking to myself that the most important part of my presentation would not be the theoretical equations that explain what I had to say, but rather that each person present be able to reproduce what I said when he or she returned home. The capability to reproduce was more important than theoretical possibility, because science is concerned with beliefs that can be established or discarded on the basis of observation. Any belief will do, provided it survives the scrutiny of everyone who tests it.

Suppose I said, "Center a green jelly bean in three hundred grams of clay, bake it for five hours at 400°F., allow to cool and bury it in six feet of sand at full moon. After eight days a little green man will emerge."

As silly as this may sound, if after returning to their respective countries each did what I had said to do and after eight days little green men emerged, the jelly bean recipe would become universally recognized as scientific truth.

Science is indifferent to *what* happens provided it is seen by all. If the Russian, the German, and the Frenchman could each create little green men out of jelly beans, and if scientists in Japan, Italy, and every other country could do likewise, then green jelly beans would become the object of intense scientific research. The reason is that the phenomenon would be universally experienced.

The problem we face in questions of origin and destiny is that our inquiry essentially involves one-time events that cannot be reproduced for our examination. We are free to design experiments whose data may be repeatedly examined, but it is an entirely different matter to realistically impute the results of those experiments to circumstances billions of years removed in time. Thus, as a practical matter, when something happens only once it becomes a matter for legal rather than scientific inquiry. We can guess at what happened and use science to gather evidence to support one or another hypothesis. But science has no proper jurisdiction in matters of origin or destiny. It can only provide evidence to a jury.

And this brings us to another dilemma. The jury—in the broadest sense, all of us who are concerned about the questions of origin and destiny— does not have a working knowledge of modern science. Large segments of the population are hopelessly lost trying to comprehend the meaning of what science says it has proved true. Most people, therefore, must depend upon the "expert" to tell them what it all means. But science can only describe things that are reproducible, like repeatedly measuring the time it takes an apple to fall. But we cannot measure yesterday or tomorrow; instead science can only confirm something in the present. Moreover, this confirmation occurs in such highly specialized fields that the rest of us are, for all practical purposes, helpless to verify the conclusions the "expert" presents as evidence.

The Bible, on the other hand, makes certain absolute statements e.g., "In the beginning, God created. . . ." Creation is set forth in the Bible as a religious doctrine whose validity depends on revelation rather than observation. Since not everyone accepts the Bible as "God breathed" and therefore trustworthy, the "knowledge" that "God created" is not universally accepted.

In effect, the two world views present us with different vehicles for deliverance—one is the God described by Scripture, and the other is the progress advanced by science. This progress is universally demonstrated in tractors for food and electric light bulbs and rockets to the moon. But although the eternal truth claimed by the Bible is selectively experienced only by those who believe, yet there is no logical reason why the two systems of truth cannot rationally coexist. However, the implicit assumption in our day is that "selective" knowledge is untrue because truth must be experienced universally.

Did the world have a beginning, or has it always existed? What of life itself? What was its origin? And how did man come to be? Taking their cues from outdated beliefs and popular stories, many will join the pieces of the puzzle and create the aforementioned box cover with little if any regard for the natural pattern that is miraculously painted across the fabric of the universe. This popular outlook is a modern blindspot that downplays "providence" in favor of attitudes mesmerized by a methodology that extols physical matter. One might accept this indifference were it not for the infinity that truly separates the thousands of biological miracles operating in just one cell of our body each second, rendering man's greatest achievements small by comparison.

How we join the pieces is determined by how we conceive reality. The stakes are really very high because the present construction concludes that science is man's best hope for the future. However, if our 5,000-year history of wars, prisons, and bloodshed means anything, then the prospect of nuclear suicide may more truly be our fate than any "inevitable" advance toward Utopia promised by present attitudes. This book proposes a box cover that gives insight into human failure, perspective on human achievement, and exposure to a destiny away from slime and through space-time. The paths we walk may at times be unfamiliar—yet they will lead us to conclusions that could prove invaluable, and that offer escape from our past, and the present hope of a glorious destiny.

ROBERT GANGE

ORIGINS
AND
DESTINY

1

WHAT CONFLICT DID SCIENCE LOSE TO SCRIPTURE?

WERE WE CREATED? Or did we evolve? These are questions of truly cosmic proportions. The reason is that they affect each one of us personally.

The labels "creation" and "evolution" have become household words. Why? Because they deal with where we came from, and where we are going. They focus on the question of *origins*. If our origins are in God, then the question of *destiny* is also raised.

More and more lives are being touched by these questions. Debates are springing up all over the country. "Old-time religion" is being tested as never before.[1] Cherished beliefs are being challenged and battle lines are being drawn. Each side is sure that the other side is wrong. But who or what is right?

This new look into origins is viewed with mixed emotions.[2] Some welcome the issue as long overdue, while others regard it as a threat to human progress. The motive behind defending creation on the one hand, or evolution on the other, is not always apparent.

Many people take the Bible seriously and are sure that God cannot be wrong. Nor would he lie. Thus, they defend creation because they're sure that it's taught in the Bible.

Others, however, are convinced that evolution is true. They are sure that science is not wrong, and that scientists would not lie. Thus, they defend evolution because they think that ample evidence has proved that it's true.

Seminaries and churches are also divided on the issue. In the home, children are asking difficult questions, and parents are searching for whatever answers they can find. Parents and young people alike, however, soon learn that many high-school teachers are not sure which way to go. Things *seem* unsettled because they *are* unsettled.

Many Orthodox Jews as well as evangelical Christians believe that the Bible has a stake in the creation-evolution argument. Yet they are bewildered as to what the facts actually teach. Many have expressed the view that both sides of the issue ought to be taught in the public schools.

The Legal Question

In March 1981, the governor of Arkansas signed into law the Balanced Treatment for Creation-Science and Evolution-Science Act. Its essential purpose was to ensure balanced treatment of creation and evolution in the Arkansas public schools. Two months later, the constitutional validity of the law was challenged on the grounds that it violated the First Amendment to the Constitution, the due process clause of the Fourteenth Amendment, and the right to academic freedom for students and teachers.

The nine-day court trial ended with a ruling in January 1982 that the Arkansas Balanced Treatment Act was a violation of the constitutional separation of church and state.[3] Although the decision was not unexpected, the differing reports of what occurred at the trial were somewhat of a surprise.

One well-known theologian wrote that creationism suffered defeat due in part to a biased judge and secular humanism.[4] Elsewhere, a school teacher published a different view.[5] He said that creation was religion in disguise, was unscientific, and, therefore, did not belong in the public schools. He also said that the judge was correct in his decision. Whom do we believe?

Thirty-five days before the Arkansas judge made his decision known, a lawsuit was filed in the U.S. District Court in Baton Rouge asking that the Louisiana Balanced Treatment for Creation-Science and Evolution-Science Act be declared *constitutional*. These plaintiffs described themselves as legislators, scientists, public school teachers, students and parents, and religious spokesmen who believe in separation of church and state, and in academic freedom in public schools for students and teachers. Surprisingly, some were reported as evolutionists who did not necessarily believe in creation-science, but who *did* believe in an open-minded approach including both the creation and evolution sides of the question.

In July 1982, a three-judge panel of the U.S. Court of Appeals for the Fifth Circuit held that the Louisiana Balanced Treatment Act was unconstitutional on the grounds that creation-science was a religious belief. Two months later, a massive 630-page brief with over 1,700 footnotes was filed under an appeal authorized by the Louisiana attorney general. And in October 1983, the Louisiana Supreme Court held that the Balanced Treatment Act was constitutional under the Louisiana Constitution. The case was then scheduled to be taken to the U.S. District Court under a motion for summary judgement filed by the American Civil Liberties Union on behalf of critics of the law. Although the Louisiana State Senate voted in May 1984 to repeal the law, the House of Representatives rejected the motion one month later. The result was another trial, and in January 1985, Federal Judge Adrian

Duplantier ruled in New Orleans that the Louisiana Balanced Treatment Act was unconstitutional on First Amendment grounds.

The Social Question

As a result of these and other similar actions in other states, creationists feel frustrated, and evolutionists feel threatened. For example, the legal battles nurtured a trend to deemphasize, or at least qualify, descriptions of evolution in public school textbooks. In response to public pressure, as well as the threat of litigation, the Texas Board of Education, which represents 10 percent of the nation's textbook market, voted as early as April 1984 to repeal the state's antievolution rules. By the end of 1985, at least five textbook publishers had agreed to revise the junior high school books to *increase* their emphasis on evolution. This was apparently done to promote the approval of the California state school board so that local school districts could receive state money to purchase the texts. California public schools are reported to be the largest textbook market in the nation.

Although the court and school board decisions have favored the evolutionists, they are not at peace because they feel that another creationist offensive is in the making. For example, a list of articles and books on creationism was announced in 1984 for readers of a magazine specializing in geological education. The magazine's purpose is to keep geologists informed—and forearmed—for the next creationist offensive. Creationist materials were grouped into six categories, including one that allows study of the original works of creationists, rather than quotations.[6]

At an earlier time when legal matters were not as prominent, the man on the street was asked to voice his opinion on the creation-evolution question. In an Associated Press-NBC News poll that was reported to have been conducted in October 1981, 76 percent said that both theories should be taught in the public schools. A study reported earlier that year of almost two thousand school superintendents, officals, and librarians revealed that efforts are made to censor books in about 20 percent of our nation's schools each year. Many of these are started by teachers or school officials seeking to avoid criticism, and about half of them succeed.

It seems clear that although the creation-evolution issue affects large numbers of people, it is not an easy one to resolve. But it also seems clear that if we are to seek an answer to this question, we must leave the legal quarrels and look elsewhere for a solution. It is doubtful that we can learn the truth about creation and evolution, the origin of life, and whether man evolved from apes, or was created by God, from a court of law. While it is true that testimony from different people can be interesting, it is also true that even the experts disagree.[7]

The truth about origins must come from *knowledge* that is based upon facts obtained by studying the physical world. Since science is a quest for such truth, it seems reasonable that science ought to be the starting point in our inquiry rather than law. Yet many people who have sought the truth about origins appear to be divided. Those who believe the Bible is true feel that they have *found* the truth there. For them, the answer is that God created. Others have turned to science for the answer. Here, the situation seems less settled because a number of people seem able to trust science and yet still believe that God created. They are convinced that the two are compatible, and that there is no problem. They feel sure that their beliefs are in harmony with the truths of Scripture and the facts of science.

Others, however, are not so sure. Some in this latter group hold that there is no God. Therefore the answer for them cannot be that God created. Furthermore, they argue, "Even if God exists, why is it necessary for him to have created the world?" When asked who did, they answer, "No one." Their reason is that they believe that *the world had no beginning.* This belief was once common on university campuses where searching minds believed that the world could not have been created by a "God." They said that God didn't create the world simply because the world did not have a beginning. Why did they say this? Because they felt that a very basic scientific law prohibited creation.

The First Law

This law is called the First Law of Thermodynamics, from *thermo,* meaning heat, and *dynamics,* meaning motion. The First Law teaches that a natural process cannot bring something into existence from nothing.[8] Since there are things all about us, the conclusion is that *they must have been here forever.* Thus it is said that the First Law forbids creation.

Why can't the world have had a beginning? Because it's impossible for things to just "pop" into existence and remain there. According to the First Law, no natural process can bring into existence something from nothing. Thus, everything in the world must be eternally existing. Although the form of things may have changed, the "basic stuff" of which they are composed is said to have been here forever.

For example, water can be seen as a liquid, a gas (steam), or solid (ice). But no matter how it appears, it is said that the atomic building blocks of water must have always existed in some way or another because the First Law implies that *everything is eternally existing.*

Another example is found in the belief that billions of years ago the universe contained very hot gases. Although these gases were in the form of a "plasma" in eternity past, it is said that they later condensed into rocks. Of course in our ordinary experience rocks appear to us as solid objects. Nonetheless, it is believed that billions of years ago their basic "stuff" was in the form of a gas.

No matter what we see or touch, the First Law would appear to teach that it is eternal. At least that's what many understand the law to say. Why? Because a natural process can't make something from nothing. Since there are "somethings" all about us, they must have been here forever.

Why Do We Care?

If the "atomic stuff" that makes up water or rocks has always existed, then this "stuff" could not have had a beginning. And if there were no beginning, then there was no creation. And if there were no creation, then God could not have "created the heavens and the earth," as the Bible says. But do the facts of science support the idea that the world is eternal?

Science has unveiled significant new knowledge over the past several decades,[9] and many are convinced that this knowledge sheds considerable light on the question of origins.[10] Thus, all that we need to do is objectively look at what has been learned. But make no mistake—the Bible is on trial. In this case, however, the verdict will not come from theologians, but instead from an international jury of scientists whose work and conclusions build upon the experience and knowledge of past generations.

For the most part, scientists as a group have one common goal. Their aim is to uncover truth regarding the physical world. The Bible also claims to be true. It identifies everything in the world as coming from a Creator, and claims that the Supreme Intelligence who brought the world into existence used human writers as instruments to pen its pages. If this is true, then what it says and what scientists find ought to be consistent. Is it? What is the verdict from science? What are the facts?

The answer to this question impacts many lives. *The Bible is on the line.*[11] If there were no beginning, then *the opening verse of every Bible in the world is wrong!* If this were to prove true, the consequences would be staggering. Millions of people all over the world regard the Bible as divine revelation from God himself. If the opening words of the book of Genesis are wrong, how could anyone bring himself or herself to trust the other words in the Bible?

The question of whether or not the world had a beginning is, in this sense, a *watershed issue.* Many people believe that the truth of the Bible rests on it. If there were no beginning, then clearly "God did *not* create."

Virtually everyone agrees that the Bible takes a clear stand on the question of whether or not creation occurred. Thus, there seems to be a genuine basis for agreement on at least two things:

First, the Bible unambiguously states that there was a beginning. Secondly, the question has only a yes-or-no answer. The importance of this particular inquiry thus lies in the definitive yes-or-no answer that the question implies.

The stakes are high and the question is clear. The challenge is to find the answer. Although scientific discovery can give rise to wrong speculations, its facts are usually trustworthy. What are the facts in this matter? And where can we go to find them?

Was There a Beginning?

What does modern science teach regarding origins? In other words, what are the actual data and their interpretations? Do the latest scientific results show that the world can be traced back into eternity past? Or do they say that it was created? Has the universe truly been here forever? Or did it have a beginning? Are the things that we touch really made of "stuff" that's eternal? Or did this "stuff" somehow pop into existence?

To answer these questions, we should first understand that scientists have taught different things at different times. Some have taught that the world had a beginning; [12] others that it is eternal.[13] But what do the facts teach? Today we have many new facts, and, in the last thirty years, knowledge has increased sixfold. What does the new knowledge teach concerning origins?

For many decades a number of scientists believed, as we have noted, that the First Law of Thermodynamics leads to a "steady state" theory of the universe. They felt that the world is eternal, and that everything in it has existed in some form or other forever.[14] They argued that a natural process cannot bring into existence something out of nothing. Today, there's a problem with this idea because *the beginning of the universe has actually been measured.* Although the measurement is indirect, it nonetheless teaches that there actually was a beginning!

To give an example of the kind of measurement we are speaking of, suppose someone fired a shotgun in another room. If we walked into the room one minute later, we would see the smoke still drifting out from the end of the barrel. In much the same way, the "smoke" from the "Big Bang" is still drifting throughout the universe. And this smoke shows that there was a beginning.

This "smoke" is in the form of microwave radiation, and scientists have measured its lingering presence from a Big Bang, which according to three independent ways of measuring the age of the universe* occurred between thirteen and fifteen billion years ago.[15] At that time, it seems the universe mysteriously exploded into existence.[16] This smoke is known as the background radiation of the universe,[17] and it was measured in 1965 by two scientists who, ten years later, received the Nobel Prize for their work.[18] Thus, the older idea of an eternally existing world is now known to have a problem. These measurements of what scientists call the background radiation that fills the universe tell us that the world is *not* eternal, but that it actually had a beginning.[19]

The measured values of the radiation also agree with the predictions of certain theoretical models.[20] These models can be thought of as mathematical pictures that describe how the world unfolded after it came into being. For example, the universe is 25 percent helium −4, the exact number predicted by the Big Bang Theory. The mathematical models can be cross-checked because they also make precise predictions about the behavior of atomic particles. Measurements from the field of science called particle physics have

---

* Globular clusters, nucleochronology, and doppler red shift in a Friedmann universe (Weinberg S. *Gravitation & Cosmology* (1972) Wiley, New York)

confirmed many of these predictions.[21] For example, experiments have been designed in particle physics that measure the neutron-decay half life; and astrophysical models of the universe have used this number to predict abundances of helium −3, deuterium, and lithium −7. The measured numbers are found to agree with the predicted values.

Today, virtually every scientist working in the fields of cosmology or particle physics is convinced that the world had a beginning. And, as a practical matter, this conviction is now shared by scientists in other disciplines. In other words, there has been a growing confidence over the past several decades in the scientific community that the world actually had a beginning.

In conclusion, it seems that the trial is over and the verdict is in. The Bible was correct all the time—the world has not been here forever. What new trial looms in the future we cannot say. But this much is sure: Based on today's knowledge and data, "In the beginning" has become scientific truth—there *was* a beginning.

2

HAS OUR WORLD
VANISHED AND REAPPEARED?

COSMOLOGICAL DATA obtained through modern and powerful telescopes indicate that the universe is getting larger and larger with the passage of time.[1] We can think of the universe as a big pink balloon with black dots along its surface. As the balloon grows larger, two things happen: The dots move away from the center of the balloon, and they move away from each other. This gives us a rough picture of what scientists mean when they say that the universe is expanding. The dots correspond to galaxies (collections of stars), and the whole system acts as though it exploded from a "point in space" 13 to 15 billion years ago.

Is the Expansion Eternal?

Measurements obtained through modern telescopes indicate that the universe is expanding, and that it has been doing so from the time that it came into existence. But despite the evidence that this is so, some have found it difficult to abandon the idea that the universe is eternally existing. The purpose of this chapter is to examine some of the ideas that have been put forth to defend an eternally existing universe.

For example, at least one person has argued that the background radiation measured by Penzias and Wilson may not have been from the Big Bang,[2] and that it can be explained in other ways.* If so, then it can be argued that although the universe is expanding, it may have been doing so forever.

The problem with this idea, however, is that as the universe expands, we

---

* The observed energy density of the microwave background radiation resembles that of other natural phenomena such as cosmic rays, galactic magnetism and starlight.

are seeing the stars destroying themselves and creating energy in the process. If the universe has been expanding forever, these stars would have had "forever" to destroy themselves. If this were true, then no stars would exist today. Since the stars *do* exist, it means that the present expansion of the universe has not been going on forever.

The only conceivable way for stars to destroy themselves "forever," and yet still be here today, is for there to be an unlimited amount of matter in the universe to destroy. One person has actually theorized as to how an unlimited supply of matter might be possible.[3] But were one to believe that the present universe has been expanding forever, it would be necessary to also believe that there is an infinite source of new matter within the universe that is participating in the stellar destruction process. Otherwise, the stars would diminish in number and eventually perish.

Unless there is a limitless source of physical matter which replenishes stars, they cannot continue to exist and, at the same time, destroy themselves forever. But is such a limitless universe rational?[4] It would be a universe of unlimited matter moving through unlimited space, and expanding over unlimited time. Yet to believe in such a thing is to believe in a universe that can neither be verified nor proven false. As such, it is an unscientific universe that has no more credibility than a child's fairy tale. At best, it is a story that one is free to accept—but certainly *not* on any scientific basis. Simply put, there is no data to support the belief that the universe has been expanding forever in this way.

Does Our World Go In and Out of Existence?

Another way to defend the idea that physical matter is eternally existing is to accept that the universe had a beginning, but to assume that it was not the only time that it began. In other words, there was more than one beginning.

As a practical matter, virtually every scientist is convinced that the world had a beginning. They have reached this conclusion not only on the basis of the background microwave radiation, but also from other related discoveries during the past decade. For example, the radio telescope at Kitt Peak Observatory in Arizona discovered a modified form of hydrogen gas (called deuterium) in the Cone Nebula three thousand light years away from earth in concentrations ten thousand times greater than that found in our solar system.

Likewise the 200-inch Hale telescope at Mount Palomar, and the 150-inch telescope near Siding Springs, Australia, both detected pure hydrogen gas in clouds believed to be billions of light years distant from the earth. These materials were discovered in space around 1980, and are regarded as the original residue from the Big Bang origin of the universe. There are also other evidences that our universe had a beginning. For example, the fact that three independent measuring techniques all yield finite ages for the universe is itself proof that it isn't infinitely old.

But even so, the question arises, why is it necessary for the Big Bang to have been the *only* beginning? Could our universe have begun more than once? Why must a beginning limit our options to only *one* beginning? The answer is that, in principle, it doesn't.[5]

Let's suppose that the universe *did* explode into existence billions of years ago. Why does this have to be the only time that it did so? For example, why couldn't this event have been the millionth explosion? Or the billionth explosion? Some have suggested that after each explosion, the universe first expands, but then undergoes collapse only to explode and expand again. It may be that this "outward explosion" and "inward collapse" have been going on *forever.* If so, it would mean that the universe has been here forever. Thus, the measurement of a beginning does not necessarily prove that the universe has not been here forever. The reason is that it may have been repeatedly exploding outward, and then collapsing inward, only to reexplode outward again. In this scenario, each explosion is a "beginning" that repeats itself over and over again forever.

The Cosmic Yo-Yo

This line of thought ultimately leads us back to an eternally existing world in which nothing is really ever created. Instead, the world is just changing its form while eternally existing. The measured background radiation is then understood as coming from the *last* explosion, so that it gives us the *appearance* of a beginning. In this picture, the Big Bang becomes just one of billions of explosions that have happened in eternity past, and that will continue to occur in eternity future. In this sense, the universe is like a cosmic Yo-Yo that is continually going out and in, out and in, and so on.

The "cosmic Yo-Yo" idea, that the world has been going out and in forever, introduces "eternity," not in terms of *one* universe that has been expanding forever but an infinite number of universes that take turns exploding into existence one at a time. Each of these explosions expands into a universe that exists for "only" billions of years before it collapses. Thus if the cosmic Yo-Yo idea were true, the present universe would be just one of an infinite number of explosions that have occurred in eternity past, and that will continue to occur into eternity future. Moreover, we are able to observe and discuss the expansion because we just happen to be living at a time when the universe is getting bigger rather than smaller.

The notion that the universe is a "cosmic Yo-Yo" is untrue. However, it has proved appealing to some because it appears to preserve the universal validity of the First Law of Thermodynamics, the law that says you can't get something from nothing. But as nice as the Yo-Yo idea may seem, it has a string attached to it (pun intended). The problem is that the Yo-Yo can't perform in the way described because, figuratively speaking, *the stars chew up its string.*

Scientists have known for over eighty years that matter and energy are different forms of the same basic "stuff"—in much the same way that ice and steam are different forms of water. When we study the matter and energy of the stars, the origin of their material shows us that the cosmic Yo-Yo can't continue to go in and out forever. Let's see why.

Stellar Destruction

Stars are made up of matter, and improved telescopes have shown us that the stars in the universe are destroying themselves. They are creating energy at the expense of the matter of which they're composed. This means that during each explosion, additional stars are destroyed in a process that accumulates "heat energy" within the universe with each new explosion.[6] Scientists have shown that because this heat energy is cumulative, the process by which the stars "sell off" their matter for energy is one that ultimately requires the universe to have had a one-time beginning.

The entire universe accumulates heat energy during expansion because the stars are destroying themselves and creating energy. And if it's hotter, then it's bigger. Thus the increasing heat energy forces the universe to grow larger with each Big Bang.

But if the universe gets bigger with each new bounce then it must have been smaller on the preceding bounce. In other words, during each preceding explosion, the universe is smaller. Thus as we go back in time, with each earlier bounce the universe must have been smaller and smaller. As we look back into the past, we find a series of explosions that progressively shrink, the further back we go.

Scientists have shown that this progression back into time converges to a beginning, so that the cosmic Yo-Yo cannot have continued forever. Moreover, scientists have mathematically studied these explosions and concluded that they converge down into a first explosion—they funnel in toward a beginning.[7] This means that there had to have been a first bounce. This is another way we know that the universe had a beginning.

The cosmic Yo-Yo idea is called the "Oscillating Universe." The theory behind it asserts that physical matter exists forever, but is cyclically transformed into an infinite number of universes, each of which first gets bigger as it expands, and then becomes smaller as it contracts. If this is true, then at the present time the universe is getting bigger in an "expansion phase," but, in future generations, it will get smaller and ultimately collapse into a "point" concentration of mass. When that happens, the theory calls for another explosion and expansion (Big Bang) to occur to make another universe.

Physical matter thus oscillates in and out with the passage of time. Although the stars destroy themselves during the expansion phase, their physical matter is alleged to be "recreated" from energy when the universe gets smaller. This is the proposed explanation for how stars can continue to exist and yet be destroyed in a universe that's here forever. They disappear into energy as the universe gets bigger, but then their physical matter returns from that energy when it gets smaller.

Can the Universe Reexplode?

The Oscillating Universe theory is based on the assumption that the universe *can* go backwards. But how do we know that it *can* reverse itself? Is it able to go out, then come back in, and go back out again, and so on indefinitely? The answer is no. In many ways, the universe is like a car that is traveling down a one-way street so narrow that it must continue in the same direction because it cannot turn around. The universe *cannot go in and out repeatedly* because the stars are destroying themselves and creating energy, and this energy heats up the entire physical system of mass and energy in a cumulative way.[8]

Were the universe to reverse itself during contraction along the same path that it traveled in its expansion phase, then the entire system of mass and energy would need to cool down in order to converge to a point from which to explode again. But the cooling process means that *the energy must change back into matter along the same path that the energy was created*. The problem with this, however, is that the reversible change of energy back into matter is prohibited by what scientists call the Second Law of Thermodynamics. This law, which is discussed in a later chapter, teaches that the universe cannot go in and out forever because there is no way for the energy, which is created when the stars destroy themselves, to convert back into mass along paths that permit another explosion to occur. This means that the system of mass and energy is not eternally existing, and that the universe must have had a beginning.

Perhaps a simple picture can help us to understand better what is being said. Imagine that the entire world consists of nothing but a gigantic ice cube. Let's now suppose that the ice cube expands and in doing so gets warmer. Two things happen: The ice cube gets bigger, and it begins to melt and change into water.

The water that was once an ice cube continues to become larger and larger until, finally, we imagine the cube to be entirely melted, and to be as large as an ocean. Let's assume that at this point the cube has expanded as far as it can; the ocean into which it has changed begins to shrink. We can imagine the ocean becoming smaller and smaller—and as it gets smaller, the water gets colder. Soon it begins to freeze. And eventually it changes back into an ice cube. The ice cube itself becomes smaller until eventually it returns to its original size. Once back to its original size, the ice cube stops shrinking and the entire cycle repeats itself. The ice cube again starts to grow and as it grows, it again changes into water. The water again expands until it reaches the size of an ocean. The ocean then starts to shrink. As the volume of water gets smaller, it freezes back into an ice cube. This cycle then repeats itself over and over and over again.

This is a picture of what some people have thought the world was doing. It is a picture of a pulsating or oscillating universe. Loosely speaking, matter can be thought of as the ice, and energy as the water. But when we take a closer look at what's happening, we can see that as the water expands, some of it becomes steam which can be thought of as energy that is unrecoverable. If during each cycle some of the water becomes steam, then less energy (water) is available to cool back into matter (ice). If the world were here forever, then eventually we would lose all of the water into steam, and no energy would remain to cool back into matter. It would all be gone because all of the water would have changed into steam. Although the ice cube picture that we've presented is intended to be tutorial and therefore incomplete, it nonetheless portrays the essence of what occurs. Thus, we conclude that the universe can't cycle in this way. It can't go in and out forever.

How Does Science Know We Began?

We have seen that the universe is not expanding forever, nor is it a cosmic Yo-Yo. When improved telescopes are used to study the stars, figuratively speaking we see that some of the water turns into steam. In a sense, this is what the stars do. When matter turns into energy, it's like part of the water turning into steam. It does not all return. In our ice cube picture, were the ocean (energy) to shrink back into the ice cube (matter), part of its water would be gone. The water that is lost as steam can be thought of as energy in a form that cannot be recovered. With each new expansion, more of the water turns into steam so that, on the return trip, even less water is available to freeze into ice.

The change of energy into a form that cannot be recovered is due to the nature of physical matter and is described by the Second Law. It results from an inability of the universe to return along the same path that it travels during expansion.[9] Once matter changes into energy, the energy cannot reversibly change back into matter. Thus, the universe can't go in and out; it can't oscillate. This means that it has not been here forever and that it had a one-time beginning.

Are There Yet Other Ways We Know We Began?

Imagine taking a motion picture of someone throwing a stone into a pond. Later, we play the movie both forward and backward to people who were not at the pond. Do they know which way is correct? Yes! But how? Because no one has ever seen ripples start from the rim of a pond, move toward the center, and hurl a stone up and into the air. It's easy to see why. We can't simultaneously start all of the forces around the rim of the pond at exactly the same time. The reason is that signals take time to travel. The universe is like a pond. Physical matter from its "rim" must ripple toward its center as we go back in time. Were the universe to contract, it would require simultaneous cooperation among all the forces at its boundary. Otherwise, material along its boundary will not later converge to a common point.

If the universe were bouncing in and out forever, it would need to shrink back each time to the same starting point. If it's impossible to simultaneously coordinate the forces around the rim of a pond, imagine trying to do it around the rim of a 30 billion light-year wide-universe! The universe cannot reverse and shrink back to its starting point because it is physically impossible to simultaneously coordinate the boundary conditions necessary to make it happen. It therefore must have had a beginning.

There is yet another way that we know the universe had a beginning. Scientists routinely study the light from stars, which consists of waves that originate from the different materials that compose a star.[10] Since the materials in the stars differ, the light waves that leave the stars and come to the earth are different. The different light waves can be thought of as the material's fingerprint. Measurements of the light coming from many stars show that the universe is made up of the same atomic materials that we find on earth.

The Second Law of Thermodynamics, a law embracing physical things on earth, and in the universe at large,[11] governs how these materials can behave. Just a short time ago, this law had limitations that prevented its application to the entire universe.[12] But recently it was modified, and the revision (called the New Generalized Second Law of Thermodynamics) is vastly more powerful than the older Second Law.[13]

The New Generalized Second Law teaches that if the universe had been here forever, all of its materials would have reached a state of rest. But we do not see such when we study the universe with telescopes. And if the universe is not in a state of rest, it could not have been here forever; it must have had a beginning.

The universe, therefore, had a beginning—a fact taught by the first verse of every Bible and now accepted by most of the scientific world. Every Bible begins with the statement: "In the beginning God created. . . ." Now science says, "There was a beginning."

3

DID A SUPERNATURAL EXPLOSION CREATE THE WORLD?

THE DISCOVERY THAT the world had a beginning is mind-boggling. Yet this verdict does not come from theologians; rather it comes from an international jury of scientists. Using only physical evidence, *they* say that the world actually began.[1] The belief is based on empirical facts that were uncovered by modern science, and these facts teach that the world actually "began." [2]

Think about it! There was a "time" when time didn't exist.[3] Neither was there any "space." But if there was "nothing," where did we come from? How did it happen? And who or what was behind it? As intriguing as these questions may be, a deeper question looms. The purpose of this chapter is to inquire whether the beginning of our universe was natural—or supernatural.

The Dilemma

If there were a beginning, then we have a dilemma because of the First Law of Thermodynamics. This First Law has been the object of considerable thought since it was first introduced to the world by William Kelvin and Rudolf Clausius. It forbids a natural process from bringing something into being from nothing.[4] This constraint was mentioned in an earlier chapter. How can a natural process bring something into existence out of nothing? Since the answer is it can't, many scientists have understood the First Law of Thermodynamics to teach that everything in the universe is eternally old. This was the law that inspired the older "steady state" theory of the universe, and for over a century it was understood to mean that the world has been here forever. But does the First Law really teach that our world has been here forever? The answer is no—and the reason for this is found in what the law actually says.

The First Law teaches that a *natural* process cannot bring into existence something out of nothing. If the First Law is correct, which seems to be the case, and if the universe had a beginning, which seems to be scientifically accepted, then one conclusion is that something *unnatural* created the universe.[5] If the world didn't result from a natural process, then it came from an *unnatural* process.

The thought that the universe may have originated *supernaturally* is unsettling to many people.[6] Yet, taken at face value, this conclusion is consistent with the total sum of evidence before us. Modern understanding of astrophysical data collected over the past fifty years or so has illuminated a profoundly important insight concerning the origin of the world. When objectively viewed, we see two complementary truths: * (1) Our world had a beginning, and (2) natural processes do not create things out of nothing. A supernatural birth satisfies them both.

But the story doesn't end there. A third element has been added. There is now reason to believe our universe came into existence out of nothing! This latest conclusion comes from recent modifications of the older Big Bang Theory—something beyond particle physics—known as the New Inflationary Theory of the Universe. However, to understand what these new insights mean, it will be helpful to first outline the scientific work that is presently underway on an international scale to unify all of nature, and which helped give birth to the New Inflationary Theory.

Scientists throughout the world are developing "Grand Unification" theories.[7] These exotic rules embrace all of nature; they link the forces surrounding the atom with those that control the stars; they tie together both the smallest and the largest things in the universe. The theories also help to explain the bewildering list of over two hundred atomic particles uncovered in the past several decades.[8] In addition, they provide insight into the results of high energy experiments. For the first time, we've begun to predict and explain what we see.[9] Thus, confidence is growing in the foundation on which the new Grand Unification theories are being developed.

The Grand Unification theories laid the groundwork for the New Inflationary Theory,[10] a new theory developed to resolve certain unanswered questions associated with the older Big Bang.

There are at least three of these questions. The first relates to the transmission of signals from one part of the universe to another. How did different parts of the universe communicate just after it began? Scientists call this enigma *causality*.

The second concerns the "shape" of the space-time fabric of the universe. What made it lose its curvature so quickly and survive longer than an infinitesimal fraction of a second? This problem is known as the *flatness* question.

---

* These truths are the result of cosmological data and understandings that are intertwined with the quantum relativistic foundations of twentieth-century science.

The third deals with the way that the stars are distributed throughout space. Why does matter cluster to form galaxies? This question is called *homogeneity*.

The New Inflationary Theory answers the first two questions and it promises an answer to the third [11] through an exotic idea called "quantum fluctuations" [12] (a new insight into cosmology about which more is said below). A quantum fluctuation can be thought of as a bubble such as appears in a pot of boiling water.

The New Inflationary Theory also gives us insight into the basic stuff from which the world was created. Unlike the Big Bang Theory, this one tries to tell us something about the raw material from which the universe was born.

In the Big Bang Theory, our hands were tied because we could not go back in time to the actual beginning. A small impenetrable interval of time, called a "Planck time," separated us from mathematically seeing the true beginning. Thus, we could never hope to know how the universe came into being. We could never see back to the true beginning. But the New Inflationary Theory frees us from this limitation and gives us a picture of the universe from the moment it unfolded. Were we to condense its implications into one sentence, it would be this: The universe seems to have come into existence out of nothing. That's right; out of *nothing*.

It's staggering to think that the entire universe began from nothing.[13] Yet there's something even more startling: *The Bible revealed that knowledge thousands of years before man ever made or conceived of a telescope.* The first verse of the Bible teaches that there was a *beginning* to the world, and that it came into existence *ex nihilo* (out of nothing).[14] The implications of this are so profound that attempts have been made to explain it away, using the idea of quantum fluctuations, the belief that the universe just popped itself into existence. However, that notion is totally inadequate. A quantum fluctuation no more explains the existence of our universe than does a bubble in boiling water explain the stove that heats it. Let's see why a quantum fluctuation cannot make a universe.

Nature's Free Lunch

Natural processes do not pop things into existence out of nothing. To explain the fact that things *do* exist, however, a few writers have tried to get around the obvious implications of a supernatural creation by saying that there may be one natural process through which we *can* get something from nothing.[15] That process is what I've already referred to as a quantum fluctuation. The basic idea is that, at times, Mother Nature is disposed toward handing out a "free lunch." But, figuratively speaking, when we open the bag to eat this lunch we find that the bag is empty.

Our mathematical descriptions of the physical world do suggest that quantum fluctuations are real. However, *no one knows in any basic way what*

they are or why they exist. This is an example of our having assigned a
label to something that no one truly understands. There is nothing wrong
with doing this provided we realize that a *quantum fluctuation is more of
a tag placed on a mathematical result, than an explanation of how something
came to be.* The idea that a quantum fluctuation evolved into our universe
is an imaginative guess; it certainly is *not* rooted in scientific fact. Ideas of
this kind are energized by a philosophical prejudice toward materialism.
Appendix 1 contains additional discussion for readers with a technical background.

In trying to describe quantum fluctuations, the most we can say with
any confidence is that they represent a natural process that *temporarily* bor-
rows energy over time intervals that are imperceptible. This is not because
of the practical limitations that ordinarily exist when we measure things,
but because what occurs within such an interval is, in principle, inaccessible
to an observer. This truth is connected with a fundamental result of quantum
physics commonly known as the uncertainty principle.

The mathematical picture can be visualized by imagining a pot of water
that's about to boil; but the pot and the water are both growing larger and
larger. In this picture, a quantum fluctuation can be thought of as a bubble
that forms at the bottom of the pot. The quantum mechanical equations
allow these bubbles to pop into existence from the vacuum of space, and
then to grow larger and larger.* However the New Inflationary Theory requires the pot and its water to grow so fast that, figuratively speaking, no
bubbles ever reach the surface of the water. This means that although, in
principle, quantum fluctuations can occur, cosmological constraints disqualify
them from becoming *our* universe.**

Thus quantum fluctuations do *not* explain how the universe exploded into
existence out of nothing. We are again left with the glaring conclusion that
since our world *did* begin, and since the First Law disallows a natural process
from creating things out of nothing, it indicates that our world's birth was
not natural, but instead had a supernatural beginning.

However, another problem remains for those who attempt to explain the
origin of the universe in terms of natural laws. This problem is more serious
than anything thus far discussed. All of our knowledge of natural processes
comes entirely from information that has been acquired after the universe
came into being. It is therefore illogical to presume the existence of originating
processes that are defined only in terms of a universe they are alleged to

---

* Even if quantum fluctuations produced edgeless, four-dimensional blobs (closed
hyperspheres) as some suggest, it is pure speculation to suppose that natural laws
inflated one of them into the universe in which we live.

** Quantum fluctuations can produce edgeless hyperspheres of the ordered phase
that inflate, but they *cannot* "percolate" into the ordered phase in which we live
because the exponential expansion exceeds their nucleation.

have created. How can the validity of such processes be defended? One must argue for their existence in a vacuum void of the world that gives them meaning! Thus to believe in such processes is a matter of faith, not science. The initial conditions that gave birth to our world belong to a realm separate from the natural laws that controlled how the universe unfolded. This distinction is rarely given the attention it deserves. At the moment of explosion, our world appears to have been tuned to a precision of over fifty decimal places. Can we hope to ever understand this miraculous event? The difference between initial conditions and the laws of nature is that whereas the latter we hope to understand more and more, the details of the former will remain far from our knowledge. Not only is this distinction true for the conditions that attended the creation of our world, but it speaks to every event we may yet experience.

Summary

The First Law of Thermodynamics is considered by many to be the citadel of science, and it warrants a prominent role in our belief regarding origins.[16] However, regardless of what we may read or hear from time to time, the demonstrable fact remains: Natural processes neither annihilate material things out of existence, nor do they bring into existence observable things out of nothing. For example, we entrust jewels to a safe deposit box because we are confident that natural processes will not cause them to disappear, and we shop in supermarkets because we're sure that natural processes will not by themselves create food on our table. The First Law teaches that natural processes do not bring things into existence from nothing. But since things *do* exist, and since scientific data teaches that the universe *did* begin, it means that it was *not* born from anything natural. Thus, recent scientific discoveries argue for a creation that was supernatural.

4

HAS SCIENCE DISCOVERED SOMETHING THAT PROVES KARL MARX WRONG?

IN THIS CHAPTER we probe one of the deepest questions that can be raised: the question of ultimate reality.[1] In a sense, the enigma of existence is implicit in our earlier discussion regarding the origin of the universe. The existence of man cannot be divorced from the existence of the universe; its origin and that of life and, thus, of man all have one common source. They are part and parcel of one reality.

Before we proceed into the rough seas of this weighty question, let me define some terms we shall be using. By *universe,* the scientist means space joined with time—two aspects of a common reality. *Natural processes* are the events, anywhere they are found, that can be observed by man to operate according to natural laws. They also include the developments in living things. *Information* may be the most difficult of these terms to grasp. We so take for granted that a molecule of water, say, has certain properties—certain "information"—that we never give a moment's thought to the origin of those properties or what happens to them under differing conditions, such as heat or cold.

When a scientist, for example, analyzes and describes a physical object, recording its constituent parts and characteristics, his description contains "information" about that object. Such information is uniquely identifiable with that object alone. If he or she is describing a hydrogen atom, the sum total of the description of the atom's particles—its bits and pieces, their location and velocity and direction—is that atom's information.

Common Misunderstandings

How does man exist? Does he belong to this universe *and* to dimensions beyond it?[2] Or is man confined to physical matter that self-assembled into atoms, bacteria, and cosmos?[3]

The latter idea is popular today. A number of scenarios have been advanced—especially in recent years, with the discovery that our universe had a beginning. These scenarios conveniently forget to take into account the fact that *natural processes on average cannot and do not produce information.*

It is accepted that intelligence produces such information. This implies that intelligence is behind every living object in the universe. For example, dust particles contain a small amount of information; an oriental rug contains a greater amount; a vacuum cleaner contains still more; and the house in which these reside still more. The laws we use daily in science demand that increased information *must* attend any increase in organization such as the sequence of assembled objects I've just described.

But those who set forth natural scenarios either ignore this or treat it superficially.[4] The layman is often unaware that the production of information is necessary; thus, he may see no fundamental problem with nature producing the self-assembly process he reads about in a popular book or journal.

The spectrum of discussion regarding self-assembly goes from one extreme to another—from the universe "popping" into existence as a result of a quantum fluctuation,[5] to a happy accident in which chemicals bounce themselves into a living object.[6] All of these require incredible leaps of faith in the light of modern scientific laws that govern the systematic production of information.

One example of an alleged self-assembly process by nature is a commonly held theory regarding the stars. This says that way back near the beginning of time the stars were essentially uniform throughout the heavens. Those who hold this view say that if you were to examine any region of space at the beginning you would see that it contained the same number of stars as any other region, giving the stars a uniform appearance. However, with the passage of time, this initial symmetry of stars changed into the increased organization we see today. This appears to us as faster stars of greater number near the center, and fewer numbers of slower stars sprinkled along the outside of the star system.

This apparent structure, we are told, displays self-organization. The previous mix of uniform stars has now changed in a way that is understood to form structure. To use an earlier metaphor, the dust particles have assembled themselves into a house that contains the rug and vacuum cleaner.

Although the idea of natural self-assembly is interesting, it is nonetheless untrue. The "structure" we see in the heavens—the appearance of asymmetry, with numerous stars clustering here and there—tells us that the stars were *programmed* to be this way in the beginning. The Big Bang had within it imbalances that foreordained the structure we see today. However, the passage of time has magnified that original asymmetry a thousand times over.

The reason stars cluster is that they were never uniformly distributed. If a star system were truly uniform, the force acting on each star in any direction would be counterbalanced by a force of equal magnitude in the opposite direction. If the system is symmetric about its center, then we expect the symmetry to be preserved. This means that no star would change its velocity without a corresponding change elsewhere. Each star with its myriad sister stars would present one uniform stellar pattern across the skies.

The remarkable thing is that we see something quite different. We see structure that was foreordained from the very beginning of the universe. This immense information is on display throughout the heavens, and it proclaims an intelligence that is *more than* the material universe—an intelligence that was present before the beginning. Otherwise, the information has no source.

Consider another example. The human body is nature's highest organized structure. We know that the information within the body—its height, weight, color, sex, voice level, temperament, and everything that makes a body—is carried within the genes, which can only be observed under a special microscope developed just twenty-five years ago.

Scientifically, we might describe in the following way how that DNA information organizes chemicals into a human body: Unbalanced electrical forces between the side chains of twenty or so kinds of amino acid residues spontaneously fold a polypeptide gene product into a three-dimensional protein structure we call a body. The resultant structure was there all the time in the unseen information along the DNA strand. The development into a body is merely the consequence of asymmetries preexisting on a smaller, unseen level.[7]

All of the information necessary to assemble the structure—whether a body, the star system, or whatever—is present in the preexisting distribution. As for the universe, the information necessary to its formation is directly traceable to the initial condition that brought the universe into existence.[8] In principle, the ability of gravitational systems to undergo self-assembly is no different from what happens when water crystallizes into a snowflake. Natural forces merely produce movement of system parts in response to preexisting asymmetries. As time passes, the unseen microstructure is magnified into something that is easily seen. The more its organization, the greater is the information that an observer needs to describe it.

However, we need to exercise care in scientifically applying these concepts. For example, when water in the atmosphere produces snowflakes, ordinarily we might think that its organization had increased. But this is untrue. We actually need *less* information to describe the atmospheric water after it has changed into snowflakes than before. Why is this so? Because when water freezes, it creates countless millions of tiny ice crystals that have sixfold symmetry. Snowflakes also have this symmetry because they are made from numerous clumps of ice crystals. Since these crystals are identical to each other, the information that describes one ice crystal describes all ice crystals. Furthermore, there are constraints on the water molecules within the volume of any one ice crystal that limit the ways they can be arranged. This means that less information is needed to describe their whereabouts. Thus when atmospheric water changes into snowflakes, the system *loses* information. This isn't only true for snowflakes. It's true for *all* natural processes.

When we try to plumb the depths of the origin of the universe, we are really searching for the source of the original specifications that produced all that we see. What brought forth the "blueprints" that foreordained the universe and man? Everything in the world traces back to the initial condition that contained information. To explain the origin of these physical structures demands insight into the *source* of that information. Natural processes are mechanisms that allow things to unfold, but initial conditions foreordain the final product that we see.

For example, physical forces push apart the cloth that is tightly folded on a paratrooper's back, but the design and shape of the fabric and the way that it is packed foreordain the parachute it produces. We don't *see* the parachute until the moment it opens, but it's there in an unseen form from the beginning. The same is true of our world. Moments before it exploded into existence, it preexisted in the information that resided in the initial condition that gave it birth. The creation of the universe aligns with the *super*natural because natural processes do not, of themselves, produce the great magnitude of information present in the initial condition from which the universe unfolded. Scientifically speaking, in order to satisfy the constraints that are involved, the galaxies must have been "preformed" within the fabric of space-time before even the atoms were made.[9]

The Question of Ultimate Reality

In the last analysis, the question of ultimate reality seems to have one of two answers: The first is *God* and what he holds in being; the second is *matter* and what results from its motion. The latter view was championed by Karl Marx.[10]

Marx's thinking suffered from wrong ideas that were believed regarding the universe a hundred years ago; the thrust of his materialistic imaginings have led to a conception of physical matter as an erratic evolution of a frothing expanse of preexisting "something." Supposedly, this material randomly contorts and distorts itself into twisted permutations of every conceivable configuration over infinite time. Its internal interplay ultimately materializes a "magic" distribution that issues forth subnuclear particles with precisely the right properties for producing all that we see and are. Clearly, to explain the origin of the universe in this way is an act of faith—and one fraught with serious flaws.

For example, as living agents we affirm that all we see and are is a useful end for *us*. We perceive the hypothetical initial "magic" that produced everything as functioning toward a useful end—namely, human life. This then implies that since a natural process produced a magical distribution, which in turn produced us, our existence was inevitable, because the occurrence of the magical distribution over infinite time was a certainty.

In simpler terms, if there is infinite time, then everything that we see and are must eventually happen. Of course, the magic word is "if." But what is the origin of this infinite time? And what is the source of the matter that is able to productively undergo infinite contortions? Anything is possible for an uncritical mind, but this kind of picture is deceptively naive for several reasons.

Time   The consensus of scientists is that the universe, and therefore space and time, had a beginning. But if time had a beginning, how can one suppose that infinite time exists? To believe this is to ignore the verdict of an international jury of scientists who have declared otherwise. In other words, to believe in infinite time is not only to believe in something not supported by evidence, but to accept something that is contrary to it.[11] Some people may accept the idea of infinite time because it provides the unending opportunity for the world and life to appear without the conceptual necessity for God. However, the evidence indicating that our world, and therefore space-time, had a beginning teaches that the notion of infinite time is wrong. The beginning of space-time *means* the beginning of time.

Pleasure and Pain   A while ago, when we considered man's existence, we noted that the human body was "written" into the genes that comprise DNA. However, man is more than his body, and human life more than what is in the DNA blueprints. For example, materialistic belief ignores the mysterious qualities of pleasure and pain. But how can nonliving matter ultimately configure itself into beings that experience pleasure and pain? What is pleasure? And what is pain? What is their source, and why do they exist? How, for instance, do concepts such as horror and paradise have meaning other than in terms of an absolute private experience of unbearable pain or indescribable ecstasy? We know of no property of physical matter that could have produced these. Pleasure and pain are things that *people* experience. They have meaning only in terms of consciousness—and not matter.[12]

Individuality   Physical matter universally interacts in a way that would seem to preclude private experience. The laws governing chemicals on earth, for example, are the same as those that control physical matter on distant stars, and the forces that connect the two span the billions of light-years separating them. Einstein's theory teaches that the mass of these distant stars contributes to the forces creating cyclones and tornados on earth; the theory identifies gravitation as the mechanism by which they do so and gives us a mathematical tool to describe it.[13]

But the exercise of conscience is an individual matter which a materialistic concept of reality does not explain. How can private experiences materialize in a universal system where each part "knows" about every other part? If we materialized from a universal system and consist only of physical matter and its motion universally interacting, each with every other part, how is it that my thoughts are known only to me? And your thoughts are known only to you? The materialistic point of view fails to explain why certain common experiences are absolutely private.

Color   We all know what we mean by the color *green*. The experience is common to all of us when we look, for example, at grass. If I say to you, "Close your eyes and picture the color *green*," you know what I mean. You can easily picture it; "green" materializes in your mind.

Yet, despite the universality of this experience, it is absolutely impossible to describe what you know as "green" in your mind to a person born blind. In saying this, we are not speaking about the wavelength of electromagnetic radiation that activates electrical signals into your brain from your retina. Instead, we are speaking of what you experience in your mind when you look at grass and see "green." [14]

The property we know as "green" cannot be communicated using physical descriptives. No numbers, labels, or measurements allow us to convey "green" to someone born blind. Instead, it must be directly perceived. This suggests that the mental experience "green" that is activated by electrical signals into the brain, and that originates from within space and time, enables the mind to access something that properly belongs to a realm outside of physical reality. Were it otherwise, the mental experience "green" would reside within space and time and thus be capable of impartation by physical descriptives. However, and as we all know, it is *impossible* to communicate this experience. It must be directly accessed.

Life   The materialistic world view fails to account for life itself. We know, for example, that the union of a human sperm and egg precipitates a new living system that then undergoes continuous development into a third human being. But what is the origin of this new life? If, in its entirety, it resides in space and time, was it dispersed throughout the physical world prior to the sperm uniting with the egg? If dispersed, then what property of physical matter preserved its identity? And what distribution nourished its existence? Were there answers to these questions, they would serve to endow physical matter with supernatural qualities.

Or was it newly created at the moment of conception? If we say that, then we are forced to believe that nucleic acids eventually acquire awareness of their own existence when they are mixed. Again we ask: What magic quality of dead physical matter produces this?

Either approach leads us into serious problems. The first picture presents us with countless billions of unseen preexisting space-time life forms that become visible when sperms meet eggs, while the second scenario alleges that batches of chemicals become conscious when they are mixed. These distasteful alternatives arise because we started with a materialistic world view. But there is another world view that avoids these problems.

Consider again a person born blind who has never experienced the color *green*. One obvious explanation for his or her failing to undergo the mental experience "green" is that "green" resides in a realm outside the physical world of space and time, and that optical defects in the body disable signals into the brain that would give the mind access to that realm. However, this implies that the life in our brain may also reside in that other realm.

If so, then the physical distribution of the brain's gray matter can be understood as an interlocking pathway channeling life from that other realm into the space and time of our world. This would explain why a person born blind could experience life, but not "green." The distribution of gray matter develops within moments of conception, at the region where the sperm meets the egg. Thus the channel would be open from the time of conception. Thereafter, all that changes is the mechanism of physical nourishment, and the means by which oxygen is delivered to metabolize carbohydrate in the cells.[15]

The notion of channeling life from another realm into the space and time of our world is, in concept, not unlike our bringing music into the kitchen by means of a radio tuned to a particular station. In this metaphor, the kitchen is our world, the music is life, and the distant station is the other realm. Music enters the kitchen because the radio is tuned to a particular station. The tuning corresponds to the distribution of gray matter in our brain, serving as a connecting tunnel that links the other realm to our world.

For what purpose have I chosen this illustration? Certainly not to explain life in so simple a fashion as was outlined above. Instead, to show that a materialistic world view is a very limiting outlook. It denies us other options for dealing with the question of consciousness and life. Materialism forces us to view everything in the world in terms of matter and its motion. Stated differently, it explains the living in terms of the dead, and it extols the dead as though it were living.

Theism, however, removes this strait jacket by allowing us to explain life in terms of the living, and the highly organized world in terms of intelligence and design. It allows us to introduce "other realms" in much the same way that a shadow moving on the earth's surface can be explained by an airplane's flying past the sun; or, ripples in a brook can be understood in terms of rocks beneath its surface. Examples abound in which the visible owes its existence to the invisible. Is not a television picture explained in terms of invisible signals through space? And a hydrogen bomb explosion as the annihilation of atomic matter too small to see? In like manner, theism asserts that our world and all that lies within it owes its existence to an eternal Intelligence whose desires are revealed in the Bible, whose designs are displayed in nature, and whose decisions are recorded in history.[16]

Consciousness   Materialism offers no explanation whatever for the empirical fact that each of us is aware of his own existence. This consciousness also causes us to be aware of the passage of time—one of the most fundamental aspects of our existence. These attributes are alien to dead matter; rocks and bookcases and wastebaskets "know" nothing of them. Yet they constitute an integral part of the very fabric of our being.[17] Majestic sunsets, beautiful music, and tender love are the exclusive providence of human life. To assert that nonliving particles bounced themselves into an awareness and enjoyment of them strains the bounds of credulity.

Free Will   If human life came from a "magical" distribution of physical matter, then the laws governing it ought to govern us. But this does not appear to be the case. All laws governing physical matter can be expressed in differential form, meaning that initial conditions are necessary to precipitate that action.

For example, these laws tell us that a bullet fired from a rifle off the horizon of the earth travels along a parabolic path. But how high the bullet will go and where it will land is determined by the angle at which the rifle is held, and its muzzle velocity at the time it is fired. These initial conditions are specified by intelligence, not physical matter; and the angle at which the rifle is held and the amount of gunpowder in each bullet are decisions made by a conscious agent. Such decisions are not subject to quantum laws governing physical matter. Does not this teach us that the two—the conscious capacity for free choice, and the *in*voluntary unfolding of physical matter—are separate and distinct? [18]

Information   The presupposition that alleges that physical matter produces all we see and are fails in a most profound way for it ignores the scientific law that constrains physical matter from systematically generating information. However, no such constraint exists for intelligence. The New Generalized Second Law of Thermodynamics (discussed in later chapters) imposes fundamental limits on the information-producing capacity of nature. [19] In effect, it relegates nature to the status of an informational eunuch. Yet, if this is so, how do we explain the advent of the universe, living cells, and man? Matter and its motion are characterized by random activity that is incompatible with irreversible evolutive processes. Of itself, this does not deny the popular evolutive hypothesis, but it *does* demand a source for the information within the blueprint that guides it. The New Generalized Second Law disqualifies physical matter as this source because it mandates that, on average, nature must lose rather than gain information. Otherwise, nature becomes a perpetual motion machine. Theism, however, suffers no such constraint because it introduces the element of intelligence—something that we *know* produces information.

Observer   The belief that reality is "matter and its motion" has a basic flaw. It forces a human being (an observer) to fundamentally consist of a special arrangement of subatomic particles and their motion. But the quantum laws that describe the location of these particles tell us that in the absence of an observer a special arrangement is impossible, because they are not confined to any one place. Instead, they are "smeared" throughout space. It is therefore quite meaningless to conceptualize man as a magical distribution of subatomic entities because to do so requires that their material substance be located in specifiable regions in space. In other words, physical matter must be "localized" in order to form a human body; but if the observer (man) is only his body, then the body must preexist in order to localize the physical matter.

Let me illustrate. Consider a large lawn with green grass extending in all directions. A boy cuts the grass and then rakes it into one large pile just off one corner of the lawn. Before he cut the lawn, the grass in the pile was "smeared out" across the whole lawn. In the absence of an observer, this is how physical matter behaves; like grass on a lawn, it is spread throughout space. But the act of an intelligence *observing* the physical matter is like the boy who cuts and then rakes the grass into a pile—observing physical matter coalesces it into a heap that is confined to one region of space.

Ordinarily we call this heap a particle. If we have a large number of them, their location and velocity in space is called a distribution. The materialistic world view reduces man to a special distribution, a magical arrangement of locations and velocities of particles. But, as we have seen, man must first exist to coalesce the physical matter into the magical arrangement that is alleged to produce man. Here we have a chicken-and-egg problem. We need man (the chicken) to coalesce particles (the egg) to produce man (the chicken).

We can illustrate the problem another way. Consider the lawn metaphor just cited, but this time assume that the boy has no rake with which to do the job. The situation now is as follows: The boy needs to put grass into piles using a rake he will purchase with money obtained after he has put grass into piles. Metaphorically speaking, putting grass into piles is coalescing particles; man (the observer) is the rake that enables this to happen. But the rake (man) is a later result of the earlier piles of grass (particles).

Or think of a horse pulling a cart. The horse is the magical arrangement of particles, and the cart is man, the observer. The difficulty is that before the horse can pull the cart, quantum laws require the cart to pull the horse. In other words, the observer must first coalesce the particles. Only in this way can we get the special arrangement. But the special arrangement is alleged to be the observer. We therefore need what we don't have—the observer—in order to get what we need—the special arrangement that makes the observer.

To say that the chaotic motion of lifeless particles eventually endowed itself with a living awareness of its own existence is to suggest the logically impossible. Such a hypothesis implicitly presupposes that an observer exists to materialize particles for magical arrangement, while at the same time alleging that such an observer is a consequence of the materializing process.[20]

One way out of this perplexing dilemma is to assume the existence of a Supreme Observer. Then, out of all of the ways that matter could distribute itself, he can materialize precisely the right distribution to produce our world. In effect, he is the gardener who cuts the lawn and piles the grass in exactly the right locations. Left to its own accord, grass grows everywhere. It doesn't cut itself into any special arrangements. Likewise, physical matter smears itself throughout space. Although he is unseen, the special arrangements of subatomic particles throughout the world bear witness to him, a Supreme Observer, in the same way that piles of grass attest to the existence of a gardener.

Two Realities   There is yet another flaw in the materialistic world view—a flaw that reaches to the very taproot of reality itself. New insights into the nature of reality from quantum physics show that everything in the world we commonly regard as physical or material obeys quantum laws. These include all that we see and touch, what we measure and generally regard as real. Such things are called "quantum objects" because they obey quantum laws. However, a second category of objects does *not* obey quantum laws. Instead, they harmonize with the system of laws that were believed to describe reality roughly before the turn of the century. These are called "classical objects." For example, a classical object is an observer or intellect, what the Bible calls "spirit."

This discovery is profound, because it indicates that reality consists of two substances, not one. The correct world view is *not* only matter and its motion (quantum objects), but observers or intelligences (classical objects) coexisting as separate components of a twofold system. Scientifically speaking, the simplest conclusion forced upon us by quantum laws is that the joint system of an observer and physical matter cannot be described by a wave function after they interact; instead, they comprise a *mixture*.[21] These new insights are the kiss of death to materialistic philosophy and to dialectical materialism. Simply put: Karl Marx misunderstood reality. He was wrong.[22]

Summarizing and Clarifying

The ten items I have touched upon in this chapter may be thought of as separate arrows converging onto one bull's eye. Namely, reality is *more* than physical matter. Scripture revealed this thousands of years ago, and now we are starting to catch up to it. Quantum physics is teaching us that there really is something beyond the physical stuff we see—something the Bible calls "spirit." We love, we fear, we experience emotions and consciousness, all because we are spirit (intelligence) as well as matter (quantum object).

It is instructive to realize what is happening today. Scientific understandings are converging on biblical truths. Although written thousands of years ago, Scripture teaches that the world had a beginning—and now science agrees. The Bible also teaches that the world came into existence from nothing—a revelation now echoed in the literature by an accepted cosmological theory.[23] The notion that man is more than his body is a biblical concept. Now quantum laws show us that the observer is indeed separate and distinct from the quantum objects he observes.

Moreover, the universe in which he lives is seen from the First Law not to have arisen of its own accord. Nature is not a magician that can make things appear out of thin air, and natural processes are not quantum burps that grow into other worlds. Nature has no free lunch, and cannot create something out of nothing. As discussed in chapter 3, quantum fluctuations can give rise to bubbles that can inflate, but they cannot percolate. Recall our boiling water and expanding pot analogy. Although fluctuations can produce bubbles that can form and inflate, the pot grows so fast that they never reach the water's surface.* However, things *do* exist. Since natural processes do not pop things into existence from nothing, the obvious answer is that some *un*natural process did it.

There is, however, another point to consider. For the sake of argument, let's hypothesize some obscure natural process that, of its own accord, produces an unlimited number of universes by means of quantum fluctuations. Let's be generous and allow the "bubbles" generated by these fluctuations to circumscribe every conceivable distribution of physical matter. However, by definition, this process, and everything that proceeds from it, is subject to quantum laws—laws that teach that *none* of the universes it creates can be ours unless we are there to witness it.** Since observers are classical objects, human intelligence is not subject to quantum laws. How then can we be the result of a quantum fluctuation that such laws brought into being?

Whoever accepts a materialistic world view ought to consider one final point. Thought processes supersede the external world, not vice versa. The reason is that consciousness is the *primary* element. In principle, the external world *can* be denied—but it is logically *impossible* to deny consciousness. Do so, and you deny the very ground of your being. If you doubt this, then the very doubt you profess has proved the existence of what you are doubting. But since you are doubting that consciousness cannot be denied, for you to deny "consciousness" is to destroy the very doubt that you profess. Thus it is logically impossible to deny consciousness. This is what led Rene Descartes to write: "I think, therefore I am" (*Discourse on Method,* 1637).

Niels Bohr understood this very well. He wrote:

> The word consciousness, applied to ourselves as well as to others, is indispensable when dealing with the human situation.[24]

Eugene Wigner, in quoting Bohr, goes on to say:

> In view of this, one may well wonder how materialism, the doctrine that "life could be explained by sophisticated combinations of physical and chemical laws," could so long be accepted by the majority of scientists.[25]

---

* An early rapid growth of the universe explains its huge entropy, homogenous mixing, flatness problem, and absence of magnetic monopoles. These are defined in the Glossary.

** *Our* universe is that distribution of physical matter whose interactions we affirm as coherent under a pattern of logical relations in our mind that align with the pattern of physical laws we discover through measurement.

5

WHY CAN'T AN ACCIDENT DESIGN A MACHINE?

WHEN WE INQUIRE into the question of origins, we are inevitably confronted with the challenge of explaining *how* a particular physical structure came into being.[1] This structure can be a living cell, or the universe itself. The difficulty in explaining the origin of such structures is that the knowledge we seek pertains to something that happened *only once*. A living cell persists by reproduction,[2] and the universe by expansion.[3] Yet both had a beginning. The question is, can we ascertain how it happened?

The Role of Science

Events that are reproducible lend themselves to scientific inquiry. Events that are unpredictable lend themselves to statistical inquiry. But *singular events lend themselves to "legal" inquiry*. The creation of the world or of life are one-time happenings, thus lending themselves to such legal inquiry. The same, incidentally, can be said of the bodily resurrection that history records for Jesus Christ (a one-time happening).[4] We must ask what role science can play in such questions.

Since science is properly concerned with reproducible events, it has no jurisdiction whatsoever in questions of origin or destiny. It can and does, however, gather *evidence* in support of one interpretation or another. In other words, it "assists the court" in gathering evidence on which the jury (you and I) renders a verdict. Unfortunately, we as jurists cannot be entirely objective because we are personally affected by the outcome.

For example, if the universe and all of life were intentionally created by an eternal Being, then the eternal destiny of "the jury" may very well depend on its response to his demands. Conversely, if an accident produced it all, then human life is the highest authority and we can live as we please without fear of damning reprisal.

What Are Our Options?

When we ask how a particular physical structure originated, we are really asking how the particular configuration of physical matter came to be organized into what we see. In principle, we can imagine countless possible ways of positioning physical matter throughout space, and of arranging for its motion. Each of these ways is called a distribution. Yet we as observers are inspecting the situation *after* any one of these particular configurations or structures is in place. How are we to know what brought about the particular distribution we see? There are at least three possibilities: causal happening, intentional arrangement, and accidental circumstance.

The first possibility, that of casuality, attributes the particular placement and motion of the physical matter to a long sequence of connected events that ultimately trace to the properties of the subnuclear parts composing the physical matter. In other words, the end product is the result of a long sequence of cause and effect happenings.

The second interpretation, that of intentional arrangement, is that an "intelligence" purposed the particular organization we see in order to produce some desired end result. This final happening thus occurs because of the way the various parts functionally interact with themselves in yielding the intended outcome.

The third idea presupposes that everything happens as a result of random events, and that neither of the above is true; instead, the particular distribution observed has occurred by pure chance through the accidental interplay of the subnuclear parts over extended or even endless time periods.

In attempting to learn which of these three possibilities is responsible for, say, the structure of the universe, we need to recognize that we have before us two, not three, choices. The reason is that causal happenings just shift the question farther back in time. If everything that we see and touch is the result of a long sequence of events caused by the one before, then we must ask how the particular physical properties of the subnuclear parts that led to the structure originated. This is really the question: Is the causal happening due to intentional arrangement or accidental circumstance? In fact, all such inquiries ultimately lead to the question: Does what we see originate from accident or design?

What Makes an Arrangement Special?

At this juncture, it's helpful to realize that of the countless possible ways physical matter can be located in space and time (space-time), *the only ones of importance are those we acknowledge to be of interest.* For example, suppose that you require a hot fudge sundae with butter pecan ice cream, whipped cream, and a cherry. If you're told that the only available ice cream is vanilla, that doesn't do it. Or you're told they have everything but the hot fudge. That doesn't do it either.

We can imagine a lot of different things that can be put into a glass cup, but if you require a hot fudge sundae with butter pecan ice cream, whipped cream, and a cherry, then *that is what's important to you.* It is likewise with these "distributions" we are discussing; the only ones of importance are those that will unfold into our universe. Nothing else will do. Everything has to be in place to produce the universe, and any departure from what's needed will *not* bring into existence the universe that we see.

This means that although accidents may, in principle, position physical matter in all different kinds of ways, the only ones of importance are those that generate our universe. But it's here that we run into an amazing thing. Compared to all of the different possible ways physical matter can be accidentally arranged, the number of them capable of bringing the universe that we know into existence is vanishingly small.

As far as we know, there is only one arrangement of physical matter that corresponds to our universe. It isn't that large numbers of arrangements are not possible, but rather, only one of them is important. Only one of them *will work.* Thus, the likelihood of an accident having created a universe suited for us is, for all practical purposes, zero. So *unlikely* is such an event that a wind storm through a junkyard would have a better chance of creating a rocket to the moon.

When a particular arrangement of physical matter interacts with itself to produce something that holds meaning for us, the arrangement is special, and the physical system is said to "function with organizational coherence." The reason is that its end result harmonizes with what we, the observer, require.

For example, we could list a number of things on earth that interact with each other to produce the stable temperature we enjoy.[5] Although these parameters are discussed in a later chapter, we can say that their organization is special because they functionally interact to give us something we need— namely, the right temperature. The particular way that these things are set up is *un*likely because, of the many possible ways that they *could* have been arranged, the way that they *are* arranged is precisely what we need. There is thus a very special relationship between the *way* we find things organized, and the interplay that precisely aligns with the needs of the life those things sustain. This means that a particular arrangement of physical matter is special not in a statistical sense, but rather in terms of the special needs of the life it serves.

Intended versus Accidental Arrangements

This important concept allows us to compare an "intended" versus an "accidental" arrangment, and leads us to the notion of design, which can be illustrated by considering an airplane. We can arrange, for example, the parts of an airplane to be distributed in a hundred different ways. We can put one wing in the front and one in the back, or we can reposition the engines to point toward the ground, and so forth. Each of these different arrangements of the airplane's parts will produce a different "system" response when power is applied.

For instance, one way to lay out the parts of an airplane is to aim the blast of hot engine exhaust directly at the fuel tanks in the wing. The system response in such a case will be an explosion. Conversely, when the parts are arranged in the ordinary way, the system response is for the plane to fly. Since this is what we *desire*, we say that this particular distribution of the airplane's parts is *organizationally coherent*. All of the parts interact in such a fashion as to produce an end result that is *harmonious with the intent of our will*, namely, the airplane flies.

Ordinarily, the specification that describes this particular distribution of the airplane's parts is called the design of the airplane. We say that something is designed when it functions *in the way intended.*

Any distribution of the airplane's parts that would direct hot exhaust gases at the fuel tanks—and thus result in an explosion—is one that obviously would not be in harmony with our intent. It does not exhibit organizational coherence because it functions to yield a useless result. End products that are of no value occur when the parts of a physical system are positioned by accidents instead of intelligence. In short, things "work well" when they are *designed* well, and the *essence of design is intent toward a useful end.*

How Do We Know When Something Is Designed?

A physical system is any distribution of physical matter—a clock, a cloud, or a cotton ball. When a living agent examines a physical system, the information contained in his description will image the way he observes its parts to be arranged. Information theory introduced in 1949 [6] made it possible for the first time in man's recorded history to quantify the degree to which he could specify a physical system. Whenever man quantifies something he assigns numbers to it, and whenever intelligence precisely specifies system quantities in this way, the description is said to contain information. In principle, a living agent is free to observe *any* physical system, but the systems we *choose* to observe are those that are of interest to us.

In other words, we choose to look at those systems that we discern to function toward some useful end (in the broadest possible sense of the word). And our descriptions of such systems contain *useful information* because the locations and motions of the system parts they specify are the *only* locations and motions that produce what we need when they interact.

In addition to systems that seem to naturally exist (sand dunes, serpents, and snowflakes), we create some of our own. For example, by arranging glass, metal, and phosphor in a certain way we can make a television set. Since this particular distribution of physical parts functions in the way intended, we say that it has purpose. The "useful information" in our description of the distribution of its parts (glass, metal, and phosphor) is called its design. Thus, a physical system is said to be designed when an observer discerns that the arrangement of its parts *functions with intention.*

Was the Universe Designed?

The question of origins is the question of whether or not natural systems that function toward useful ends were *intended* to function that way. For example, the universe is a physical system that functions toward a useful end. Was it *intended* to function that way? If so, then *it was designed.* In principle, all physical systems can be observed and therefore, described. But does each description contain useful information? Does what we see have physical parts that interact and function toward useful ends that are aligned with our desires? And if so, do we say they were *designed* to do so, or do we say that their existence is the result of an accident?

For example, the bateleur (snake eagle) ordinarily flies at speeds above fifty miles per hour, and in wind currents it glides without effort at speeds in excess of a hundred miles per hour. One would think that the severe turbulence identified with thermal updrafts would disrupt its flight. Yet once aloft, although the bateleur scarcely beats its wings, it flies for hours on end covering distances of over two hundred miles a day. Moreover, it performs impressive aerobatic feats, including full rolls.

The reason for its great success is its highly functional way of reducing turbulence in the immediate vicinity of its wings. Separate feathery protrusions along the trailing edge of its near six-foot wingspan reduce turbulence to very tiny eddies. As it turns out, this reduced turbulence is exactly what we desire for our high speed aircraft. Therefore, the same technique has now been incorporated into later versions of airplane wing designs. But are we to regard the structure along the bateleur's wings as *intended* to function that way, or do we say it is the result of an accident?

At this point, one can choose to believe that it is the product of "natural selection." But that is not an explanation; it is only a *label.* For the sake of discussion, even if natural selection were true, the question we would then need to ask is, who or what is the origin of this miraculous catchall named "natural selection" that transforms confusion into design? Why should dead cosmic dust create living organisms with wonder-working machinery that self-assembles molecules into miraculous biological systems exhibiting technology that dwarfs human ingenuity?

Or consider a shark, when it bites the sand to catch a flounder. Hidden below the surface, the flounder is motionless. How does the shark know the flounder is there? The answer is neither sound nor vibration nor odor. Instead, the shark possesses a fantastically sophisticated three-dimensional electric field detector that senses the muscle and body potentials of the floun-der. The high sensitivity of this system can be compared to our knowing the precise whereabouts of a single flashlight battery located about two thousand miles away (fifty nanovolts per cm).[8]

Or consider the black warbler. Here is a bird that weighs about one-third of an ounce; it loads up on fat half again its weight, and takes off from northeast Canada to fly past Bermuda and on toward the African coast. From there it flies to South America, reaching the Venezuelan coast after four days and five nights of nonstop flying at a fuel economy of over seven hundred thousand miles per gallon.[9] We might ask, "If natural selection produced so wondrous a flying machine, why did it deny this little bird oil for its feathers?" Since it flies over oceans, one might think that nature would have provided oil for its feathers so that it could have "pit stops" along the way. As it is, its flight *must* be essentially nonstop.

One reason that natural selection is an empty phrase is that we can create any story to defend it. For example, we can explain the absence of oil in the black warbler's feathers by saying that it's nature's way of keeping the bird out of the ocean, and therefore from drowning. Conversely, if it turned out that its feathers *did* have oil, we could argue that the oil is there to keep the black warbler from sinking, since it flies over water. The point is that one can always create a story to explain something after the fact. Given any fact, the human mind can conjure up any number of reasons to explain that fact.

Biological miracles are everywhere, but natural selection provides no sober insight into their origin. Rather, it is an ill-defined concept of "fitness" that decades of research have failed to operationalize.[10] Natural selection no more explains living systems than does natural affection explain the people who express it. Stories are fabricated *after* the fact, and its failure as a research tool stems from the recent discovery that it has *no explanatory power.*[11] These points are more fully discussed in a later chapter.

Nature's miracles are found not only among the fish that swim and the birds that fly, but also among the creatures that crawl. The bombardier beetle (*Brachinus*), for instance, is a bizarre insect with a defense system that's a cross between a gas bomb and an automatic rifle.[12] Externally, the beetle has two rear nozzles that can be rotated like a bomber's gun turret. Internally, it has two chambers, each with chemicals that are harmless when kept apart (24 percent hydrogen peroxide and 10 percent hydroquinone). But when an enemy approaches, the chemicals are internally mixed into an explosive gas, which the beetle pumps out its rear nozzles at temperatures above 200 degrees Fahrenheit. And it is able to perform this feat up to twenty times a day!

Or, consider the porpoise. Special fat cells resembling machine oil (isovaleric acid) are distributed throughout its forehead (melon) to form a very complex three-dimensional acoustic lens.[13] High-frequency sound waves generated at the base of its blowhole are focused by this lens into a very narrow beam, which is then reflected back to the porpoise, thereby allowing it to navigate through the water at high speed. Some evidence suggests that this lens also functions as a "stun gun" by channeling large bursts of sound energy into the water to immobilize prey, which the porpoise then rapidly overtakes.[14] The reason that a porpoise can swim so fast (over forty miles per hour) is because spongy material within its loose, finely-laced, layered skin rhythmically vibrates with movements that virtually match laminar flow, and that reduce its drag by 90 percent. We don't use the idea in our submarines because, as a practical matter, we can't reproduce the material.

The Cosmic Dust Religion

But how can the random interaction of nonliving matter produce structures so sophisticated that our most advanced technology seems pale by comparison? How did such magic originate? Even if we say that it ultimately traces to the physical properties of subnuclear particles, we are then led to ask, "How did they arise?" [15] Why, for example, does an electron have *exactly* the electrical charge and mass that it does? [16] Why is it that light travels at precisely the speed it does? [17] And who or what dialed the value of the gravitational "constant"? [18]

Some suppose that these things are the result of natural processes, *but there is not one shred of factual evidence to support such a belief.* [19] As a matter of fact, the physical universe in which these processes express themselves is itself the result of mysterious origin. The belief that this origin is "natural" is an act of faith because the word *natural* only has meaning in terms of the existing world—not in terms of the ill-defined realm that preceded it. Yet, if a Supreme Intelligence is behind it, are we able to accept that? If God actually designed and created our world, could we ever believe it? Or is our nature disposed to invalidate anything produced by an Agent outside our control?

Is the Best Explanation Intelligence?

The "machines" that I chose to discuss were the snake eagle, shark, black warbler, bombardier beetle, and porpoise. But these biological wonders are just the tip of the iceberg. There are approximately 11 million species of life on earth, and *each one is a living miracle.* They are the result of mind-boggling organizational intricacies at the molecular level that leave us in awe. The thirty-sixth edition of *Gray's Anatomy* contains 1,578 pages, each with a superficial description of a subsystem of the human body. I defy any honest, rational person to open that book to the first example, examine it, say it happened by chance—then turn and examine the next page, say it happened by chance, and so on. See how far you get! The point is that these organic structures present us with a degree of complexity we cannot explain mechanistically.

The most heroic attempts to explain life by many brilliant minds are akin to "explaining" that a car moves because it has four wheels. To a child this *is* an explanation because it describes the extent to which he can see. Likewise, the biological hypotheses we create make sense to us because they align with the shallow depth to which we see. But a superficial understanding of even the simplest of structures unveils stupendous levels of microscopic cooperation among physical interactions found throughout the universe. These interactions depend upon myriad unseen locations, motions, and subatomic parameters so precise that our attempts at explaining life resemble a blindfolded monkey throwing darts at the moon. This is not to say that we shouldn't try to explain things, but to plead for sobriety when claiming that accidents create machines.

Everything we know tells us that machines are structures intelligence designs, and that accidents destroy. Therefore, accidents do not design machines. Intellect does. And the myriad of biological wonders that sprinkle our world testify to the design ingenuity of a Supreme Intellect. This is the simplest explanation—yet the one that is most rejected. The English scholar William of Occam formulated a principle known in science as Occam's Razor. Succinctly put, the principle states that the simplest theory that fits the facts corresponds most closely to reality. In our case, the simplest theory is that Intelligence rather than accidents designed the living structures that populate planet earth.

6

WHAT ROLE DOES ENTROPY PLAY IN DESTINY?

THE NEXT TWO chapters deal with some heavy material. They are concerned with an unseen quality that all physical things possess, called entropy. Although perhaps unfamiliar, the word is over one hundred years old. This chapter has been included to explain what it is—and what it is not.[1] Understanding its meaning will prove valuable to all readers, both technical and nontechnical alike.

The word *entropy* is used to describe a certain mathematical quantity [2] that is quite important in any discourse on origins; [3] as such, it is mentioned in later chapters as well. Hopefully, presenting it here will give most readers a clear and accurate picture of its meaning, along with insight into changes that occur in our world. Although this chapter may require some effort, it is worthwhile in our quest for knowledge about origins.

As scientists learned more about the universe, the meaning of the word *entropy* underwent change in our century. Today it is widely misunderstood, even among technical people. Although it is my purpose to clarify the misunderstanding as we proceed, the changes in meaning are discussed in a later chapter.

Entropy is a mathematical quantity that allows scientists to measure the way physical systems change. It doesn't matter whether we're talking about a tennis ball or the sun, a galaxy or a razor blade. Everything possesses entropy which changes with the passage of time. As we have seen, the First Law teaches that mass and energy are conserved.[4] *The Second Law teaches that, on average, the entropy of any physical system increases with the passage of time.* [5] But what is entropy?

Some Old Ideas

Entropy was recognized when Nicolaus Carnot pioneered fictitious engine cycles in 1824.[6] Rudolf Clausius stated the earliest version of the Second Law in 1850, and in 1865 he coined the word *entropy* [7] to describe an unusual mathematical quantity that he had discovered.*

In 1896 Ludwig Boltzman recognized the close relationship between this quantity and the way gas molecules move at differing speeds. He showed that the molecular velocity distribution had all of the observable properties of Clausius's "entropy." However, Boltzman identified it with spontaneous heat change.[8] This concept underwent further refinement in the early decades of the twentieth century, leading to the notion of entropy in terms of heat exchange.

However, widespread confusion persisted concerning entropy's real meaning, and this led to the misuse of the term by a number of authors, even in recent times.[9] But despite the confusion, scientists agreed that it was important, and showed a growing awareness of its utility in expressing the way physical things change with the passing of time.[10]

How Do We Know That Entropy Always Increases?

Entropy is simply the *name* of a mathematical expression that measures the degree to which energy becomes less available for useful work with the passage of time. In this sense, entropy is a measure of the deterioration of the energy that an observer deems useful—and it is the observer who gives meaning to the term "useful." Entropy always increases because as time passes, the kinds of energy that do useful work continue to change into a form that is less available for such work.

For example, air that is released from a balloon exhibits pressure that could be channeled to do useful work, such as turning a windmill connected to an electric generator. But air randomly distributed throughout a room cannot do useful work because it is as likely to move in one direction as the other; each movement is canceled by an equal but opposite movement, giving zero net pressure, on average, in any one direction.

Early in the twentieth century there was scientific consensus that nature moved in one direction—entropy always increased during any physical change. But here an error developed: Entropy began to be identified with *disorder.* The reason was that nature was observed to change from states that were well defined to those that were confused and in disarray. This seemed particularly true when, for example, water changed into steam. But to see *why* nature moved in this one-way direction, we need to look at things on a much smaller scale.

Scientists are convinced that everything in the physical world is composed

---

* The mathematical function discovered by Clausius was a "differential" whose integral vanished around a closed path.

of tiny elements called atoms. We believe that there are ninety-two useful kinds, and that different combinations are organized into "building blocks" called molecules. This picture allows us to understand the materials that we see and touch, such as glass or wood. For example, water is made from molecules that contain hydrogen and oxygen atoms. A glass of water contains many billions of these molecules, which are always moving around and bumping into each other. The hotter the water, the more collisions among the molecules and, therefore, the greater the confusion in this tiny molecular world. Water molecules that are used to make a hot cup of tea are, therefore, in greater disarray than those used to make iced tea.

In the case of iced tea, the water is colder so that the water molecules move more slowly and collide less; this means they are more ordered. If they are made cold enough, the water changes to ice and they almost stop moving altogether. In this case, each water molecule remains more or less in place, a picture very different from when the water is hot and the molecules are colliding helter-skelter. Thus, unlike ice, the molecules in hot water are very disordered.

Many people wrongly identify the word *entropy* with the disordered state [11] (e.g., colliding water molecules in hot tea). Since the Second Law teaches that entropy increases with the passage of time,[12] they conclude that disorder must do likewise and the result is a wrong understanding of the Second Law—namely, the erroneous idea that entropy and disorder are the same, and that since entropy always increases, disorder must do likewise.[13] Let's illustrate this with an example.

In your mind's eye, picture an ice cube slowly melting from heat flowing into it. As water forms and as more and more heat raises the water temperature, its molecules move faster and faster. Since heat flows from hot to cold, the colder parts of any system become more disordered as they heat up. But what about the hot parts that supply the heat? They, of course, cool down. This means that their molecules are moving slower and are therefore becoming more ordered, whereas the colder parts that heat up from gain of heat become more disordered.

The Second Law requires that, *on average, the total entropy must increase.* However, if the entropy increase required a net increase in disorder, it would force us to believe that the increase in disorder as the colder parts heat up exceeds the decrease in disorder as the hotter parts cool down. Many people believe that the Second Law teaches this. But they are wrongly identifying entropy with disorder, and they wrongly understand the Second Law to require that the total disorder in both the cold and the hot parts (the total system) must increase.

A Popular Yet Naive Fantasy

What has entropy to do with disorder? The truth is, practically nothing. Yet a common belief is that the two are one and the same. Entropy can be *correlated* with disorder, but not *identified* with it. For example, think of entropy as rain and disorder as your umbrella. Each time it rains your umbrella gets wet, thus rain and wet umbrellas correlate; they both appear at the same time. But although they are correlated, they are not related; i.e., there is no direct connection between your umbrella and rain clouds. Should you decide to stay home when it rains, your umbrella won't get wet.

Entropy can be correlated with disorder in the same way rain can be correlated with your umbrella—but even that correlation is valid only in three special cases: ideal gases, isotope mixtures, and crystals near zero degrees Kelvin.[14]

Not only is entropy wrongly identified with disorder; the error has caused some people to introduce a nonsensical thing called "negentropy." [15] This idea assumes that negative entropy exists, and that it can be identified with order. It says that the onset of life was accompanied by a change in negentropy that just balanced the increase in entropy, and that this change explains the order found in life.

However, the idea of negentropy is quite wrong because it is defective in several basic ways.* Nevertheless, over the past twenty years a number of people have used this erroneous concept in an attempt to justify the creation of life by natural processes.[16] To understand how they do this, picture water in an ice cube tray in a refrigerator. Let the tray represent the earth, the refrigerator represent the sun, and the transition of water into ice, the creation of life. The order that arises when water becomes ice is said to be balanced by the disorder that occurs when the liquid refrigerant changes into a gas (molecules are in greater disarray in a gas than a liquid). The spontaneous creation of life is then justified by saying that the increased order in life corresponds to negentropy that is offset by the greater increase in entropy (disorder).

But life is *complex,* not ordered; and the basic natural process that changes water into ice is counterproductive to the creation of life because it results in a *loss* of complexity. The reason that ice is ordered and not complex is that ice is made up of millions of tiny atomic units that are identical to each other. This means that if we describe one of them, we will have described all of them. When water changes into ice, we actually need *less* information to describe the ice because its molecules no longer behave in an independent manner. It is less complex because we need less information to describe it. But unlike ice, life is vastly complex because we require staggering quantities of information to describe even the simplest of cells. Negentropy is thus an erroneous concept.

---

* (1) It is *conceptually flawed*—order and disorder are not identified with entropy.[17]
(2) It is *physically flawed*—it violates one-sided conservation laws.[18]
(3) It is *mathematically flawed*—the function describing our intuitive notion of disorder is unique when positive.[19]

When something becomes ordered, it becomes less complex. On the other hand, a living cell is a highly complicated structure whose description requires a vast amount of information. To explain life's origin we must explain the source of the information that resides in each cell. Whatever brought life into being involved an act which, rather than losing information, created it.

Notwithstanding the confused analogies between "life" and "crystals" that are sometimes found in books on origins,[20] the fact is that the latter are ordered whereas the former is complex. Therefore, to explain life's origin one must identify the source of the information (algorithms) embodied in the complexity along DNA. Yockey is particularly lucid on this point.[21] However, some writers, in their zeal to dissociate entropy from disorder, have inadvertently contributed to the confusion they sought to eradicate by also dissociating entropy from the concept of "information."* This latter error is very widespread[22] and is the reason why so many intelligent people mistakenly believe that nature can create life. The entropy that is germane to life concerns the distribution of *nucleotides* along DNA—and *not* the distribution in the levels of energy.**

The important truth for our discussion is that life isn't ordered; it is complex. We saw that clearly in chapter 4 in our consideration of the materialistic world view. An increase in organization of a structure—from simple dust particles to the oriental rug to the vacuum cleaner to the house (to repeat an earlier metaphor)—requires the systematic increase of information, but information is not produced by natural processes in the magnitude necessary to explain the origin of life.

Let's summarize what's been said thus far:
1. The Second Law requires entropy to increase.
2. Entropy cannot be identified with disorder.
3. Negentropy cannot be identified with order.
4. Ordered molecules (ice) present less information.
5. Living cells are not ordered—they are complex.

The Meaning of Entropy

If entropy isn't disorder, then what is it?

We said earlier that it's the name of a mathematical expression that measures how the form of energy changes with the passage of time. However, we can gain greater insight into the nature of this change by considering

---

* Although this latter term is commonly understood in the general sense of knowledge, the word is used in science to mean the logarithm of the probability of the corresponding state of a physical system.[23]

** All natural distributions exhibit entropy, but the entropy of one distribution has *nothing whatever* to do with that of another. Thermodynamic and genetic entropy respectively describe the energy *path* and *plan* of an organism. They've been confused for decades.

the most modern sense of the word's meaning. Picture in your mind a nurse operating a slide projector displaying an eye chart on a large wall screen as in an eye examination. At the top is a very large letter, followed by two somewhat smaller letters below. Each subsequent line on the chart contains greater numbers of letters, but of diminishing size.

Now suppose that while viewing this white chart with its black letters, you are asked by the nurse operating the slide projector to take an eye exam. You agree to take the test and after doing so the nurse reports your score as 20:20.

Distrustful of so perfect a result, she asks you to retake the eye exam. Again you agree, and your score is 23:23, a result almost the same as the first. Certain that your eyes have not deteriorated over the short span of several minutes, you request a third exam and are given one. This time your score is 27:27.

Perplexed, you discuss the matter with the nurse. You wonder whether her telling you the score affected the result of the test. Although skeptical, she agrees to withhold future scores until four additional tests are completed. Now you score, in sequence, 30:30, 34:34, 39:39, and 45:45. Despite the larger numbers, these scores convince you that your eyes have not deteriorated, for why should both eyes change in exactly the same way? Also, how could so large a deterioration in eyesight occur in the short span of time over which the tests were administered? Yet the scores also convince you that each time you take a test, you do more poorly than the time before. Something is changing, but what?

The answer, of course, is that the eye chart is changing. Looking over at the projector, you see smoke rising above the lamp. Heat from the bulb was ever-so-slightly warping the slide, causing it to gradually go out of focus so that the image on the wall screen was losing its sharpness and becoming progressively defocused.

This is precisely the concept of entropy. With the passage of time, the physical world undergoes gradual "defocusing" to an observer. The way this deterioration manifests itself is that energy becomes less available for useful work with the passage of time.

Useful work is accomplished when physical objects undergo *directed* motion in space. An observer's act of describing the motion of the objects produces information—information that is true about the movement of the objects at the time the observation is made. However, with the passage of time, the motion continues, now unobserved, rendering the observer less able to direct the objects in the way desired—and thus accomplish useful work—because of his growing uncertainty of the objects' whereabouts.

In the words of the New Generalized Second Law, an observer functioning within a closed system will lose, but never gain, information.[24] In essence, this result follows from the fact that all measurements yield incomplete information; an observer's uncertainty increases with the passage of time (your scores on the eye test). *Entropy is this uncertainty.* These simple words come from some rather deep physics, parts of which are outlined in simplified ways in other chapters. (For further discussion of the more technical aspects of entropy and its relationship to the Second Law, see Appendix 2.)

In summary, entropy is a mathematical expression that allows scientists to assign numbers measuring the degree to which energy deteriorates into less useful forms with the passage of time. This decay corresponds to the progressive decline of an observer's ability to extract useful work from the system due to his growing uncertainty of the whereabouts of the physical objects described by him at an earlier time.

When rigorously formulated with all of the "bells and whistles" the observer must be included as part of the system that is described. The mathematical expression that assigns numbers is found to measure also the observer's uncertainty of the location and velocity of every object within the system, and at each instant of time. The New Generalized Second Law is a formal mathematical statement showing that the decline on average of an observer's information is an inevitable result of the passing of time, and that the total information available to an observer cannot exceed what exists in the system's overall description.

These considerations impose important constraints on the theory of the chemical origin of life, and the commonly held belief that natural laws can energize biological structures into increasing levels of complexity. Virtually all attempts to justify these ideas have focused upon the thermodynamic flow of energy in an organism, rather than on the genetic blueprint by which the flow is controlled. This unfortunate confusion has created the false impression that living organisms sprang from dead chemicals, and that their progeny prospered under processes which, under any other circumstance, would be regarded as the inspired product of intellect.

WHAT ELUSIVE NEW LAW
GOVERNS ALL LIVING SYSTEMS?

WORTHWHILE PURSUITS require effort, and to probe reality requires heroic effort. But it is worth it, because destiny is our goal. The material in this chapter may stretch the reader at places—but I encourage you to follow through. Examples will be given that will, hopefully, illustrate the ideas and illuminate their meaning.

What Is the Second Law?

The Second Law of Thermodynamics can be an intimidating phrase. We can view it as the Second Law of Science (the First Law was discussed in chapter 1). I've studied the Second Law for over twenty-five years and I am convinced that it's the most misunderstood and misused law in all of science. Creationists (wrongly) use it to say that evolution is impossible,[1] and evolutionists (wrongly) use it to show that natural processes are equivalent to the activity of intelligence.[2] With the discovery of new knowledge,* the Second Law underwent revision, and was replaced by the *New Generalized Second Law* of Thermodynamics. The older Second Law is a special case of the New Generalized Second Law.

In the thirties and forties,[3] the Second Law was expressed in terms of the ability of a physical system to spontaneously change its heat content, e.g., water freezing into ice. This old idea was perpetuated by some authors into the fifties and sixties.[4] Other writers, however, grasped the part played by "intellect" in physical reality, and either implied[5] or introduced[6] the role of the observer in the Second Law. The result was the union for the

---

* Information Theory and Quantum Statistical Mechanics

first time of "uncertainty" with the thermodynamic variables of a physical system. For the time being we can think of the elusive concept of uncertainty as akin to guessing at the shapes of treetops with satellite photos as our only source of information.

In the seventies, however, a field of science known as Quantum Statistical Mechanics developed, and what emerged was a far more general and sweeping law of which the older law was a special case. Twenty years earlier, information theory appeared. Its insights allowed man for the first time in human history to quantify his participation in the system that he measured. This interaction between intelligence and measured objects is the focal point of the New Generalized Second Law,* and, while in principle biological evolution is not forbidden, this law does impose severe contraints on how natural structures can change.

In this newer and truer way of describing things, heat content is expressed in terms of a microscopic world that involves the *location* and *motion* of atomic particles. As discussed in the preceding chapter, entropy is identified with the uncertainty of an observer taking measurements and is a barometer of the one-way direction of natural processes. Although this may be unfamiliar to some people, the reader need only understand this: Modern science has shown that the older law is merely a special situation of the New Generalized Second Law, which, in simple language, can be summarized as follows: *On average, things mix.*

The Old Versus the New

We can contrast the traditional Second Law with the New Generalized Second Law using the following example: Imagine that we're in a park beside a quiet pond and someone takes a picture of it. Then, I take a rock and throw it high into the air over the pond. The rock comes down and makes a big splash in the center of the pond; and ripples emanate from the pond's center and travel toward its circular bank. Fifteen minutes later, with the rock now at the bottom of the pond, everything is quiet. Again, someone takes a picture of the pond.

The things described by the old law are very much like what we see in the two pictures. The traditional law can only describe things that are at rest, just like before and after the rock was thrown. But it can make no pronouncements and can draw no conclusions while the rock is being thrown or while ripples are moving. However, the New Generalized Second Law has no such limitation and can continuously describe things at each instant of time—before, during, and after the rock is thrown. Another difference is

---

* The formal expression of the New Generalized Second Law is given in Appendix 3. Although rigorously formulated by Hobson,[7] the generalized canonical entropy had been previously developed independently as a generalized entropy by a number of authors.[8]

that the old law can only describe these "rest" or equilibrium states using thermodynamic variables, for example, pressure and temperature. However, the new law has no such constraint and is valid for *any observable* whatsoever.

Can Accidents Make Patterns?

We have said that the New Generalized Second Law can be understood to say that, on average, things mix. This means that with the passage of time, natural processes will destroy patterns. Conversely, if we wish to create a pattern, things will need to be separated—an activity of intellect. This is true because patterns are created when things are separated, and destroyed when they are mixed. For example, suppose there were many rocks around the pond. Of themselves, they formed a pattern of one kind or another along the bank. This pattern disappears if flash floods wash the rocks into the pond. Moving rocks into the pond means that they will have "mixed" with the water. Likewise, ripples by the rock thrown earlier can be thought of as waves mixing with the bank of the pond.

If later we were to play back a motion picture of my throwing the rock, with the film running backward, we would see a rock flying out of the pond up into the air, and ripples starting from the bank and disappearing into the center. In other words, we'd see a physically impossible event: things *un*mixing of their own accord.

With these considerations in mind, let's reconsider the basic idea that dust moved through space millennia ago to produce all that we see and are. The question is, on average, do dust collisions unmix to produce patterns? Or do they mix to create chaos? Suppose we shook a container that originally had salt at one end, and pepper at the other. Soon we'd have a speckled mixture of salt and pepper; we would see that mixing produces chaos. But were we to shake the container continuously, the *possibility* exists that on one very magic shake we could find all the salt once again at one end of the container and all the pepper at the opposite end. This is the concept which says that every now and then a very special accident can happen that will generate a pattern.

Statistical Interference

The belief that accidents can generate patterns is flawed, for it presumes something regarding physical matter which, in general, is untrue. In the particular example considered, to say that a lucky shake can produce the desired pattern presumes that when the salt and pepper were homogeneously mixed, somehow, on our magic shake, each particle would be free to move toward a separated state (salt at one end and pepper at the other) *without colliding with each other*. In other words, to assume that the salt and pepper can be unmixed on a magic shake of the container *is to presume that a statistically feasible future state of physical matter is unconstrained by the history of its past distributions.* But the mixed state of the pepper and salt *disallows the desired pattern on one shake.* Even if the magic shake occurs, collisions between the salt and pepper will keep them from separating into opposite ends of the container. The only way that shaking the container will produce such separation is if a series of magic shakes occurs.

How feasible is the occurrence of a sequence of magic shakes? Not very feasible at all. The problem with the statistical generation of patterns in this way is that, on average, our physical laws *mandate* that the salt and pepper must mix, not separate. The point is that not just *any* pattern will do, but only the one that is desired.

In this trivial example, we've made the desired pattern a separation between salt and pepper. But in actual fact, the desired patterns are near random distributions with vast functional coherence. Yet the simple example illustrates the difficulty in accidentally producing even a trivial separation of salt and pepper because on average the Second Law constrains them to mix.

Can Intellect Explain Earth's Patterns?

We might ask: Once mixed, how can we generate a pattern with all salt on one side and pepper on the other? The answer is that you, as an intellect, can observe where the black specks of pepper are and proceed to pick them out by hand with tweezers. If you were you to do this, you could generate any pattern you desire. These kinds of patterns are generated by intellect, not by chance.

Unlike pepper and salt, the actual state of affairs in the cosmos involves dust that is free to adhere to itself as it moves about. Because of this, some have argued that a series of fortunate accidents can build, one on the other, to produce the desired end pattern. But this idea fails on two counts. First, most of the distributions, if left to chance, will be the wrong ones. Thus, the adhesion merely removes from the cosmic commutative game material dust that is already in short supply. Second, successive lucky accidents are so *un*likely that even if some lucky, transitory, "in-between" combination occurs, the combinations that follow will act to destroy the prior psuedo-pattern. Because on average, *things must mix!*

Some have argued that the adhesion is a function of the "right combination," i.e., only those particles stick that intermingle in the right way. But this takes us back to the idea of physical matter somehow coming into existence with magical properties that over billions of years manufactured the blue sky, red wine, and green grass, along with us to enjoy them.

These intellectual excursions, though heroic, that seemingly attempt to replace God with sod as the source of our world's patterns, are not warranted by the empirical data of science. The fact that some people are motivated to defend them indicates that the academic exercise exists for reasons other than the pursuit of the world's true origin. People who logically pursue truth focus on facts and propose what those facts teach. But in the question of origins this is not the case. Here it is assumed that matter and its motion are all that exist, and ingenious stories are proposed that are consistent with the philosophical presumptions.

A good example of what natural processes do can be seen by watching a small child on the beach on a warm summer day. As the child tries to build a sand castle, the incoming waves repeatedly pound on the structure, washing the sand into the ocean and destroying its shape. If the child builds the sand castle elsewhere, then, over a period of time, the action of the wind will also destroy it. Both wind and waves destroy patterns. In this simple example we have an accurate picture of how natural processes pound away and destroy complex patterns. We can stand on a beach of our choosing until the day we die, but we will not see the ocean water or wind position sand so as to restore the complex pattern of the child's sand castle. It doesn't happen because nature is a destroyer, not a builder.

The example of salt and pepper illustrates that the natural flow is for things to mix. However, many events in our common everyday lives also illustrate the one-way direction of this universal law. Let's consider several of these experiences that affirm the universal truth that, on average, things mix.

How Does the Second Law Affect Our Lives?

The Second Law affects our lives in many ways. For example, soap and water will mix to make suds. A burning log mixes with oxygen to form fire and ashes. Sugar put into coffee mixes to sweeten it. Did you ever drink a sweetened beverage that sometimes tasted sweet and sometimes tasted bitter as you sipped it? Of course not. Why? Because the Second Law forces the sweetener to rapidly mix throughout the drink so that it is either sweet, bitter, or in-between, depending on the amount of sweetener. *It will be the same throughout the cup or glass.*

The truth of the matter is that on our scale of observation, things do not unmix. Soap suds will not unmix and return to a bar of soap and drinking water. If we have ashes, they will not unmix to become a log and oxygen. If we have sweet coffee, it will not unmix to bring back the sugar and the original coffee. But another thing happens when things mix. The patterns in space that previously existed when they occupied separate locations now cease to exist; i.e., when things mix, their patterns are destroyed. This is illustrated through what may be a familiar example.

Let's assume that you have purchased a brand new car and have taken it home from the dealer. Admiring your new car you examine the fenders, seeing that they are shiny and appear to be made of iron. But that's soon forgotten as you use the car and other things begin to occupy your mind. Several years go by, and you recall the time when you brought the car home and examined the fenders. You remember how shiny they appeared, so you decide to reexamine them. You now notice that the same fenders have begun to rust; i.e., the iron has mixed with the oxygen in the air. But, as disheartening as that may be, were you to wait long enough, the rust would begin to flake away and the entire fenders would disappear. Moreover, with the disappearance of the fenders they would lose their "pattern" (shape). When iron mixes with oxygen, the result is rust; and, given enough time, the rust will eventually flake away and the entire pattern that previously existed in space will be lost.

This kind of process in which iron and oxygen mix to form rust reflects again the universal law that "on average, things mix." Here we begin to appreciate the mystery surrounding the many complex patterns that exist on the earth. Were you to attempt to separate salt and pepper that had previously been combined, you could not do so by shaking the container. The combination would not unmix because, in nature, things do not separate of their own accord. But to explain the origin of the world we must explain how things separated into complex patterns. And this is not as simple as some suppose. Thermodynamically speaking, the systematic production of patterns is equivalent to making a perpetual motion machine!

The Observer's Role in Reality

The New Generalized Second Law mathematically describes the distribution that atomic particles will assume when put in the field of an observer's awareness. This New Generalized Second Law teaches that their location in space at each instant of time will be the distribution that maximizes the observer's uncertainty, subject to the predicted values of the observables. In simple language, nature provides intelligence with *minimum information*. All the older formulations of the Second Law are special cases of this fundamental, universal truth.

One interesting sidelight of these new insights is that the word entropy used in the older expressions to describe nature's one-way flow through time is now understood to be the *uncertainty* in an observer's description of the physical system. That is, entropy is the observer's uncertainty at an instant of time concerning the spatial pattern of objects measured at an earlier time. Since these objects assume positions that yield minimum information to the observer, the structures that materialize in space are those that, at each instant of time, yield maximum uncertainty (entropy).

These considerations apply to the *entire* system, and, when applied to the closed system of the universe (as indicated by modern understandings of its origin), the New Generalized Second Law has profound implications not only for the origin of the earth, but for the life that we find on it, and for the mechanism of evolution that is alleged to explain it.

Our new understandings also dovetail quite nicely with some of the deeper implications of quantum physics, which teach with growing vigor that the reality of measured objects finds ultimate existence *only in the information contained in its description by an observer*. These and other insights are new to the twentieth century and are what set the older ideas apart from modern knowledge. So that we can understand some of this in more familiar terms, however, it will prove helpful to return to our simpler picture.

Suppose we poured a box of salt into a tub of water. The result would be no mystery—we'd quickly get salt water. Now let's enlarge the tub to the size of the Pacific Ocean, and in your mind's eye imagine that we're stranded in a rowboat far out at sea with nothing to drink. We can't drink the ocean water, because it's a mixture of salt and water, a solution not unlike the result of pouring the box of salt into the tub of water. If we wait, and wait some more, and continue to wait even longer, we find that the salt in the ocean water will not unmix to become drinking water and a cake of salt. Were we to wait for drinking water in this fashion we would die of thirst long before the salt and water unmixed of their own accord.

When we apply this consideration to the origin of planet earth, we find this mystery: If on average, things do not *un*mix, who or what produced the vast unmixed states that permeate all the earth? The book of Genesis says that it was Intelligence. Considering that this book was written thousands of years ago it is astonishing that its author explained earth's patterns in terms of six supreme acts of separation by some stupendous Intellect. Being unaware of the scientific fact that things don't *un*mix, why didn't the writer explain earth's origin in terms of natural forces? Why did he invoke a Supreme Intellect?

The Mystery of Information

Modern science has shown that patterns contain information that can be measured and quantified (assigned numbers).[9] When we ask where this world came from we are really asking for the *source* of the information that exists in the form of these complex patterns. The patterns are produced when things are separated. To explain their origin and, therefore, the source of the information within them, we need a way to unmix things. Natural processes make poor explanations because as things become unmixed, they do so at the expense of other things in the system that get mixed. The universal law works in such a way that when the total package is considered, *more things must end up mixed than unmixed.*

For example, suppose we were to put a walnut at the center of a pancake. Nature can unmix things in the walnut provided that in doing so greater mixing occurs elsewhere. Since unmixing produces patterns, we might imagine a natural process making both a pattern near the pancake center and producing information in the walnut. But, since mixing destroys patterns and, therefore, information, we think of the information produced in the walnut *as coming from other information located throughout the pancake.* This "other information" is lost as things become mixed in the outer regions of the pancake. The New Generalized Second Law of Thermodynamics teaches that nature cannot create more information in the walnut than was originally available throughout the pancake. We can produce information in the walnut, but only at the expense of information that exists elsewhere. The pancake is our universe, and the walnut is a living cell. The mystery that confronts us is that the information in the walnut vastly exceeds that available in the pancake. Were we to believe that a natural process created life, this would mean that nature brought more information into existence than is available within the universe (under 270 bits [10] versus over a million bits [11] for just a simple bacterium).* A similar concern exists if we imagine that nature produced planet earth.

Too Small and Too Young

Few people realize that only since the early fifties have we been able to quantify the information resident in patterns. When we examine the numbers, we find that the random action of the "bits and pieces" of the universe in the form of cosmic dust cannot explain it. Some answer by saying that it *is* explainable if we give it enough time; they say that the random action of the dust *can* explain it.

When this idea is carefully examined we find that even if the universe is 13 billion years old and 30 billion light-years wide, it is still too young and too small to explain what we see. We touched on the basic reason why this is so earlier, in the concept of statistical interference.

If you put hot and cold water into a tub, you observe that they obey the universal law—they mix to form lukewarm water. Now it's our experience that lukewarm water does not unmix to give us back hot and cold water. To get these, we need an intellect to design both a refrigerator and a furnace. But what if we were to wait long enough; is it not *possible* for all of the fast-moving water molecules (the hot water) to move to one side of our tub, and all of the slow-moving ones to the other side?

The problem with that argument is that, as in the earlier example of salt and pepper, it ignores the basic properties of physical matter and presumes that if the fortunate circumstance were to statistically occur, each of the molecules would be free to travel along their randomly ordained paths *without interference from all the others*. Thus, to perform the feat, we once again find ourselves needing a fortuitous sequence of magical accidents that somehow allow the desired end result to materialize. But physical laws predestine such hope to despair because *on the average we must get more mixing than not*. Given the properties of physical matter, were we to wait long enough we would lose the water through evaporation long before it ever unmixes.

What Patterns Does Nature Produce?

But do natural processes ever produce *any* kind of pattern? The answer is yes. We can look at snowflakes or at the way different kinds of salts form crystals. These things are patterns, but they are very *simple* patterns.

---

* These concepts are discussed in Chapter 13 and Appendix 6.

For example, if you were to walk inside a salt crystal, you would be able to look in any direction and essentially see the same thing. The reason is that a salt crystal contains nothing more than a very tiny pattern that repeats itself billions of times. Let's look at this from a different point of view.

Many years ago, when I was in grammar school, a teacher said to me, "For your punishment, you shall write 'I will be good' a thousand times." Now, I could write that phrase over and over again, and I might cover the front and back of ten sheets of paper. But that does *not* mean that I had produced ten sheets worth of information. In fact, we have virtually no information simply because I took the one small phrase, "I will be good," and repeated it over and over again. Nature does that with the very patterns that occur naturally. They repeat over and over again and actually contribute very little information. In fact, information is *always lost* in natural transitions of this kind, including the crystallization of water into ice. This is what the New Generalized Second Law teaches—and this is what is observed.

But in inquiring about the world's origin, the real question we need to ask is, "What is the origin of the complex patterns we see and experience in the world?" If I took those ten sheets of paper and began to cover them with Einstein's theory of relativity, I would have a far more complex distribution of symbols than by my repeating a simple phrase over and over.

This is the situation we find in the world. All the natural processes that produce patterns do so with virtually no information in them. Yet despite this fact, teachers for decades have convinced many, both young and old alike, that the world can be explained in terms of natural processes. Even some biochemists are convinced that they can mix chemicals and produce life. But it's a futile exercise because to produce life you need the source of information contained in its blueprint. The information contained in a living cell is much greater than what is available within the universe through natural processes. The margin between the two is so vast that, were we to recite the difference in terms of printed letters, we'd need the volume of forty thousand universes just to store the paper on which the letters were printed.*

8

DID INTELLIGENCE
DESIGN THE EARTH?

THE BOOK OF GENESIS describes the inception of the world in terms of a series of six successive acts of separation. In doing so, it ascribes the origin of earth's patterns to the activity of a Supreme Intelligence—a description that is in remarkable alignment with our modern insight into the *in*ability of natural forces to produce such patterns. But how often do we pause and consider the interplay of the vastly complex patterns of physical matter that enable the earth to function as a sophisticated life-support system? This interplay, known as "coherence," is *what keeps us alive.*

To explain the origin of these complex paradigms, we must uncover the source of the *organizational coherence* that they manifest. But this goal can be easily misunderstood, because in seeking the root of these four-dimensional, space-time configurations, we are not seeking *whatever* can generate a complex pattern. To be sure, this is a necessary condition; but it is not a sufficient condition. Complexity is only a small part of the story. It is not so much that the patterns are complex, but rather that they are *complex in a coherent way.*

Useful Patterns

Using our minds, we can create countless near-random, complex patterns. But *virtually all of the patterns thus created will display no functional coherence.* If we are going to explain the origin of the world we must be able to logically explain how this functional coherence came into existence.

From the perspective of complexity, many patterns may qualify. Yet of the near infinite number of almost random patterns that can be envisioned, as a practical matter, *one* produces the self-consistent functional coherences that harmoniously sustain the 11 million species alive on earth today.[1]

It's easy to suppose that other patterns may exist that are capable of sustaining this many species. But the definition and demonstration of *just one other* is an impossible task. The point is that we *know* planet earth exists in the way described, but we know of no other! Some have engaged in wishful thinking and romantic speculation on this point, but that won't do. What we need is knowledge based on facts, not intuition rooted in supposition. If we are to rationally explain the origin of the stable life-support system called planet earth, then we must explain the production of functional coherences intrinsic to the distribution and nature of the parts comprising it.[2]

We perceive this coherence in this planet's mountains, oceans, and land distributions. We see it in the relative kinds of gases and the pressure of the atmosphere. We find it in earth's tilt angle and spin rate, and in the eccentricity and size of its orbit. These and other planetary and solar parameters display cooperative relationships that stagger the mind—not only in terms of the tolerances with which they are assembled and the intricate ways they interact, but in the provisions and protections they provide.[3]

Ours is the only planet with significant water, and with all ninety-two useful elements available at its surface. What other planet offers trees for fuel and caves for shelter? Earth shines as a Garden of Eden in an otherwise hostile and barren abyss.[4]

Earth's Astounding Temperature

The sun is 92,900,000 miles from the earth, and yet its 12,000 degree surface temperature radiates precisely the correct amount of energy for the proper intensity to reach this planet.[5] Moreover, it arrives with the right "color" distribution for the gases through which it must pass. This is remarkable because radiant energy decreases with the square of the distance, and arrives with different strengths for different colors.[6] Yet the situation is much more involved. The earth's diameter is 7,900 miles (North to South Pole) so that it intercepts one two-billionth of the total solar energy that reaches us. Yet if its diameter were slightly smaller or larger, we would either freeze or roast to death.[7] But this, too, is only part of the story.

The comparative sea-to-land mass; the one-to-five silica/water specific heat capacity; the lunar mass, distance, and orbit in relation to the ocean tides and surface area and other influences collectively interact to cover this globe with a shifting cloud cover. In conjunction with still other factors, these control the thermodynamic emissivity and reflectivity of the upper atmosphere so as to stabilize earth's temperature by radiating and/or reflecting more or less heat back into space.[8] The importance of this lies in the fact that the more or less stable temperature we enjoy essentially all over the earth is determined by the *difference* between the amount of heat the earth catches from outer space and the amount it loses due to radiation and reflection from the cover of its outer atmosphere.[9]

Or, consider something as simple as the question, How deep is the sea? The oceans have an average depth of just over two miles. Yet were they much deeper, the 0.03 percent carbon dioxide in the atmosphere would be absorbed into the oceans and decrease to the detriment of earth's plant life.[10] Were they shallower, however, their ability to store heat would decrease, resulting in violent temperature excursions and gradual polar ice accumulation.[11] These and other global parameters constitute complex patterns of physical matter that are functionally intertwined with physical properties to produce the organizational coherences responsible for the stable temperature we enjoy. And lest we take the thermal environment for granted, we might recall that the moon is only 239,000 miles away. Yet its surface temperature varies each lunar day (15 earth days) from a high of 214 degrees *above zero,* to a low of 243 degrees *below zero!*

The Miracle of Survival

The patterns we find on earth not only harmonize to guarantee the temperature; they also act to ensure our very survival. Consider one example: Near the equator, the troposphere (the air we breath) is about ten miles high (five miles at the poles). Since volcanos are stabilized by a balance between pressures above and below the earth's crust, if the atmosphere's height were appreciably lower, the decreased air pressure would act to promote increased volcanic activity attended by increased earthquakes.[12] Moreover, atmospheric protection against five hundred large meteorites that are estimated to strike earth's surface each year would be lost, and our population would be exposed to their devastating consequences. Some of these meteorites weigh thousands of tons and impact the earth at speeds of 150,000 miles per hour.

But consider what would happen if the atmosphere were significantly *higher* than it is. The unshielded radiation and reduced collisions along the outer troposphere would energize leakage into space of the lighter nitrogen molecules. Were this to continue, breathing difficulties could result for us near the earth's surface due to an enriched oxygen mixture. Breathing problems would also occur as we tried to exhale against the higher atmospheric pressure. The reason is that we empty our lungs primarily by the elasticity of lung tissue, and not by moving the diaphragm muscle (used to inhale).[13]

The enriched oxygen mixture would also begin to oxidize important elements available on the earth's surface, elements needed by vegetation. Were this to occur, plant life would rapidly die off,[14] and animal life would soon follow.[15] These and numerous other planetary factors are inextricably interrelated in ways that conspire to keep us alive. Moreover, they testify not to "order," but rather to a *functionally coherent complexity* whose central thrust is to sustain not only human life, but things as tiny as a single-celled amoeba.[16]

Though one of the simplest of life forms, this creature contains a vastly complex structure with patterns that are anything but simple. If we used a microscope to look inside, we'd realize very quickly that it performs all the essential functions that an elephant performs. For example, it gets food, processes oxygen, eliminates waste, reproduces itself, moves around, and interacts with its environment. This single-celled creature is just one of a myriad of life forms we find in the world.

This world is saturated with patterns that interact harmoniously, function coherently, and sustain themselves indefinitely. For example, there are growing seasons and dormant seasons for plant life. These are activated yearly by a small shift in the strength of sunlight at different colors, and this shift occurs due to the 3 percent eccentricity of earth's orbit.

Or consider our planet's water system. Water circulates from the oceans and goes over land to deliver rain so that food can grow; then it returns back to the oceans. There is also a complex exchange pattern between plant and animal life. Plants need carbon dioxide and produce oxygen as a byproduct; animal life needs oxygen and produces carbon dioxide as a by-product.

This is a world of complex patterns harmoniously interacting so as to sustain themselves. Such patterns are never produced on our scale of observation by chance processes. We see them only produced by intelligence. What experiment has ever shown that functionally coherent complex patterns are produced by the chaotic motion of dust? There are none! Just the opposite is true. Experience abounds where such motion produces patterns with virtually no complexity or information at all.[17] Where then is the empirical warrant for the faith that presupposes that lifeless particles first made a home for themselves (the earth), endowed themselves with a living awareness of their own existence (us), and then proceeded to build art museums, music halls, and bowling alleys?

Patterns in Our Life

Have you ever compared the patterns produced by chance processes with those we generate in the machines we build? Would we believe that, given enough time, random motions could produce the engineered systems we design and build? For example, when we examine an automobile engine we notice that the piston goes up and down and at regular intervals.

Why doesn't it go sideways? Or move at arbitrary times? The reason is that the up-and-down motion of the piston exists in harmony with valves located at the top, and a crankshaft positioned below. Furthermore, the intervals of its motion are synchronized with the opening and closing of valves so that gasoline enters and exhaust gas leaves at the correct moments of the engine cycle. In fact, so critical are the shapes of these parts and is the timing that small variations can produce severe power loss. Thus, the timing is carefully orchestrated to satisfy design requirements, as are the shapes and location of each part in the engine.

Or consider a television receiver and the complex patterns that make up its picture. Do we believe that natural chance processes could ever generate this? We know that when we look for TV stations late at night, we see "snow" on some of the channels because the stations have gone off the air. We can also duplicate the snow during the day by disconnecting the antenna. This underscores what we all know: A television picture exists due to signals received by the antenna, and the program we watch makes sense because the signals are related to one another in a coherent fashion.

In other words, it is the coherence among the signals that allows us to assign meaning to the picture on the screen. The coherence comes from a studio scene composed of complex patterns that functionally interrelate in a meaningful way. The coherence is preserved in signals sent to your antenna where they are processed to replicate the studio scene on your television screen. The tolerances in this system are extraordinary, and the slightest imperfection in its picture-making parts is picked up as a blemish on the screen.

Few of us would believe that, given enough time, interstellar particles would eventually collide to create an automobile engine or a television receiver. Yet many have no problem accepting the idea that such particles created human beings. I understand that the Saturn missile is thirty-six stories high, and yet has a fuel tank whose wall is only eighty-thousandths of an inch thick. I have learned that it took the collective resources of over ten thousand companies to build the missile, and that it was constructed over a five-year period using thousands of trained, skilled, thinking people. It consists of incredibly complex and intricate chemical, mechanical, and electrical subsystems that must all function together at precisely the right moments and in the right ways. But if I were to drag that missile into the thoroughfare of a major city and tell people that some chance sequence of fortunate collisions among atomic particles caused it to assemble itself, I'd be laughed out of the city—and rightly so. Yet we are asked to believe something that's infinitely more ludicrous: that the human body came into existence that way.

The Mystery of Information

What's really at issue in the question of earth's origin is the source of the informational specification that organizes the atomic parts into a life-support system. For example, suppose you were to get into your car and I were to instruct you how to reach a particular location in the middle of our country. I might write out seventeen pages of instructions containing much information. Someone else might say to you: "I can get you there a much easier way. All you have to do is *turn right*—whenever you're in doubt, just turn right." Impressed by these simple instructions, you put them to the test. But very quickly you realize that you're driving around in a circle.

Angry over the time you've wasted, you turn to the seventeen-page specification. To be sure, these instructions are very complicated and they contain much information, whereas the other specification, "Turn right," had hardly any information at all. But the complex set of instructions successfully functions to direct you where you need to go. This simple example crudely illustrates the kind of problem we must address in our search for insight into origins. Natural processes are limited and the only specification they can ever produce is, figuratively speaking, "Turn right." But to explain the origin of the world and the complexity of patterns within it, we have to explain the origin of a set of extended instructions—specifications, figuratively speaking, that can take us to "the center of the country."

One pattern we find on earth is life itself. In the past two decades, science has uncovered bits and pieces of life's blueprint that we have begun to analyze with new and powerful mathematical tools. What they tell us is that in looking to nature for the source of life, we've been driving around in circles. Careful studies of the vast magnitude of complexity uncovered by electron microscopes probing living cells indicate that natural forces acting in the time and space of the universe are inadequate to explain the information revealed, and that a Supreme Intelligence is the only known logical explanation for what we see. Simply put, materialism is an inadequate world view to explain what modern tools have disclosed. A similar viewpoint has been expressed by a biochemist who won the Nobel Prize for discovering DNA in 1953. His answer is that we may have been planted here by a supercivilization out among the stars.* Aside from there not being one shred of physical evidence to support such a view, the question of where *they* came from is unanswered.

The Bible teaches that the world was created by a Super Intellect, whom it identifies as God. This is consistent with the simplified earlier example with salt and pepper, and the need for an intellect to create functionally coherent patterns by performing acts of separation. If salt and pepper are thoroughly mixed, there is no pattern. A pattern is created by a person or an observer—an intellect—observing specks of black pepper and separating them from pieces of white salt. Intelligence can create complex patterns this way.

An application of this principle might be one of the very valuable original Rembrandt paintings. Rembrandt took colors and, after separating them, located them in different strengths at different places on a canvas. In other words, Rembrandt created complex patterns (paintings) for which he became famous. He was a person, an intellect. Only thus could he create timeless and world-acclaimed art patterns. In recent times some have tried to produce "art" by randomly throwing paint blobs against a canvas. It's fair to say that these efforts have proven much less successful.

Or consider a seamstress who makes a dress; she uses the same basic

---

* F. Crick, *Life Itself,* published by Simon and Schuster, 1982.

principles. First, she takes cloth and separates it into different shapes. She then proceeds to sew the pieces together, thereby creating a "grand pattern" (possibly copied from another pattern) out of all of the separate shapes. The dress she creates in this way "functions" to fit a person of a particular size and shape and the reason is that intelligence designed it that way. But had the separate shapes been assembled at random, the dress would have turned into a cloth of dubious value.

Or consider yet another example. Before you write a letter with a ballpoint pen, all the ink is located within the pen. But after you write the letter, some of the previously-pooled ink has been separated from the pen and is now located onto paper. Thus, letter-writing does two things: It separates ink and forms a complex pattern over the sheet of paper, and it creates information in terms of the relationship of the symbols to one another. The information contained in the complex pattern on the sheet came from your *intellect* creating letters by separating and then distributing ink across the paper. Moreover, by organizing the letters into words and the words into sentences, the "complexity" of the ink pattern increased.

The message or information in your letter *is* the pattern of ink that exists across the sheet. But were your letter exposed to the elements by accidently dropping it onto the sidewalk, or inadvertently leaving it on a park bench, nature would undo your letter-writing. Natural forces will act over time to "mix" the ink on the paper and destroy the pattern, and the information created when you wrote the letter. The point is this: Nature is a *destroyer* of patterns and, therefore, of information.

Were we to examine the pattern displayed by a complex rock formation and then return to the same place many years later, we would discover that natural forces had eroded the formation and dissipated the pattern. This simple example, like so many others, is in agreement with the facts of science, and shows that random, chance processes erode rather than create complex patterns. Natural processes are, therefore, a poor explanation for the complex patterns of this world. These patterns are better explained as the product of Intellect.

It is more logical to believe that planet earth functions to sustain life because it was designed to do so. This is the best explanation because it aligns with all of the facts as we know them. If we inquire into the origin of the Intelligence who designed earth, that's a different question—but we have answered the question as to earth's origin. If we speculate that this intelligence resides among the stars in the form of say, some supercivilization, then we ask: "What is *its* origin?" Conversely, if we say that God designed the earth, then to inquire into his origin is an entirely different matter. The reason is that "God" belongs to a different category, i.e., supercivilizations *have* life, whereas God *is* life.

Were we foolish enough to inquire into the origin of "God," we would first need to presume that our inquiry was meaningful—that "God" *had* an origin. If we somehow pass this hurdle, we must next assume that our minds are capable of comprehending the answer. In this case killifish have a better chance of learning the origin of manmade satellites falling into the ocean.

It seems all that can be said with sobriety is that intelligences (you and I) exist on earth. Therefore, it's not unreasonable to suppose that we originated from a higher Intelligence. This is much more logical than to suppose we came from dead dust.

9

HOW DID LIFE
ORIGINATE?

Ants danced last Summer
and flies flew through Fall:
Winter bred its berries—
but Spring made them all.

IN A SIMPLE WAY that expresses what we all have come to know about
life: each year at springtime it buds anew. Indeed, life on earth is *so* prevalent
that we encounter it no matter where we go. For example, do you remember
the last time you had a picnic? If it was like mine, there was a struggle
between eating the food and its being eaten by the ants and bees. The ants
crawled all over the table, while the bees attacked the sweets. Then, as the
sun went down, mosquitoes came in droves from nowhere. But a picnic
isn't the only place where we encounter life. An annoying fly can buzz the
dinner table while a spider weaves a web near the ceiling. A cricket's chirp
can break the quiet of a summer night or a bug may hit the windshield
while traveling down a highway. Roosters crow at dawn, cows graze at noon,
and gnats swirl at dusk. But where do all of these things come from? Who
or what is the real source of their life?

This planet teems with life. Trees produce countless leaves and support
nests that accommodate all kinds of birds. Moreover, the birds can be found
in every country and in any climate. Some hop on lawns, and others fly
across oceans, which themselves contain so many life forms that we have
yet to catalog them all. The variety of sea life is so enormous that it's difficult
to know how to describe it. For example, not only do fish come in a large
number of colors and shapes, but their sizes range from ones so small that

they resemble paperclips, to those so large that they are longer than some driveways! The diversity is not only true of life on the land and in the sea; it is also seen in the 10 million kinds of insects and worms that live below the earth's surface.

But where did it all come from? How did these living things get here? Many believe that they came from a chemical accident.[1] The idea is that billions of years ago lightning passed through different gases in the earth's early atmosphere and created a living object.[2] Thereafter, that object supposedly evolved to produce all the life that has ever existed on earth, including what we see today.[3]

It may surprise you to learn that a number of scientists no longer believe that the occurrence of life can be explained as the result of a chemical accident on this planet.[4] New evidence has been discovered which shows that sparks traveling through gases do not make life. As we shall see, the new evidence teaches that living cells appear to have been *designed;* and if they are designed, then a Supreme Intelligence created the blueprint.

How Many Kinds Are There?

An estimated 1 million species of animal life inhabit the earth's surface while an additional ten times this number are estimated to live in subterranean environments. These 10 million insects and worms can be thought of as having a "bashful" existence in hidden levels not directly visible to us. The 1 million that exist above the ground (plus an additional half million species of plant life), though visible, depend upon the 10 million we don't see. This is because the invisible life forms continuously perform countless thousands of subterranean chemical operations that enable the visible life forms to live.

It is easy to miss this underground activity. Although elephants are easily seen with the naked eye, tiny insects aren't so readily apparent. Yet all of them exist together on one planet and work in beautiful and astonishing harmony. One seems to offer exactly what another needs. Where did they come from? And why are their activities so perfectly correlated?

When we consider how easily this precariously balanced system could become unstable, we are awe-stricken with the many and varied reciprocal feedback mechanisms that sustain it. The very structure of this system is woven with safeguards that keep it from catastrophic collapse.[5] What is the origin of these mechanisms? And how could they have come into being under conditions for which no one of them has any discernible survival value apart from the existence of the others?

We can pose that question from an entirely different perspective. Where did *you,* the reader, come from? If you say, "From my parents," then I'll ask, "Where did *they* come from?" We both know that your parents didn't create you any more than my parents created me. Our parents *pro*created us. It's like striking a match to light a candle. Once lit, we can use the candle to light another candle. In human terms, people beget people and we know this is how our parents brought us into the world.

Thus, when we inquire into our origin the question can be understood to ultimately trace back to the deeper question, Where did the *first* life come from? That doesn't necessarily mean that you or I *came* from that first life, but it certainly is a good place to start. If we can't uncover the origin of *one* living cell, how can we have any hope of discovering the origin of the 70 billion body cells that comprise each of us? In the case of a candle's flame, it's easy to state its origin. The match did it. But what "match" gave rise to the first life? Where did it originate?

We know that each generation of life grows to a peak in strength and vigor, then withers and dies. This cycle enables the next generation to be born anew. But, as a practical matter, the seed that makes it all happen doesn't change. And it seems never to tire or die. Instead, each generation creates new seed from the blueprint found in the old.[6] The miracle of life is the miracle of its seed. Many people find it easy to imagine that atomic particles bounced themselves into some magic combination to make it happen. But though such imaginings are easy, recent scientific data shows that they are not sensible.[7] To see why this is so, it's helpful first to look at history, and the folly of old ideas, and then at what we've discovered that shows something more than chance is at play.

The History of Life

Five thousand years ago people thought that life came from grain. They would see rats running from piles of wheat and they thought that the wheat had given rise to life. They also thought that water was the source of life. For example, when they saw toads hop out of ponds, they sincerely believed it was the spontaneous generation of life. Today this sounds very amusing; but if we had lived then, we would probably have come to the same conclusion. Of course, they changed their minds when they sat around the pond and studied it. Eventually, they realized that toads hopped in before they hopped out. The same thing occurred with the wheat; they saw rats running in before they ran out. We can learn a lesson from all of this: Generally speaking, it is easiest to believe and accept whatever we know the least about. In essence, our minds can make anything seem plausible in the absence of knowledge to contradict it. Later, when our knowledge increases, it points us away from the earlier, mistaken ideas. History regarding human ideas about the origin of life [8] has taught us this lesson several times over.

The idea that life comes from nonlife didn't stop with rats and toads. Afterward, it was supposed that life originated with worms, i.e., the next unseen smaller level. Each time a worm crawled out of the mud, man thought the mud had spontaneously created life. Of course, today that seems silly, but back then they believed it to be true. Eventually, they learned that mud doesn't make worms, at least not the big kind. But other, very tiny, wormlike creatures appeared which caused them to believe that the mud made insects.

Have you ever seen the eggs of a fly? They hatch into larvae that squirm and look like tiny worms. Insects were laying eggs on the ground, and the eggs were hatching into maggots that squiggled like tiny worms. The big worms were said to have come from the small ones, and maggots were thought to be the spontaneous generation of life. Again man was sure he was right, but again, he was wrong. Yet the same thing more or less was happening in bowls of meat. When they put meat into a bowl, maggots soon crawled all over it. Thus the creation of life was again transferred to the next, unseen smaller level.

No further proof seemed necessary. Put meat into a bowl, and presto!—out comes life. That worked until someone had the good sense to cover the bowl. Then the life from the meat suddenly disappeared. What happened was simple. Flies and other insects had been laying eggs on the meat, and when the eggs hatched, life appeared. But we know that this life didn't come from the meat, but from the eggs that had been deposited onto the meat. Once again, people sincerely believed they had discovered the spontaneous generation of life, but it proved to be only a disappointment. Yet when that hope was spoiled, they repeated the error of the past. As you can probably surmise, they projected that life was spontaneously generated at the next unseen, smaller level. This time it was *really* small—the tiny living specks known as bacteria.

How Small Can Life Be?

Bacteria are single cells of life that are plantlike in character, and they're so small that millions of them can fit on the head of a pin! What better choice for the spontaneous generation of life? Furthermore, this idea flourished in the eighteenth century, when science was seen as an invincible ally of those who believed that bacteria were the actual beginnings of life. Several felt that definitive biological tests could be performed, and many were sure that these tests would demonstrate the spontaneous generation of life from nonlife. Furthermore, virtually all of the prominent thinkers of the day were sure that these tests would truly resolve the question. However there were dissenters, and among them, Louis Pasteur. He believed otherwise, and his scientific investigations that followed proved he was right, and that the others were wrong. Yet the proposed tests presupposed an ability to see things no one had ever seen before. But how could anyone see bacteria—especially at that time?

The microscope, invented in 1590, provided the answer. It was used to unveil plantlike bacterial specks eighty-six years later in Holland. Then, in the late 1800s, a controversy raged in Paris over broth that was spoiling. Bacteria were making it cloudy, and again people believed they were witnessing the spontaneous generation of life. Yes, we've been here before. It's the idea that life can come from nonlife. The facts again proved the experimenters wrong, and demonstrated that to get life one needs life—a lesson that persists to the present time.

Most everyone agreed that the broth had become cloudy due to bacteria, but how had the plantlike specks spontaneously come into existence (for that was the predominant opinion)? Pasteur disagreed, and to prove his point, he put clear broth into a bottle and sealed the opening. But when his broth remained clear, his adversaries shouted, "Foul!" They claimed that life didn't appear in Pasteur's broth because he had done something improper, such as preventing the essential ingredient from reaching it, which, at that time, was thought to be air. They actually believed that air was a magic ingredient necessary to the spontaneous generation of life, and that the broth needed air for life to appear. This seemed reasonable at the time because nothing happened to the broth when the bottle was sealed, yet it had become cloudy when exposed to air. A remark typical of the thinking at that time was: "No wonder the broth is clear; the bottle has no access to a fresh air supply." But Pasteur invented a way around their objections and, by doing so, demonstrated once again that the idea that life can come from nonlife is wrong.

Pasteur was sure that broth didn't create life. He believed that life came from God. And to show others that it didn't come from broth, he invented the Pasteur flask, which looked very much like a big, hollow, glass ball. The only way into the ball was through a glass tube connected to its top. The tube went up and away from the ball, then curved back down toward the bottom of the ball, where it again reversed direction and curved back up, terminating with its end hanging open in space. Air entered the tube through this open end, and, passing through the tube, eventually reached the broth in the bowl. But the dust particles on which the bacteria were riding became trapped in the lower curved neck of the tube. Thus, the tube allowed air to reach the broth, but trapped any particle that may have been suspended in the air. Therefore, even though air entered the bowl, the broth stayed clear. (It is reported that this broth remained clear for decades after Pasteur's experiment!) What was the lesson? That, like the rats, toads, and worms that had gone before, the bacteria *had to go in* before they could come out.

Life's Incredible Blueprint

Since man had again failed to find the source of life, the time was ripe for a new idea. But the next idea wasn't really new; it proved to be the same thing all over again. Once again the cry was: "Life comes from nonlife . . . and at the next unseen, smaller level." But this time man chose the smallest thing imaginable. The spontaneous generation of life was said to occur on the scale of the "protein molecule"—a level of structure many regarded as the basic building block of life itself. The reason is that when submerged into the same chemicals of which the protein molecule is made, they can be chemically instructed to assemble another protein molecule.

Thousands of years came and went, and yet the source of life eluded humanity. Then came the twentieth century and we were told science had the answer. And many believed the new story: "Life was created by a chance combination of chemicals." But was it true? Had we finally found the level at which nonlife spontaneously generated into life? As long as this level remained unseen, people could believe the answer was yes. But, with the advent of electron microscopes and information theory, the answer changed to no.

When we pause and consider the "trend line" that threads through life's history, the new answer shouldn't surprise us. Man once thought that wheat hatched rats and ponds made toads. Then he said mud bred worms. Later, he believed meat formed flies and broth spawned plants. Now the story is that slime made cells that crawled out of a bath of nutrients. What is fantastic isn't the story, but rather that so many people believe that it's true. Why do we do this? Part of the answer is that it's always easy to believe the things we know the least about.

Each time, the spontaneous generation of life from nonlife seemed assured. But when the consequences of such beliefs were actually studied, they were found wrong. Now the story is that life originated from a chemical accident. Some even believe science has already created life in a test tube, or that science has proved that life began accidentally when this planet was very young. As we shall see, none of this is true. Stories are fun and can be convincing, but facts are hard to come by.

Here, it is important to realize that the accidental explanation of life's origin is not a *scientific* explanation. Regardless of what you may read [9] or hear, *all scientific explanations are falsifiable.* [10] But the idea that life came from some fortunate accident millennia ago is not a falsifiable hypothesis. No one has duplicated the event in a laboratory, and all work being done to create such life must fail because modern science has declared nature to be an informational eunuch. Careful scientific calculations show that natural sources cannot produce the information we find in life's blueprint. [11] The universe is simply too young and too small to have produced the information found in even a simple bacterium. Furthermore, the accidental story of life is believed, not because the facts of science have shown it to be true, but rather because no other alternative is plausible without recourse to "God."

The concept of "God" as an explanation is offensive to some people for two reasons. First, "God" is equated with religion, which many believe has no place in science. And second, "God" implies an authority under whom one must arrange his or her life. But while this latter concern is something we all may wrestle with at one time or another, the notion of "God" does not have to equate to religion. Instead, the concept is more properly identified with intelligence.

Since about 1950, scientists have been able to evaluate material structures in the physical world, using a mathematical tool called information theory. [12] This tool allows us to quantify the degree to which we can specify a physical system. The unit that we use to measure these systems isn't inches or pounds or seconds, but rather *bits of information*. But information is something that ordinarily comes from intelligence, not natural processes, and the truly astonishing thing is that the latest discoveries show that the structures that make life what it is are just jammed full of this "stuff" called information.[13]

Since the universe is simply too young and too small, to account for its appearance, (even at 13 billion years and 30 billion light-years across) we are forced to ask, "From where did it come?" The logical answer is that it came from a Supreme Intelligence! Not only is this logical, but it's also the *simplest* answer. If this implies religion, then this is something the individual will have to grapple with. But the irrefutable fact is that information theory and the data from electron microscopy, when applied to living cells, force the conclusion that they have been *designed*. Why do they force this conclusion? Because they are jam-packed with information that cannot be logically explained as the issue of natural processes within this universe. The next chapter begins our exploration as to why this is so.

10

IS PROTEIN GOD'S
FINGERPRINT?

A POPULAR EXPLANATION for life's origin is that a fortuitous chemical accident brought it into being. But although this miraculous accident idea is
fashionable, it is out of step with the actual data of science. Calculations
on the idea have been done by a number of investigators, and their conclusion
is unanimous: It is simply too unlikely to be credible.[1] Prior to the practical
development of the electron microscope the true extent of the complexity
of living cells was unknown. However, when facts began to accumulate and
data analyzed, the results suggested that believing in the Great Pumpkin
might be more credible than the "miraculous accident" idea. Although this
might sound silly it really isn't. The calculations show that the belief that
life arose accidentally is statistically impossible and intellectually outrageous.

The Mystery of Protein

Mankind's track record at explaining life's origin has been consistently
poor. Historically, we've *always* been wrong, so no one should be surprised
that our current idea appears also to be wrong. As we have said, the current
theory pushes the spontaneous generation of life to the level of the *protein
molecule.* How small is that? To answer this question we need to ask, what
is protein?

Consider the following illustration. A string of railroad cars, each connected
to the next, is lined up. There are petroleum cars, cattle cars, coal cars,
lumber cars and others. This gives us a rough idea of what protein looks
like under an electron microscope—a string of "chemical railroad cars" called
amino acids.

For example, if we picture two kinds of trains composed of 574 cars in
all we have a good picture of hemoglobin, a protein in our blood that carries

oxygen throughout our body. Iron is located within hemoglobin in a special way that allows the molecule to carry oxygen more efficiently than anything else known. Were it not for hemoglobin, our heart would need to pump fifty thousand gallons a day just to keep us alive. As for our blood pressure, would you care to guess? It would be almost seventy pounds per square inch, or about five times the pressure of the atmosphere.

Protein is made of building blocks called amino acids. We can picture them as the links in a chain, or we can think of them as wooden blocks connected end to end in the same way that railroad cars are connected. Imagine trying to assemble a "hemoglobin train." We would need a total of 574 railroad cars, each "car" being an amino acid. There are twenty different kinds of useful amino acids in our body. If we are to simulate protein, then in designating the first car we can select from among twenty different kinds. In designating the second car, we must also select from among these twenty kinds, and so on!

Ways to Assemble a Train

With twenty selections for *each* of the first two locations, we have twenty times twenty ways of choosing the first two cars of our train. We can assemble the first and second cars in four hundred ways (combinations). If we were to make a train with three cars, we would choose from eight thousand combinations.

Hemoglobin contains two "trains" totaling 574 cars—each selected from among twenty kinds of amino acids. The number of ways we can assemble these hemoglobin trains is so vast that it is a trillion, trillion, trillion (repeat twenty times more) *times the entire number of stars in the universe.* Yet despite this, *only one combination known to man carries oxygen most efficiently in your blood.* Moreover, if just one railroad car is changed in the sixth position of one of the trains, the result is sickle-cell anemia. Consider this: 270 million of these hemoglobin protein molecules of just the right combination reside in *each* of the 30 trillion red blood cells in your body. Did this just happen by chance? Some people have enough faith to believe that it did. Faith can be good if it's based on evidence. But where is the evidence that this system came into being by chance? There is none!

Was the Human Body Designed?

Can we calculate the certainty (inverse probability) that hemoglobin could not have happened by chance? No, because hemoglobin is so complicated that we can't fully describe it. We need to settle for something much simpler. The argument then is that if a simpler thing couldn't have happened by chance, then neither could the more complicated structure of hemoglobin. One protein that is much simpler than hemoglobin, and which scientists have extensively studied, is a "string of cars" called "cytochrome C." It's a much shorter protein than hemoglobin in that the length of its "train" is only 101 railroad cars.[2]

Cytochrome C is also of interest because it is basic to all of life. Among other things, it controls both the respiration and energy transfer in the living cells of a broad spectrum of life.[3] Let's recall that the calculation necessary to learn whether life could have come about through an accident was not possible until very recently. That's because the calculation needs two things: insight from information theory and data from electron microscopy.

The first image ever made with electrons instead of light occurred on April 7, 1931, on a thin metal grid.[4] Five years later, electron microscopy was used for the first time to magnify a living cell.[5] Thereafter, serious work began on the development of an electron microscope,[6] and a series of rapid technological advances [7] made it a working tool by the 1950s.[8] Further developments enabled definitive application of electron microscopy to the fine structure of living cells. By the early sixties its use as a practical research tool in the biological sciences was unquestioned.[9]

Although the mathematical tools necessary to interpret the data from electron microscopy had been discovered a decade earlier,[10] as a practical matter realistic knowledge of the microstructure of cellular systems wasn't available until the early sixties. Thus if we believed life was an accident, before 1960 no one could prove us wrong. Today that's changed. For the first time in history we can *calculate* the "next unseen, smaller level." The result is this: To get life, you need life. Nothing less will do. Anything else is wishful thinking.

When scientists calculate probabilities showing that cytochrome C could not have been produced by an accident, it's a little more complicated than just asking the question, How many ways can we assemble a train? But the basic idea is the same. Of course, many technical details must be carefully taken into account. When these calculations are done, a variety of factors must be considered, including the fact that not all "railroad cars" are equally available (residue probability) or significant (codon degeneracy). Likewise, when selecting the "railroad cars," it is necessary to distinguish among those choices that are selected from comparable locations (homologous protein lineage) and the extent to which they may be similar (synonymous amino acid residues).

Suffice it to say that all of this has been carefully done, and the calculations published in the scientific literature.[11] The result is staggering. In terms of the railroad train, *the calculations show that the longest train that an accident can produce is fewer than fifty cars.* This is mind-boggling when we remember that a hemoglobin protein molecule consists of two trains totaling 574 cars! At this point you may be thinking: What's so staggering about limiting a train (protein chain) to fewer than fifty cars (amino acids)? Since we only needed 101 for cytochrome C, isn't that only missing the mark 50 percent? No, we've missed the mark by a *huge* percent. It's deceptively naive to think that the certainty that this can't happen doubles with the length of the train, for it doesn't work that way. When the train length doubles to the 101 amino acid residues of cytochrome C, the numbers are such that, as a practical matter, it's impossible for an accident to have produced it. It is so unlikely that the odds cannot be easily explained.

A Look at Some Staggering Numbers

The certainty that an accident did not create cyctochrome C has been carefully calculated.[11] Yet this small protein corresponds to a "train" containing only 101 railroad cars. We can't even fathom the complexity of hemoglobin with 574 cars. We're only looking at the certainty that cytochrome C didn't happen accidentally. But here I as a writer have a problem. The certainty that we know chance did not produce cytochrome C is so vast that to communicate it in simple terms isn't easy. The problem is illustrated by the following example.

Picture an 8½ × 11–inch sheet of paper with letters printed on both sides. Let's allow eighty columns by sixty-six lines of letters, giving us just under 5,300 letters on each side of the paper, or 10,600 letters per sheet. Putting the sheets into piles, we can stack about 320 sheets per inch, giving us just over thirty-six thousand letters in a cube one inch on a side. Now, what volume of space do we need to store enough sheets whose total number of letters equals the certainty that chance did not produce cytochrome C? When I first did the calculation the answer astounded me. *We need the space of almost forty thousand universes, each 30 billion light-years wide!*

Light travels at a speed of just over 186,000 miles per second. This means that in one second light can travel seven and a half times around the earth. If light can travel that far in one second, imagine how far it will go in a year. Scientists call the distance light travels in one year a "light-year." It is roughly 6 thousand billion miles. We believe that the universe—out to the visible horizon—is about 30 billion light-years wide. Yet the certainty that an accident did not create cytochrome C is the number of letters filling both sides of 8½ × 11–inch sheets packed into the space of forty thousand universes!

Consider this. You and I are both aware that we exist. Yet we're told that all of life, including you and me, bounced itself into existence eons ago by a fortunate accident involving cosmic dust. But if we honestly face what we've uncovered in the past thirty years or so, we find ourselves up against the following question: When we believe, in the light of modern knowledge, that lifeless particles eventually endowed themselves with a living awareness of their own existence, do we not engage in the secret and irrational worship of interstellar dust under the guise of atheism? In short, do not the scientific calculations outlined above point to God rather than to sod as the source of our life?

What Do We Mean by "Proof"?

The magnitude of the numbers outlined above can be put into perspective by asking, How sure are we that an accident could not have created life, as over against our confidence in other conclusions that are commonly held?

In approaching this question, it's helpful to realize that modern knowledge, and therefore science, is synthetic. This means that our conclusions are never known with absolute certainty. They are only held to be true to a certain level of confidence. As a scientist, I personally participate in the process. It's just that we're never *sure* that what we think is true today will be true tomorrow. In science, we routinely measure things, but there's always room for reinterpretation because tomorrow we may find something new. But does that mean we can't prove anything? Surprisingly, the answer is no.

How is it possible to prove something while at the same time saying that tomorrow it may be wrong? What kind of proof is that? If something that is believed to be true today can be shown to be false by some future discovery, how can *anything* be proved? The answer to such questions lies in carefully defining *what* is being proved and in realizing that the basis for accepting the proof is a set of events that are *reproducible* within the space of an advancing time. Specifically, what we say is this: By mathematically analyzing reproducible events, we can prove that the truth of one belief *is more inevitable than another.* As a practical matter, when the belief becomes "almost certain," we then accept it as "true."

How Confident Are We of Gravity?

Is there a "truth of science" that almost everyone is willing to accept? While there are several contenders, almost everyone would agree that the inverse square law of gravity is true. But how sure are we that this law is true? Newton introduced it about three hundred years ago [12] and numerous experiments have confirmed its validity ever since. Had only one experiment been performed, the belief could be seriously questioned. But because the inverse square law has been confirmed by *many* investigators in various countries over an extended time period, our confidence in the law is high. How high is this confidence? It's *not* 100 percent. [13]

We can estimate the highest possible confidence anyone can rationally have in the law of gravity and when we've got the answer, we'll compare our confidence in this belief to the belief that an accident could not have spontaneously generated the "simple" protein discussed earlier. When we have done this, we will see that the confidence calculated for the inverse square law is far less than our confidence that an accident could not have created life.

Let's maximize our confidence in the law of gravity by transforming all 5 billion people on earth today into instant scientists. We'll allow them three hundred years (the time since Newton) in which to do experiments in the inverse square law of gravity. We'll also endow them with superhuman powers so that they only need *one second* to start and complete each experiment. This means that they don't eat, sleep, or do anything except bring in another confirmation of the inverse square law every second of their lives. And they do this for three hundred years. At the end of this time, how sure would we be that the law of gravity is true? It's actually far *less* sure than we are that something other than chance created protein.

To compare the two, we'll again fill both sides of our paper with letters and ask: What volume of space do we need to store all the letters whose total equals the certainty that the inverse square law is true? The answer is surprising. It's a cube less than two miles on a side. Now think about it. Forty thousand universes, each 30 billion light-years wide, would be needed to store the paper with a letter total that equals the certainty that chance cannot produce even simple protein, while our corresponding assurance that the inverse square law remains true for the next experiment is a cube less than two miles on a side!

What Is "Occam's Razor"?

Although this example is necessarily oversimplified, it nonetheless illustrates something that is quite true: *It is nonsensical to believe that an accident created life.*

To compare a cube under two miles with forty thousand universes is to liken the finite with the infinite. The groundless belief that life spontaneously arose from nonliving physical matter was rationally defended for centuries because no one had any information to the contrary. Now that is over, and we know better. Today, we can see inside living cells and study the resplendent majesty of a structure so awesome that it reeks of divine fingerprints. It's one thing to defend wrong beliefs out of ignorance, but it's quite another to perpetuate the folly when the light of day shows a more truthful way.

In science we use a principle called "Occam's razor." It can be explained as a rule that "cuts away" complicated explanations when a less complicated one will do. Succinctly put, it means that *the simplest explanation is the best explanation.* What can be simpler than the thesis, "intelligence designed life"?

What motivates us to deny the clear direction of new scientific insights in favor of more complicated, but less likely, explanations? Why do we deny that intelligence designed life? Our world is full of "intelligences." You are an intelligence, and so am I. Since the human body is the most sophisticated and complex machine known to man, what would motivate us to deny that a Supreme Intelligence designed it? Are we able to accept the existence of an Authority higher than ourselves? Or are we committed to beliefs that perpetuate man as the highest authority? Either way, one thing is sure: Scientific data do *not* support the thesis that life arose by chance. The calculations could have come out differently, but they didn't, so the likelihood of life having occurred through a chemical accident is, for all intents and purposes, zero. This does not mean that faith in a miraculous accident will not continue. But it *does* mean that those who believe it do so because they are philosophically committed to the notion that all that exists is matter and its motion. In other words, they do so for reasons of philosophy and not science.

11

WHY CAN'T NATURE CREATE LIFE?

THE BELIEF that life spontaneously generated from nonlife has dominated the history of man's quest for an answer to his origin.[1] And yet as popular as this belief has been through the centuries, it came under growing attack soon after the Renaissance in the 1500s. Up to this time, philosophy had guided the tenor of human thought. But, with the advent of science, a small group of thinkers began to systematically investigate the reproduction and life cycle of living things. These were men whose beliefs were based not on philosophy, but rather on the results of actual experiments they performed.[2]

Prior to the Renaissance, human thought regarding origins was focused either upon God or an intuitive, mechanistic mysticism that supposed that the motion of physical matter had in some way created the life existing on earth. But the advent of science brought a third focus whose basis for belief was neither Holy Writ nor biased thought, but rather the logical conclusions of empirical fact. When scientists working in the field of biology pursued their investigations into life's origin, they continued to draw the same conclusion after numerous and repeated observations. As they studied many different kinds of life forms, the repeating conclusion came to be known and accepted as the "law of biology," namely, that "life comes from other life." [3]

This law asserted that there is something special and distinctive about life; it has a peculiar quality, a unique attribute. This special trait was identified only with living things. If you wanted life, you needed other life to get it. Life could only come from other life. This was believed for a simple reason: It's what everyone *observed*. It was an experimental truth, and yet, despite the scientific warrant for such a law, it clearly stood in sharp contrast to the philosophical impetus that had driven large numbers to believe that life could be spontaneously generated.

If one wants life, he or she can only get it from other life. This is true in a park, on a farm, or in a laboratory. What's startling is how many people are unaware that it's *still* true. Despite all that one hears and reads, no one has ever produced life from nonlife. You and I may have come across a story on radio or TV, or an article in a magazine or journal that communicates the distinct impression that at one time scientists produced life of some kind in a test tube, i.e., from chemicals, but such impressions—though even "intuitive" for some—are simply untrue. No one anywhere has ever created life from chemicals. And although you may have heard that it was done somewhere, or may be thinking of something you've read that you feel proves the opposite, *it simply isn't so.* Neither can it *ever* be so.

The Importance of "Information"

All experiments that have ever been done to create life fall into two categories: those that start with life and those that don't. If you start with life and get life, it doesn't count because everyone knows that life makes life. But when it's tried without life, we *don't succeed, because we can't succeed.*

Accidental miracles and inevitable assembly are romantic ideas, but neither is true. Modern scientific insights into the nature and origin of biological assemblies effectively outlaw self-organization of the kind needed to create life.[4] There are times when nature *can* and does form *structures,* just like winter can make snowflakes. But nature can't create *life* any more than a snowflake can survive the heat of summer. The reason is that Mother Nature is impotent, i.e., she loses more than she wins. What does nature lose? Scientists call it "information," and it resides, among other things, in an observer's overall description of a biological structure.[5]

The greater the complexity of the living object, the greater is the information necessary to describe it—and *we* bring our own complexity to the process of observation. Recent scientific work has shown that this fact is quite important, because an observer and the object he describes are separate components of a common system (our world).[6] New scientific laws teach that the information present in an observer's description within the universe (for example, a living or fossil object) has meaning for the *entire* system. The new laws indicate that the information within an observer's overall description of a living object is as much a characteristic of the object as it is of the system in which the object resides.[7]

The scientific concept of information is a difficult one to discuss, yet it is vital if we are to understand life's origin. The concept is also fundamental to a true understanding of the physical laws governing the universe. The reason is that each one of these laws is nothing more than *our* description of how the universe and everything in it behave *for us.* Our perception of physical reality *is* what is real, and the only things we can logically show to be physically real are the things we are able to observe (directly or indirectly measure).

In the last analysis, natural law is our description of what we observe

the behavior of things in the universe to be. Information is thus common
to our description *and* to natural law. It is the umbilical cord that ties us,
the observer, to the placenta of physical reality. Information is something
that intelligence produces, nature loses, and life uses to assemble its parts
in the process of reproduction. Moreover, vast quantities of information were
utilized by the source of life at the time the first living object was created.
Scientific evidence now indicates that this "source" was not nature.[8]

In terms of a simple yet descriptive picture, the calculations show that
nature's seeds fall through the holes in her evolutionary purse faster than
she's able to gather them up. That is, on average, physical systems *lose* information with the passage of time. If only natural processes are at play, then
on average the complexity of physical structures should *decrease* and not
increase with the passing of time. Yet when we examine the fossil record
we do not see complexity decreasing; we instead see it increasing.

The New Generalized Second Law of Thermodynamics indicates that the
production of information evidenced by the progression of increased fossil
complexity did not arise from natural processes. These processes can, of
course, degrade previously living forms into fossils, but they cannot be the
womb from which these life forms originate. Were we to suppose that the
properties of physical matter produced and sustained the systematic growth
in biological complexity that we see in the fossil record, then we will have
prioritized intuition over insight. The biological structures that nature destroys
cannot originate from her processes because on average these processes destroy
information. The limitations of natural processes are further discussed in
Appendix 4. Were we to accept the claim that natural laws explain life on
earth, then faith must supercede fact.

Can Life Be Made in a Test Tube?

Biochemists who do avant-garde work in laboratories routinely make bits
and pieces of special chemicals that are found in living cells.[9] But they don't
make life. Even so, it's easy to get excited when one looks through a microscope at these tiny chemical wonders. At first glance, the bits and pieces of
some of the chemicals appear to multiply in ways that give the appearance
of life.[10] Thus, these chemicals are reported by some to resemble fragments
of a tiny part of a living cell. Another reason for excitement is that some
have thought that a portion of the chemicals may actually be a piece of
life's protein.[11]

The questions we need to ask are: Do the fragments actually qualify as
life? And, are the look-alike chemicals really protein? The truthful answer
to both questions is no. When we hear about test-tube babies, the experiments
involve fertilizing an egg with a sperm.[12] But the egg and sperm come from
other life. Therefore, it's a situation where life makes life. Or else we may
read or hear about how RNA—the "template" on which life's protein is
assembled—has been made to multiply in a test tube. Some claim this is

how life may have started. But the chemistry used in these RNA experiments is of two kinds: one that starts with life, and another that doesn't. The first kind doesn't count, and the second one produces chemical structures that contain essentially no information.

When enzymes (life) are used (in the first kind of RNA experiment), they contain information that can control which chemical goes where. Thus, it's possible for a string of chemicals to *strategically* grow in length, much like linking together words by selecting different letters of the alphabet. But if the enzymes are absent, what are produced are a number of look-alike fakes similar to random splotches that resemble letters, but which really are not. When examined, their length is pitifully short, they are structurally impoverished, and they are biologically sterile. Why? Because they contain virtually no information.

Did Life Self-Organize?

Prigogine won the 1977 Nobel Prize for mathematically showing that under certain conditions physical matter can undergo a change from a disorganized state to one of greater organization.[13] He later inferred (without proof) that life could have come into being this way; and he also failed to identify any source for the information that it required.[14] Furthermore, in discussions regarding the question of life, his equations do not account for the vast magnitude of *information* existing within biological structures, which enables them to coherently function as efficient oxygen-burning organic machines.

Natural combinations are totally inadequate to organize chemical parts to live, and when physical matter alters its distribution in the way described by Prigogine's equations, the overall information contained in the system decreases. This means that whereas local pockets of organization (increased information) are possible in principle they can only occur at the expense of disorganization (information loss) elsewhere in the system. Although scientific data indicates that the universe is about 13 billion years old and 30 billion light-years wide, it nonetheless is too young and too small ever to have produced the information needed to create biological structures.* Even the simplest of structures contains information whose magnitude far exceeds that of the entire natural universe.[15] Thus, rather than explaining life, Prigogine's analysis deepens the mystery.

What about experiments that involve the discharge of electricity through special gases? Has anyone ever tried to make life's protein this way? Did they succeed? Yes, they tried; and no, they failed.[16] Lightning can't create life any more than duststorms can make airplanes. For many years people experimented with different kinds of exotic chemicals, and much of this work continues to be in progress even today. The special chemicals chosen for

---

* Discussed in Chapter 13 and Appendix 6.

the electrical discharge are fragments of material that we find in living cells. In this sense they are biological chemicals.

The things these biochemists produce, however, are no more biotic than the granite used for tombstones. Both are expensive, and yet deader than a doornail. Virtually everything imaginable has been done to the chemicals in an attempt to create a biomolecule. This includes massaging them with energy, mixing them with gases, and exposing them to electricity under a variety of special arrangements. But functional biomolecules are chemicals organized to live. They contain information that comes from intelligence, not electricity. The first makes the second, not vice versa.

The Ink of Life

Suppose we find a lengthy story in a newspaper informing us that a hurricane is on its way. The story describes the hurricane's size, when it will arrive, the speed of the wind, and where it will strike. In other words, the page of newspaper contains information. That's because the ink is shaped into letters that in turn are arranged into words. The words are organized into sentences, and these in turn are grouped into paragraphs.

But if the ink were a big blob, *there would be no information.* It's the way that the ink is organized that creates the story about the hurricane. Likewise with life. It's the way in which the chemicals are organized that creates the material called protein. If the chemicals are uncoded then there *is* no life. Why? Because life does not consist of the chemicals in a molecule. It consists of the coherent and harmonious interplay among millions of microscopic parts that have been mysteriously organized to live.

To illustrate the point, imagine a tiny elf the size of a flea. Furthermore, imagine that he hops onto a sheet of newspaper and peels off, one by one, every letter on the page. We continue to watch as he throws each of the letters into a barrel. When he's finished, we see that all the letters are in the barrel, so that we're left with a big, white, blank sheet of paper.

Next, the elf proceeds to mix up the letters by repeatedly turning the barrel. Then, he removes the letters from the barrel and—one by one *at random*—pastes them back onto the otherwise blank sheet of paper. When he's through, the barrel is again empty, and every letter is back on the newspaper page. But this time the letters are helter-skelter, randomly located all over the page. We have a hodge-podge of ink in the form of letters. We have letters, but we don't have any words or sentences, i.e., *all the information is gone.*

At a distance of twelve feet away, our printed page looks like an ordinary sheet of newspaper. But when we get close, we realize that something is wrong because we can't understand anything. It's all jibberish! Nothing makes sense because there are no words. The story of the newspaper is the story of life. Man-made chemicals no more resemble protein than do confused blobs of ink resemble our hurricane story. The reason is that the story isn't the ink, but *how the ink is organized.* Likewise, life isn't the chemicals but how *they are organized.*

Making protein-like blobs by passing electricity through gases is akin to pasting random letters on a page. Neither the page nor the blob has information. In the laboratory, materials called amino acids are used as the chemical ink. Experiments are then designed in the hope that these chemicals will coalesce into life's protein. It would be like putting ink bottles on a white bed sheet during a thunderstorm in the hope that lightning may splatter the ink into Einstein's theory of relativity. But Mother Nature won't cooperate. The ink must always splatter into lifeless blobs because the needed information exceeds what nature can obtain from the inorganic universe.[15]

Were we to pass over the bedsheet in a low-flying airplane, the blobs of disorganized ink would be unreadable. Almost any story could be told in the plane as to what they really mean—just like viewing the disorganized newspaper sheet at twelve feet. But upon landing and examining the bedsheet close up, we would see that the ink was totally disorganized. Living structures contain chemicals organized to live. But the chemicals in the blobs generated by the electrical-discharge experiments are in disarray. What is important is not the chemicals, but rather how the chemicals are organized. Many people wrongly believe that scientists have created life's protein in the laboratory by passing electricity through mixtures of gases. But to identify lifeless chemical blobs with life's protein in this way is the same as calling ink flung by blindfolded monkeys a newspaper.

In many ways, nature is like the little elf who pastes random letters on the page. They both destroy information. Imagine a handwritten, personal letter that has fallen under a dripping faucet. The ink has smeared and only bits and pieces of the letter are legible, for the dripping water has slowly washed away much of the ink. Most all of the information is gone.

This illustrates in a simple yet clear way how *all* natural processes work. Natural processes *destroy* the way things are organized. And in doing so, they *annihilate* information. This means that if life evolved on earth at the mercy of natural processes, then the fossil record would show a *decrease,* not an increase, in the complexity of biological structures. This does *not* mean that life could not have evolved, but it *does* mean that if life *did* evolve, then it did so by a process that included all of the needed information from the very beginning. In other words, if each of the species originated as the issue of the one preceeding, then the thermodynamic constraints imposed by the sheer magnitude of the information contained in just one human cell (see Appendix 6) disengage nature as the energizing agent. The reason is that otherwise, thermodynamically speaking, nature becomes the equivalent of a perpetual motion machine.

12
WHY DO WE NEED LIFE TO CREATE LIFE?

LIFE EXISTS because of information along DNA. This information is in the form of groups of chemicals that are strategically positioned to create life's blueprint. The blueprint is composed of extraordinary patterns that organizationally function to sustain and perpetuate life. In the last chapter we examined how natural processes destroy patterns and therefore information. In this chapter we examine the belief that natural processes created these patterns and show why this is a practical impossibility.

Order versus Complexity

When someone tries to conceptually create life using only natural processes, he or she is trusting that nature will do just the opposite of what dripping water does to ink on a letter. The belief that life assembled itself requires faith that the chemicals self-organized and, in terms of information, that an ink blob wrote a letter by itself. Were this to happen, the chemical arrangement would be a kind of blueprint. That's because life's blueprint (DNA) instructs other chemicals how to assemble themselves.[1] The idea that dripping water will rearrange ink to produce a blueprint is a neat idea. However, the difficulty is that only a miracle can account for the kind of blueprint needed to explain the creation of life.[2] The basic problem is that accidents aren't miracles—they are accidents. But we need a miracle of the kind that dust, dirt, and slime cannot deliver. Lightning bolts notwithstanding,[3] chemically ordered blobs don't make life—they make crystals.[4] And this is where much of the confusion has been with regard to the question of life's origin.

Numerous books have been written over the past several decades that promulgate one central theme: Natural processes brought life into being.

But these authors have confused order for complexity, and have misunderstood the thermodynamic quantity called entropy.[5] We discussed both the history and confusion over this word in an earlier chapter.* It's easy to get natural processes to create ordered arrangements. It is done whenever a winter storm creates snowflakes.** But when considered as a total system, these processes *lose information.* If we are to learn how life was created, then we require a process that *destroys order and creates complexity.* In other words, we need the exact opposite of ordered arrangements—we need a natural process that will produce a near-random arrangement. But these requirements are not as simple as some have supposed.

For example, were we to take a deck of playing cards and examine whatever sequence of fifty-two cards a particular shuffle might produce, it could be argued that the specific arrangement of cards seen would have had a near impossible likelihood of occurring. And yet, there in full view it exists for all to see. It is then said that this is also true for an unlikely chemical sequence appearing in the DNA strand of a primeval cell. But this kind of rhetoric is deceptively naive and is hardly a convincing illustration that life could have so easily overcome the statistical impossibility of its appearance on earth.

The Magic Shuffle

The problem that confronts us in explaining the origin of life is that we must explain the appearance of a *particular* nucleotide sequence, mainly, the one found in the DNA of living cells, and this is *enormously* more difficult to explain than the appearance of *any* sequence from a pristine shuffle of fifty-two cards. In the latter case, the probability is 100 percent that *a* sequence will appear, whereas with life the probability that the *necessary* sequence will occur is, as a practical matter, zero. Yet we find the playing card example along with other similar illustrations in books written to convince the uninitiated that, as a matter of principle, natural processes not only *can* produce life, but most likely *did.*[6]

The argument that a near-impossible arrangement can easily appear (some sequence of the fifty-two cards) is erroneous because it presumes that *each* of the many trillions upon trillions of ways that the cards can be arranged *** organizationally functions to satisfy life's requirements. But this is hardly the case. For example, to explain the origin of life we must explain the origin of a *particular* sequence of nucleotide bases in the DNA blueprint

---

* Writers on origins wrongly present entropy in terms of a distribution in energy levels instead of the nucleotide bases that constitute the genome's ensemble of genetic messages.

** It also occurs when chemists make adenine molecules by shining ultraviolet light on hydrogen cyanide.

*** A random shuffle of 52 playing cards can yield over 8×10^{67} possible arrangements.

that instructs cells to manufacture protein, including the production of three thousand vastly complex enzymes that supply the "workmen" responsible for doing the actual assembly.[7]

The blueprint also contains detailed specifications that produce the heart, stomach, kidneys, and gall bladder, along with every other organ and gland in the body.[8] It also instructs the manufacture of muscles, nerves, and skin, together with the myriad body parts including eyes, ears, and brain.[9] And if that isn't enough, the blueprint contains additional instructions responsible for the manufacture of reproductive organs that perpetuate the blueprint by producing new human beings! Yet as impressive as this may be, what is staggering is that, as a practical matter, only one kind of protein will work in each case.[10] *All* the others tend to be worthless, not only because they function improperly, but because they self-destruct! Figuratively speaking, this includes the particular fifty-two card sequence that our random shuffle delivers.

Some people have argued that if we kept shuffling long enough, then the required magic sequence must appear. But what they fail to understand is that the magnitude of the information (complexity) found in even simple cells is so vast, that to suppose it was produced by natural processes in a universe as young as 13 billion years and as small as 30 billion light-years is to abdicate one's cognitive faculties—not because we can't accede to its occurrence in our minds, but because the constraints imposed by the limited space-time "fabric" render the event aberrant. Although oversimplified, we can express the difficulty by saying that the cards will wear out long before the magic combination can occur!

Did Life Assemble Itself?

People are divided on the question as to whether life assembled itself. A large number believe that life is a miracle created by God, but many others avoid the idea by believing that life assembled itself. Regardless of one's persuasion, however, either belief requires faith. No human being saw how life developed; yet, surprisingly, those with the most to say sometimes behave as though they did. If we're to believe that life assembled itself, then let's at least identify scientific reasons for doing so. But when we look for hard data we find not facts but materialism, i.e., a philosophy that *impersonates* science. This philosophy champions the idea that only matter and its motion exist and, therefore, concludes that life must have assembled itself because there are no other options.

If you are one who believes that nothing exists except matter and its motion, then you believe in this philosophy—you believe in materialism. For you, self-assembly is a must. It happened because, if it didn't, life wouldn't be here. The reason for your belief is you've assumed that nothing exists except matter and its motion. This assumption is obviously related to the discussion in a preceding chapter where we noted that scientific calculations based on data from electron microscopy of living cells show that the belief that life accidentally arose is an act of faith and *not* science. Likewise with self-assembly—it too is an act of faith.

For example, suppose we needed a computer to control traffic flow in and out of New York City, How would we acquire it? The answer is we'd first carefully analyze the auto traffic in and out of the city, and then give the data to a team of engineers. When the design phase was complete after, say, several years, they would select a company that constructed computers using complicated electrical devices and integrated circuits. These devices and circuits would be manufactured by other companies using technology developed over half a century by thousands upon thousands of trained, skilled, and thinking people. But let's stop and consider that the neurological pathways controlled by the brain in a human body are so much more complicated than auto traffic that the biological control defies description.

For example, a single nerve cell can be many times thinner (four microns) than a strand of hair, yet have up to 100,000 electrical receptors that receive messages from many hundreds of other nerve cells—and at propagation rates up to 250 miles per hour. The total length of these neurological wires in the human body is estimated to be several hundred thousand miles. As for the brain itself, its complexity lies beyond anything that can be imagined. By way of perspective, the brain of even the simplest insect exhibits a level of complexity that exceeds all of the human relationships possible on earth today. Where then is the basis for believing that interstellar debris eventually assembled itself into human civilization? Everything we know shows that natural processes destroy information. Therefore the notion that they systematically amassed unfathomable quantities of it makes no sense whatsoever. It would be different if we had evidence to the contrary, but we don't.

With this in view, consider the kinds of beliefs regarding life's origin presently rampant in our society. The notion of biological self-assembly is growing in popularity.[11] Life's blueprint is becoming increasingly accepted as the inevitable result of natural processes within the physical world. The belief is that these processes transformed nonliving matter into living, loving, and laughing people over a time period of billions of years. Some people require very little evidence to accept such ideas, and the source of greatest comfort for such thinking has come from studies on bits and pieces of a substance called "RNA"—a chemical template used by cells to manufacture protein.[12]

Can Man Create Life's Template?

Many experiments and theories have been proposed in an attempt to understand life's basic chemistry.[13] Some of these studies involve the use of enzymes, which are proteins that speed up life's chemical reactions. Enzymes are loaded with biological information, and to include them in any experiment that seeks to "make life" is equivalent to creating life from life.

However, other experiments are done in which enzymes are *not* present.

These investigations thus attempt in some way to simulate the chemical environment that may have existed on our planet when it came into being. These experiments have shown that under very special conditions certain chemicals will combine to create *short* RNA. These short segments of artificially created RNA can, in turn, be made to procreate other *short* RNA, and the chemical reproduction has given rise to the belief that this is how life may have begun.[14] It has also created the false hope that life may one day be artificially created. It's easy to see how the experimental results reinforce such beliefs. Whenever something self-replicates it presents a lifelike appearance. It's thus easy to think that one may be looking at the onset of life as one observes these tiny RNA segments chemically reproducing in a laboratory environment.

However, the experimental results can be very misleading. It's instructive to realize that *many* nonliving things multiply. Crystals do it all the time. And dust, for example, interacts with water-laden clouds to create snowflakes. But RNA growth is not identical to snowflakes, and segments of RNA have been created in the laboratory that procreate other short RNA segments. Yet despite the different mode of replication, snowflakes and RNA are *not* dissimilar. The reason is that each shares something in common that explains why neither can ever produce life. Let's see what this is.

The first thing we recognize is that when natural structures come into being—e.g., a hurricane—they undergo an *increase* in complexity. Many authors have siezed upon this tendency of natural systems to spontaneously form structure to support the belief that natural processes could have similarly produced the biological structures that manifest life.[15] But this is not true, and to see why it's not true we need to clearly understand the role that complexity plays in the physical systems of the universe.

When scientists mathematically describe a physical system that spontaneously forms a structure (e.g., a snowflake, a crystal, or a hurricane), the equations tell us that in a very literal sense the complexity of a structure can only grow at the expense of the complexity of other structure in surrounding regions.[16]

To recall an example of a previous chapter, the complexity of the walnut at the pancake's center can only grow if the complexity of the surrounding regions decreases. This is equivalent to saying that the walnut acquires information at the expense of information elsewhere. In other words, they grow in structural complexity at the expense of the complexity that is available from their surroundings. We can think of these physical entities consuming information the way we consume food. But if we ask what is the source of the ultimate information that is drawn upon in this growth process, the answer is that, except for intelligence, we *don't know.* Random motions of physical matter are possible. Although unlikely, they may produce patterns and, therefore, *some* information. But such motions cannot produce the *magnitude* of information needed to explain life.

Natural things can only multiply complexity by destroying the complexity of their surroundings. This is how the biochemists are able to create the short segments of RNA discussed above. As a practical matter, the amount of information present in these abbreviated molecules is derived from the information present in the chemical bath used to generate them, and *cannot exceed the information content of this bath.* This criterion defines the maximum information that can ever be produced in artificially generated RNA in the absence of enzymes.

As discussed above, if enzymes are present, the chemical bath produces significantly longer RNA chains because "life" is effectively being used to generate "life," i.e., the enzymes are derived from other life and carry genetic information otherwise unobtainable by the chemical bath. However when the enzymes are absent, the RNA strands are much shorter.*

The implicit assumption that apparently inspires these and similar investigations is the belief that RNA molecules of much greater complexity can be experimentally created if the "right chemicals and conditions" can be found. The principal reason for this hope seems to rest in the basic misunderstanding between thermodynamic and genetic entropy discussed in a previous chapter.

In summary, the confusion between crystallography and biology has nurtured the illusion that chemicals can self-assemble themselves into meaningful structures. This is particularly true in studies with RNA.[17] However, what actually occurs in these experiments is that the *total system* undergoes a *loss* of information, and no amount of chemical manipulation can make it otherwise.[18]

Of course the temptation is to believe that if the right chemical "seed" can be found, then it will ratchet itself into higher structural levels through self-assembly. The problem with this goal, however, is that the magnitude of information needed to regulate life is unavailable to the chemical bath. The reason is that the information content of the entire inorganic universe is much too small. This is why we need life to get life. And the mystery which confronts us is that there is no known *natural* source that could have produced the needed amount of information in living structures.

Further Implications

Aside from the new insights that relate complexity to information, a very basic difference still separates modern science from the older ideas, and it would do us well to review the division; namely,

The independent existence of the physical world apart from human observers cannot be logically defended. The reason is that quantum laws are statistical

---

* In the absence of enzymes, a poly-C template in a 50:50 mixture of activated A and G monomers with lead ions yields 10:1 ratios of G:A showing over 90 percent correct base pairing; if zinc ions are present, a poly-C template with activated G monomers yield G chains with about 40 bases-cytosine (C), adenine (A), guanine (G).

descriptions of *observations*—they do *not* describe an "independent physical reality."

Let's now apply this twentieth-century insight to a fossil. We can assign numbers to the biological structure of a fossil that quantify the size of the blueprint totally describing it. Furthermore, our description of the fossil will contain information that measures the fossil's complexity. If now we examine, say, three fossils of separate species that existed over different time periods, we will produce three blueprints, one for each of the species. We will discover that each is more complex than the one before, and that the simplest contains far more information than what exists within the entire natural universe. This then raises two questions: (1) What is the source of the biological information, and (2) why is it increasing with the passage of time.

The New Generalized Second Law speaks to the magnitude of this complexity and states that, on average, the observer must *lose* rather than gain information. This implies that the fossil record should show a decrease, rather than an increase, in the complexity of the biological structures it preserves. Since this is not the case, it suggests that the appearance of greater and greater information is not the result of its natural production, but, instead, a progressive revelation of information previously programmed into the entire biological system. The sheer magnitude of the information, and the systematic growth of fossil complexity with the passage of time are not explained by natural hypotheses—whether natural selection or otherwise.

The ordinary Second Law could not address this question because it can only describe the state of a fossil at times of rest (equilibrium). When the complexity of the biological structure of a later fossil was observed to be greater than that of an earlier one, we knew of no reason why natural machinery could not exist between these two equilibrium or "rest" states to permit it to happen. Furthermore, our older science did not allow us to *quantify* complexity; nor was there awareness of the fundamental importance of the observer's informational role in regulating the "locations and speed" (phase point) of physical matter. Thus, there was no reliable way to know whether the magnitude of the information available to an observer through natural processes in the universe was inconsistent with the fossils.

This is now changed. Today, we know that the complexity found in biological structures is too large to have been produced by a natural process. In addition, the ordinary Second Law is now replaced by the New Generalized Second Law which is not limited to the before and after rest states, but is valid *between* the two. Moreover, it is not limited to "thermodynamic variables" (such as temperature and pressure), but is valid for *any* observable. The New Generalized Second Law imposes constraints on the changes that are possible between an earlier and a later fossil (the before and after rest states), and it tells us that natural machinery does not exist to *systematically* increase the complexity of biological structures with the passage of time.

What's important about this conclusion is that it does not rest upon a particular explanation (such as natural selection). Rather, it is the basic result that regulates physical matter. This indicates that regardless of what we might conjecture to be the alleged "natural" explanation for the progression of increased complexity in the fossil record, it will be untrue in the same way a patent examiner in Washington, D.C., knows an alleged invention for a perpetual motion machine is untrue.

The Meaning of the New Second Law

What *does* the New Generalized Second Law teach regarding the natural flow of information? It teaches that nature is a sieve whose structures undergo deterioration and, therefore, information loss with the passage of time. Since physical processes are not able to retrieve this information, and since intelligence is the only known "pump" that can reverse the process, intellect could hardly have resulted from processes that lose what it produces.

Quantum physics teaches that intelligence exists in *disunion* from the things it measures, and that the sum total of physical reality is composed of two entities: quantum and classical objects. The first are subject to quantum laws, whereas the second (spirit) are exempt from them. The New Generalized Second Law is the result of quantum laws, and teaches that an observer in the universe *loses* information as time passes.

Why is information lost with the passage of time? Because if we measure physical things and then allow them to change in a natural way, they take on forms that minimize the information in our description subject to predictions based on earlier measurement. When we apply this consideration to living systems, we expect the fossil record to contain biological structures that decrease rather than increase their organization. The reason is that if the sequence of these structures is identified with natural change, they represent distributions of biological components that *minimize* the information in their description by an observer. But the fossil record does not show an information loss; instead it reveals an evolutionary process that, *on average, produced information.* Thus the systematic growth of biological complexity recorded in the fossil record cannot be understood in terms of natural processes in the light of the New Generalized Second Law.

The concepts of information and uncertainty may seem elusive to us because unlike our older science, these new insights have no simple mechanical interpretation. Likewise it's not easy to visualize an observer undergoing a loss of information. This too has no simple analog. Therefore, let's try to understand these important new concepts in a more familiar setting. It's worth the effort because the information loss taught by the New Generalized Second Law regulates every physical thing in the universe.

Picture a one-room schoolhouse with a window along an outer wall. Looking through the window from the outside we see a room with seven rows of desks, five to each row; they are all empty. Inside, thirty-five children are running helter-skelter, and from outside the building the teacher hears much noise and commotion. Looking through the window, she tries to see who's doing what, but the situation is complex because each child is doing something different. Upon her return to the classroom, how will she possibly recall the independent activity of the thirty-five children that are running helter-skelter inside? That's a lot of *information* to remember. But as she ponders this, all of a sudden one of the young people inside notices that the teacher is looking! He shouts and the loud warning is heard by all of his classmates. One by one, each child returns to a desk, and within moments all of the children are seated. Order returns to the classroom, and now it's easy to describe each child's whereabouts. In other words, what previously was complex has now become ordered. To describe the whereabouts of thirty-five children that are quietly seated in seven rows, each with five desks, requires less information than when each is up and running around.

We can liken the schoolroom to a crystal whose atomic particles are neatly lined up into rows. It resembles the ordered schoolroom and it's easy to describe. But when each of the particles is moving around helter-skelter, more information is needed to describe what's going on because the location of each particle is different at each instant of time.

Holding each piece of the system in easily identified fixed locations considerably reduces the needed amount of information. That's because ordered systems are less complex and, therefore, easier to describe. What previously was moving in complex ways is now quiet, still, and calm. And whereas we previously needed to call out each child's name and location at each instant of time when he or she was in motion, once seated, their location is specified by the position of his or her desk for *all time*. Moreover, since there are five desks in each row, we can even use one row number to identify each of five children in that row.

Now suppose that the teacher randomly selects groups of five children each and instructs them to form circles by holding hands. The information needed to describe each of the seven circles would increase because we could no longer use the same row number to specify the location of the five children. These seven groups, each with five children in a circle, can be likened to the production of small RNA molecules in a chemical bath. As the children change from a state of running helter-skelter into a state of seven circular groups, each with five children, the complexity of the schoolroom, and therefore the information, *decreases*. An observer's description of the room contains less information with the children organized into circular groups than with them running helter-skelter around the room.

In a similar way, when atomic ensembles crystallize into small RNA molecules in a chemical bath, the molecules are more complex than the ensembles. This was also true when the children formed circles; a group of five children is more complex than any one of the children considered separately. However *each* of the seven circles can be described by the *same* information. This is also true of the RNA molecules, because all of the molecules are essentially the same. Thus the overall information needed to describe the chemical bath *decreases* when RNA molecules form, because when *all* of the atomic ensembles are considered, their description as independent entities is more complex than when they coalesce into RNA molecules.

The more children we collect into groups (RNA), the less information we need to describe the schoolroom (chemical bath). That's because a complex situation has become less complex (more ordered) due to the repetition of seven identical groups of children (RNA). This is what happens in a test tube with a chemical bath. As the RNA multiplies, the complexity of the chemical mixture, taken as a whole, decreases. The key point, however, is that the maximum complexity one can obtain in any RNA molecule is limited by the inherent complexity that the phase change (crystallization) can draw upon within the overall system (chemical bath).

In systems that are void of life, the final product is pitifully small (on the order of ten to twenty informational nucleotides). The reason is that the reservoir of information that must be drawn upon to produce even a primitive component of life is so vast that it far exceeds the corresponding level of complexity of the "chemical bath" filling the volume of the universe. This is why test-tube experiments that produce RNA lengths of the order of one hundred informational nucleotides must be "primed" *with* life (e.g., enzymes); these proteins then become the source of the needed information that produces the longer lengths of meaningful RNA. But the lesson is the same: To get life you need life—nothing less will do!

13

WHY IS LIFE
A MIRACLE?

IN PREVIOUS CHAPTERS we noted that natural forces destroy information. We saw how they erode patterns, and we illustrated how a natural process can produce information in one location (the walnut) only by losing it elsewhere (the pancake). We referenced experiments that attempt to make bits and pieces of life's molecules, and explained that the complexity of these chemical patterns (short RNA) is limited by the information available to the bath. We also noted that thermal entropy is commonly confused for genetic entropy and said that snowflakes and ice cubes have very little information because they are ordered, whereas large amounts of it reside in living cells because they are complex. We saw how decades of ignoring this distinction led authors to pursue crystallography rather than biology, thereby nurturing the false belief that nature can create life. We also observed that to explain life's origin demands that we find the source of the DNA information that instructs the manufacture of life's parts and controls the biological processes by which the parts organizationally function. We explained that the New Generalized Second Law regulates the flow of information in an observer's description of the physical world, and that on average this information can never increase, but instead will decrease.

Can We Measure Information?

The reader will note that the word *information* appears seven times in the above passage and that it is a common thread throughout our discussion on life's origin. Therefore, let's turn our attention toward this word and see if we can gather more insight into the concept of information. Had this concept been more clearly understood in older writings it's doubtful that order would have been confused for complexity. In the past, confusion between complexity and order was widespread, and it led to the erroneous belief that life's origin could be understood through an exchange process involving physical matter in other parts of the universe. This false notion still appears, even in recent times.[1]

Today, we know that life is *not* ordered—it is *complex*. Thus, to explain life we must explain the origin of complexity. It is easy to see why this is true. Living structures are atomic particles organized to live. Were we to find the wing of an airplane in one corner of a junkyard, its tail in another, and the engine buried beside a windshield, we all know that the parts couldn't fly. But when assembled into a plane, they *do* fly. The same is true of atomic particles. Just as an airplane consists of parts organized to fly, in the same way our body is made of atomic pieces that are organized to live.

We can think of the degree to which something is organized as its complexity. What's important about the time period in which we live is that several decades ago, scientists learned how to measure complexity. In scientific lingo, we discovered how to *quantify* the degree to which we can specify a physical structure and, therefore, the degree to which we can measure its complexity. But our yardstick doesn't have inches. It's a measuring rod that has units called "bits" of information.

In previous chapters we discussed how life makes life; of course, examples abound to illustrate the point. People make people, plants make plants, and pugs make pugs. But the question is: How small can something be and still make itself? Loosely speaking, the answer seems to be, as small as a large protein molecule. This protein structure can be thought of as an organic machine composed of chemical parts. What's significant is that if we submerge this organic machine into a bath composed of similar chemical parts, the protein's structure can direct these parts to assemble another organic machine just like itself.

The information contained in our description of the structure of protein can be likened to the decisions it would need to make were it to successfully supervise the assembly of another organic machine just like itself. Therefore, the minimum amount of information needed to describe protein is found by answering the following question: What are the *fewest* decisions that a machine needs to make in order for it to assemble itself? Not too long ago, a famous twentieth-century mathematician, John von Neumann, asked the same question. He discovered mathematically that a machine would need to make about fifteen hundred correct decisions, one after the other without error, in order to reproduce itself.[2]

We can measure the amount of information present in the structure of a protein molecule by thinking of each decision the machine must make as a bit of information. If we do this, von Neumann's answer can be expressed another way. The least information needed to describe a machine complex enough to guide its own reproduction is fifteen hundred bits. Thus, as an inch is a unit of length and a pound a unit of weight, a bit becomes a unit of information.

Phrased in this way, a bit of information becomes a measure of consecutive decisions between two alternate courses of action. When we say that the amount of information needed by a machine to reproduce itself must be at least fifteen hundred bits, what we *mean* is that the machine must make at least fifteen hundred consecutive decisions *without error* to faithfully replicate itself. If one decision is wrong, it's doomed, and its structure terminates in extinction.

Maxwell's Mysterious "Demon"

The organizational intricacies of protein reflect information on a scale that a Supreme Intelligence can produce, but that nature cannot. To see why this is true, let's think about a small imp who became known as "Maxwell's Demon." [3] We will allow the imp to control a tiny window that connects two adjoining compartments. In your mind's eye, imagine two boxes joined by a common wall. In the middle of the wall, picture a tiny window that connects one box to the other. On one side of the window there's a shelf where the imp is perched.

The imp is able to open or close the window at will, and without effort. Both boxes contain air and from time to time, as a result of this air, a gentle breeze blows against either side of the window. The imp is told, "Open the window if the breeze on your side is strong; otherwise keep it shut."

Now this may seem like a simple request, but the question is, can the imp obey the instruction? Although it may seem like something he can do, it turns out that were he to successfully perform the required task, he would violate one of the most fundamental laws of science. It's worthwhile to learn why this is so, because we will not only uncover a fascinating insight regarding the origin of life, but we will also discover the answer to something that stumped the whole world for over half a century regarding Maxwell's demon.

We've said that each of the two boxes contains air. But air consists of tiny molecules which are atomic specks so small that about 10 thousand billion will fit onto the head of a pin. Furthermore, these minuscule dots are in a state of constant motion; we sense them each time we feel a breeze. A strong breeze means that they're moving fast whereas no breeze means that they're hardly moving.

Now suppose the imp opens the window each time a strong breeze occurs. If he consistently does this, all the fast-moving molecules will pass through the open window and into the box on the other side. But since he keeps the window closed when there is no breeze, the slow molecules will remain in the box where he's standing. Thus, the imp has succeeded in separating the fast and slow air molecules, putting the fast ones into the one box, and keeping the slow ones in the adjoining box. From a scientific point of view, faster air molecules mean a higher temperature and an increase in pressure.

Therefore, our imp has created a pressure and temperature difference between the two boxes; i.e., he has created energy!

But how can Maxwell's demon work? How can he create energy? This question baffled the world for many years, and no one was able to offer a satisfactory answer. Scientists asked, "Why can't an imp open a window?" If he could, he certainly could separate the fast- and slow-moving air into separate compartments. The fast-moving molecules will travel to one side, and the slower ones will remain in the other.

No one questioned the fact that, at least in principle, the imp had created energy. Let's see how we know that this is true. To show that the imp has created energy, we can wait until he's collected all the fast-moving air on one side. When that is done, we'll open the window, but this time keep it open. Air from the high pressure side (box with the fast-moving molecules) will rush through the opening and into the other side. If a generator wheel is located near the window during the time it's open, the resulting gush of air can be made to turn the wheel of the generator and, thereby, make electricity. Therefore, the imp *does* create energy. But here's our dilemma: *It's impossible to create energy in a closed box!* So no one could figure out how the imp could do it!

Death of a Demon

Maxwell invented his demon in the 1800s, but not until 1929 did a scientist named Leo Szilard find the answer. The imp can't create energy—not because he's unable to open and close the window, but because he doesn't know when to do so. In other words, he doesn't have the information necessary to identify which air molecule is moving fast and which is moving slow. But what's even more important, it *costs him energy to acquire the information he needs!* In fact, Szilard did a careful analysis showing that it costs *more* energy than the imp can recover.[4] Simply put, the process of creating energy forces you to lose it! We can phrase it yet another way: *Information is equivalent to energy in the sense that to have one means you can create the other.*

Let's now recall what makes biological structures live. It isn't the existence of their basic atomic particles, but rather the *way* these particles are organized. To create life is to create information that defines and controls organizationally functioning harmonies among nonliving parts; what's remarkable is that these harmonies "interplay" to produce a stable structure manifesting biological qualities that preserve, through self-replication, the information that defines and controls them.

In its simplest expression, to create life is to organizationally compose a living song from nonliving notes. Yet were we to bring the living melody of a pulsating structure into existence, it would mean that we would have also created the sheet music that imaged its organized tones. This sheet music is analogous to the information in an observer's description of a living structure. Just as the sheet music contains all of the notes of the song, so also does the information that describes a biological structure capture and image all of its complexity. But the magnitude of this information exists on so vast a scale that its origin defies logical understanding through any natural process within the space and time of the universe. In short, it has no rational explanation other than as the fingerprint of a Supreme Intelligence. The reason is that Mother Nature's IQ is much too low for her to have been the Genius that created life's near infinite blueprint.

We now catch a glimmer of the importance of the constraints that kept Maxwell's demon from acquiring unlimited information. How could the imp know how fast the air is moving? In some way or another, *he must look.* But when he does that, it costs him energy; "looking" involves the transfer of light energy for when he looks, at least one unit of light (a photon) will bounce off an air molecule, and into his eye. Light energy is used up in this process. Careful calculations show that the energy lost as light enters the imp's eye is more than the energy obtained when he traps the molecule.

Thus acquiring information to produce energy is not cost-effective. The energy spent by the imp for the amount of information he acquires *exceeds* the energy he can create when he uses this information in knowing when to open and close the window. But had our imp somehow gotten this information for free, he could have freely exchanged it for energy, i.e., *he could have created energy.* In this sense, the substance of what's real *is* the information that describes it. Although this concept might be new, the assurance we have that it's so stems from the fact that modern quantum laws do *not* describe independent physical things, but instead are statistical relations of our observations.

Modern science has given us a new and profoundly important tool by which to understand the world. For the first time in the history of mankind, we are able to measure the information needed to describe an object's complexity. But it costs us energy to acquire this information. The energy exchange connects us, as living agents, to the physical stuff we observe. Since physical reality is what we describe it to be, what we know to be real is the information in our description of it. This insight may be unsettling to the reader, so let's see if we can understand it from a somewhat different perspective.

First, let's note that "physical stuff" is composed of energy. Atomic bombs work by exchanging a tiny piece of physical stuff or matter for an enormous amount of energy. This energy is released in the form of light, heat, and wind. We saw earlier that Maxwell's demon could have exchanged *information* for energy. The reason he didn't is because he lacked the information that he needed to perform the exchange. Furthermore, to acquire this information would have cost him more energy than he would have been able to obtain by using it. This conclusion is something we said earlier and it bears repeating: The energy we spend to acquire information always exceeds the energy we can create from it. This discovery is new to our century and it has deep implications and profound ramifications.

The Miracle of Life

Physical objects are described by information. Without it they are indescribable. The more complex the structure, the more information we need to describe it.* Since the complexity of the object is measured by the magnitude of the information in its description, we can think of the information as "resident" within the object. In effect, one is synonomous with the other. This means that the information used by an observer to quantify complexity can be understood as the object's ultimate reality. In the absence of an observer, the object's existence *cannot be logically defended.* Appendix 5 provides further discussion on this point.

But how much information is needed to describe the things about us? Were we to calculate the information in our descriptions of things, what magnitude of complexity would we find in the numbers? What do the calculations reveal? For example, how much more information is in a jet airplane than in a roller skate? And how does the universe compare with a man?

In order to establish a basis for answering such questions, let's return to self-replication by a machine. We've seen that a machine needs at least fifteen hundred bits of information before it can assemble itself. Thus, since life makes life, the fifteen hundred bits is a measure of how small a living structure can be. With the invention of the electron microscope and its comparatively recent practical development, it has been possible for the first time in recorded history to actually study the interior of protein. The results in the two decades following such pioneering investigation have been startling. The mathematical result showing that fifteen hundred bits is the minimum information needed by a machine to replicate itself is consistent with the astonishing discovery that fifteen hundred bits is roughly the information existing in a large protein molecule.

Now, isn't it remarkable that protein just happens to possess enough information for the fifteen hundred consecutive decisions it must make without error to be replicated? It *is* remarkable, for the following reason.

Fifteen hundred bits is so vast that its origin from a natural process cannot be logically explained. For example, we might ask how fifteen hundred bits compare with the information content of their physical objects in our world? But it's so large that it doesn't compare. For example, the information stored in the world's largest library is under fifty bits, and all of human knowledge is of the order of sixty bits. How much information is present in the solar system? The answer is about one hundred seventy bits. And what about the universe? What is its information content? Here the estimate is two hundred thirty-five bits. These and other related matters are discussed in greater detail in Appendix 6.

---

* All descriptions can be reduced to a one-dimensional sequence of symbols whose complexity is the information content of the shortest algorithm that completely describes it.[5]

If the physical structure of all nonliving matter embraces about two hundred thirty-five bits, where did the fifteen hundred bits of a large protein molecule come from? The sensible answer is that it came from a Supreme Intelligence. But lest we lose our frame of reference, let's remember that *life is more than protein.* The smallest system of self-sustaining life isn't protein—it's a living cell. How much information does *it* contain? To answer that, let's consider something simple—a plantlike, one-cell entity called a "bacterium." What would you guess its information content to be? The answer may stagger you. It's *millions* of bits! This is why life is a miracle (see Appendix 6).

There is no rational basis to explain the source of so staggering an amount of information on the basis of natural processes in a universe as young and as small as ours, though it is 13 billion years old and 30 billion light-years wide. Yet, are not human beings more than simple, one-cell plants? And aren't you more complex than even a tiny assembly of cells? As to the origin of these things, the simplest answer imaginable is that a Supreme Intelligence who the Bible calls God designed it all. Why is so obvious an answer never even considered in ordinary publications dealing with life's origin? Just as we see animals existing at a higher level than plants, and we higher than animals, is there any logical basis for not explaining the miraculous organization of biological structures as the design of an Intelligence who exists at a level incomprehensible to man?

The physical world bears witness to design in virtually every structure about us. Yet as guppies in the fishbowl of space-time, we still ask for proof that there is water! But is the proof not in the butterfly that flies and the flower that blooms? Does it not present itself in a starlit sky and the morning dew? Some can and do reject these things as proof. But what do they offer in its place? Can nonliving matter explain the very human experience of majestic sunsets and the time-tested music of Bach and Beethoven? Do these things not imply a designer whose most intricate of all structure challenges every physician who performs surgery on a human body?

Even the simplest of structures implies design. For example, earth's temperature depends upon light from the sun which in turn comes from intricate nuclear processes that work in part because a neutron weighs slightly more than a hydrogen atom. But were it the other way around, the sun along with all other stars in the universe would collapse and bathe earth with deadly radiation that would destroy all life.

Some believe that everything that we see and measure came into being by itself, including this particular mass relationship. But what is the basis for such belief? Certainly not the facts modern science has uncovered with regard to the information content of biological structures.

The most primitive organism implies the prior existence of at least two thousand enzymes—each a fantastically complex protein of its own—and in a human cell these produce additional protein chains that number one hundred times this total. But people are more intricate than protein chains and biological structures more complicated than enzymes. Moreover these structures share unusual relationships with the physical constants of the universe. The human eye, for example, has its peak response at the one part of the spectrum where sunlight penetrates earth's water vapor (the water window). While survival pressures could have played a role, the fact that the sun has its peak emission in the same spectral region cannot be explained this way. When one examines the details, there is a mysterious relationship between the structure of the eye, the gravitational constant of the universe, the atomic unit of electric charge, and the quantum constant of Planck.*

The very young believe in the Easter Bunny, Santa Claus, and the Tooth Fairy. But what are we who are not so very young to believe? The materialistic myths of a prior century? Or the modern indications that an Intelligence has made itself known?

---

* The gravitational constant undergirds the sun's density; the latter in turn is the principal parameter behind its temperature and its emission. Conversely, the electric charge and Planck's constant underlie the molecular structure of water and, therefore, its absorption.

WHY ARE MEN AND APES PHYSICALLY SIMILAR?

ANTHROPOLOGY is the field of study concerned with man's origin. Anthropologists, the people engaged in such study, tell us that when we look in a mirror and see ourselves, what we see is an ape after several million years of evolution.[1] Does that bother you? It does some and yet others are less concerned. The basic idea is that through the course of time, evolution gradually changed wild beasts into human beings. It's like replacing successive slices of salami with baloney. Gradually over the course of time the apes (salami) change into men (baloney). The question I'd like to explore from a scientific point of view is this: Did such a transition occur? We need to realize that many intelligent people believe abundant evidence exists proving that man came from the ape.[2] We need to look at this evidence from a scientific perspective and with an open mind.

History is replete with ideas that once were believed true but today are known to be false.[3] In the case being considered, the evidence is so poor that two published papers suggest that apes actually evolved from man.[4] The basis of this argument is that all known fossils are ancestral to, or precede, chimpanzees, gorillas, and man. If these three species split apart from one another in the distant past, the fossils cannot tell us when it occurred. Instead, we need to study genetic material for the answer.

Genetic dating and serological (serum) techniques indicate that it could not have happened prior to 5 million years ago,[5] a time when the fossil record teaches that the ancestor "common" to the three species *resembles man more than ape*. Others have published a number of reasons why they believe that if man evolved, it's more logical that he came from the sea.[6]

One of their arguments is that man's salt intake is independent of his body's salt requirement; another argument is that human babies are "plump." They also note that the human nose has muscles and that on occasion "webbing" appears between fingers or toes. These ideas are not cited here because they make sense, but rather to illustrate that the idea that man evolved from apes is not as clear cut as some would suppose.* It's important to realize that the people who propose other ideas on man's origin are quite intelligent and well aware of many of the facts that are available on this question, perhaps even more aware than those who believe man came from apes. Yet these people reject the theory of human evolution. Why? How can intelligent scientists reject what every one "knows" is true? The answer is that the case for man's evolution is not based on hard facts, but on a surprising number of assumptions.

Common Parts

It's obvious that at a distance men and apes look alike. So do typewriters and computers. Does this mean that computers evolved from typewriters? We might say yes if we include their common designer, but typewriters don't evolve, they wear out. A typewriter can't produce a computer any more than a light bulb can make a star. On the contrary, machines rust and light bulbs burn out. Where then does the notion come from that man evolved from apes? We know that they share common features. Both have eyes, ears, arms, and legs, but so do countless other life forms. They both have a nose, mouth, and stomach, but does this mean that any one of them was *produced* from the other? If every part of our makeup is simply an advanced version of an ape's, and if the ape itself comes from some other animal, either living or dead, then how different can we be from all the other life forms in the world? The question is really, is there anything truly distinctive about mankind as compared to the many hundreds of thousands of species that exist on the planet earth?

A common belief as to why man differs from the other primates on earth is that he has great reasoning powers that enable him to enjoy life at a higher level of existence. Basically this idea holds that man is simply another animal at a much more advanced stage, which evolved from apes after the apes evolved from something lower. If this is true, we are animals that differ from other animals in *degree* but not in *kind*. There is no absolute disunion between us and the animal world. They are what we once were, and we are what they will become.

---

* The term *apes* is commonly used to denote pongids and their presumed Miocene ancestors. For ease of writing we will refer to human evolution as man coming from apes—meaning Miocene apes, the surmised progenitors of both pongids and hominids.[7] Recent work has dethroned *Ramapithicus* in favor of chimpanzees and gorillas; other conjecture puts man on yet another line.[8]

How true then is the claim that we came from apes?[9] Where does honest inquiry lead us in this matter?

Taken at face value, it would almost seem evident that man is simply another form of animal life. For example, man has two eyes just like a horse, a dog, and even a rat. Likewise, man has a heart that pumps blood just like so many of the animals that we see around us. A cat has a nose and a man has a nose, each with two nostrils. Rabbits and people both have two ears and animals have mouths with tongues and teeth similar to man's. Moreover, both have lungs which breathe oxygen and both would die if all of the oxygen were to disappear from our planet. We have reproductive organs and so do they. Man has two front limbs and so do animals; muscles and a skeleton and so do animals. They eat food and digest it with their digestive organs, as does man. The similarities are endless, and when expressed in this way make it seem that man must be just another animal, at a higher level of existence. Clearly, this would seem to be the case when viewed in the way that we have expressed it. But, it is precisely here that we must stop and take a closer look at what we have stated.

For example, one question that might be asked is, do we have any indication that man is intrinsically different than the animals? Is there anything that we can point to that shows a fundamental separation between man and the animal kingdom? One thing we might observe is that whereas man lands on the moon, monkeys land in trees. Whereas chimps use their arms to travel from tree to tree, man uses his jets to travel from continent to continent. And whereas apes beat their chests to send noise through the jungle, man orbits satellites to send radio signals through space. There are many more examples that one could note, but the main thing this all suggests is that man is *not* just another animal on a higher plane, but rather a *separate* level far above the animals.

There is a grand and regal distinction about human life which transcends the instincts by which animals are bound. There is within man a self-evincing majesty, reaching out for purpose and meaning in the hope of immortality. Whereas animals seem consumed with the natural impulse for their next meal, we find that, as the Bible and five thousand years of human records confirm, within the heart of man lies *eternity*.* This is why there are so many religions all over the world today.[10]

If this be so, then what of the anatomical similarities between man and animals? What of the two eyes, the two ears, the tongues and teeth? What of the common physical structures found in the lungs and the reproductive organs, the muscles and skeletons? Isn't this sufficient proof that man is simply another animal, but at a higher level of existence? The answer, of course, is yes, if the sum total of man's existence is the same as that of an animal. If a man is nothing but his body, then the anatomical and physiological

---

* Ecclesiastes 3:11

similarities as the lever arm in a frog, a bat, and a man might be considered evidence that man is nothing more than an animal at an elevated plane. This kind of argument, however, is analogous to saying that an airplane is merely an automobile at a higher level, because they both have wheels and engines; or that a television set is simply a radio at a higher level, because they both use the same transistors and speakers and operate by electricity. The point is that both human and animal life do share a common existence regarding physical things, such as running and seeing and hearing and breathing. But that's where the similarity ends.

A lever arm performs the same function in a frog, a bat, and a man. So do the heart, lungs, and muscles. Each of these organs are structures that express themselves under the constraint of *physical* laws. What's important is to realize that whenever one needs to do something in the physical world, there is always a best way to achieve the desired result. There is always an optimum design that best delivers the outcome needed. Pumping blood, breathing, or moving are functions, and these organs are designed to function in the best way possible.

Scientists and engineers have a special phrase to describe this optimum or best way of doing things. All physical systems exhibit an "optimum gain band width product." This is true in mechanical systems, optical systems, electronic systems, and in the body itself. For example, were we to go around the world and inspect the way engineers design radio receivers, we would find that virtually all of them "mix" the incoming signal with another signal that's generated within the radio. This produces a "difference signal" which, when amplified, gives the highest signal for the least noise. There are other ways to design radio receivers, but this is the *best* way if the desired result is maximum signal with minimum noise.

Likewise, think of the automobile made in Europe, Japan, Australia, and America. All have four wheels. But *must* they? Obviously not. We could make a car with three, or five. If that's true, why do most have four wheels? Because that is the best way to produce the desired function we want. Also, look around the world and you will find, for the most part, that airplanes have one wing. They don't have two, or three. Many years ago they had two, but we soon learned that it wasn't the best way to build aircraft for the function we wanted.

Another example of optimum design is found in television. Virtually every TV receiver throughout the world produces a picture through a device known as a cathode ray tube, or CRT. Is this the only way we can make a television picture? No. There are several ways of doing it. But the CRT is the best way, so in virtually every country where television sets are made, they are built this way. Recently, the need for a very tiny television picture has developed. The device to be used to make that very small picture will probably not be a CRT; another mechanism appears to be better suited. The point is that there's always a best way to design physical things. The reason apes and men have parts designed the same way is because each of the designs is the best way to do the jobs they perform.

Interim Summary

In summary, the first thing we noted is that throughout the world today there is an idea that man is nothing more than an animal living at a higher level of existence than the animals around him. This idea holds that man evolved from an ape and that when you examine an ape's body and a human body, the similarities are so strong that you are tempted to believe man is just a more advanced "animal" on the evolutionary ladder. We pursued this theory by surmising that, by the same token, an airplane is nothing more than an automobile at a higher level because they both have wheels and engines. We could have added that they are both made from metal, use glass windows and hinged doors, and have people at the controls.

However, although an airplane and an automobile share these similarities, it's clear that their *differences* are what's important. Although an automobile must travel on the ground, an airplane is free to do otherwise. A plane can travel on the ground like an automobile, but the automobile cannot travel in the air like the plane. It's the same with the television set and the radio. Both have speakers and transistors and operate by electricity, but although the television set can make sound like the radio, the radio cannot produce a picture like a television set. In all these examples, there are both similarities and differences. Again, the important thing is the differences, not the similarities. The similarities exist at the same functional level, whereas the differences introduce a completely new dimension.

Let's apply these identical considerations to animals and human beings. Animals eat food and people eat food; animals walk on the ground and people walk on the ground. People can do most everything that animals can do, but people are not in bondage to such behavior. Let's look at the belief held by so many people that man is nothing more than a social animal, with behavior that manifests itself at a higher level of existence. We see that, although man's body has many parts that function or operate in ways similar to those of an animal, that does not mean that man himself is an animal any more than a television set is a radio or an airplane is an automobile.

Optimum Design

It is true that man has limbs for motion, eyes for seeing, and ears for hearing, as do animals, but this is because *the function which each of these performs in the physical world is the same.*

Since there is always an optimum way to design things to obtain a desired result, we find that the physical structure that performs a given function in animals is similar to the structure that performs the same function in humans. If you take any of the earlier examples, such as digestion, you find that the structure that performs these functions in an animal can be virtually the same in a human being.

Take the stomach, for example. We can find this thing called a stomach in monkeys, in dogs, and in man. If you are going to operate an oxygen-burning, organic machine through chemical energy stored in such things as proteins and sugar, the best way to do it is to get it into a storage sack of some kind, where digestion can take place, where food can be converted into a form suitable for the body to process, regardless of whether the body belongs to an animal or a man. Therefore, all of these physical structures we see in common in animals and man can be understood as optimally designed structures by which their function is best achieved. In a sense, it is like looking at different paintings by the same artist. These paintings are functional masterpieces that perform wondrous tasks, and in ways we cannot improve upon.

For example, consider the various organs of the body. Few understand the intricacies of these organs; those familiar with them have only first-level understanding. We cannot duplicate them, and our comprehension of what they do is at best quite limited.

Thus, it is quite easy for someone unfamiliar with these things to believe that they just evolved. After all, why not? Such a belief isn't based on detailed, sober inquiry into the mechanistic details that produced the organizational marvel before us. Rather, it is based on one's ignorance of the degree of the miracle necessary to produce the structure in question. An engineer, for example, would never say that an internal combustion engine materialized of its own accord. Yet the heart—a wonder whose mechanical cycle dwarfs the thermodynamic internal combustion counterpart, which on average reliably pumps about two thousand gallons of blood daily over a period of seventy-two years—is glibly said to have "just happened."

What has been done to improve the structures procreated every time a newborn baby comes into the world? Has man made a camera better than the human eye for the function it performs? The eye can look at something very close and then almost immediately focus on a far object. In both cases, the object seen remains in focus. Why? Because the eye is a self-focusing camera. Furthermore, it has virtually no spherical aberration or astigmatism, and it has a color spectral bandwidth second to none.

Consider the ear. Many years ago a scientific paper described an experiment in which scientists carefully recorded both the size and location of all the tiny bones in the human inner ear. They then put this distribution of bone structures into a computer and scanned one side of the filter they had modeled with all the acoustic frequencies normal to human hearing. They reported that the human ear is the world's most perfect mechanical frequency discriminator, of all those they investigated, doing its function with virtually no attenuation or phase distortion. The ear is an optimally designed structure that performs a function unique to human communication better than any other structure known. Our ability to discriminate frequencies enables speech between humans, yet this miraculous structure was given to us free of charge at the time we were born.

Each of the animals also has ears suited to its needs. Does this mean that a human being is an animal at a higher level of existence? Of course not. Did a radio evolve of its own accord into a television set? Did an automobile change by itself into an airplane? Yet, this is precisely where our conclusions would lead us, were we to use the logic of anthropologists in a fossilized electronic junkyard. *Common structures represent optimum designs.* The structures that perform these functions are essentially the same in an animal and a human because man and animals share common functions in the physical world. We know, however, because human experience bears witness to the fact, that man exists as an entirely different dimension of being than does an animal. Common parts between man and apes do not identify one with the other; rather they show that the two are *correlated.*

Animal Usage

Consider the functions animals perform. They walk, see, hear, smell, eat and so on. Each of these functions is merely part of a list of things necessary for animals to survive. What then is the purpose behind an animal's survival? What functions do animals perform beyond merely breathing air in order to live? We immediately recognize at least three things they do. The amazing thing is that in each of the three cases, what they do is related to, and necessary for, the survival of human life.

First, animals are food for other animals, which in turn are food for humans. Thus, one thing animals do is provide food for human life. Second, they provide clothing for humans, not only from their hides but also, in some cases, from their fur. Third, animals provide humans with a source of convenient and inexpensive labor. When we examine the five-thousand-year record of advance of human civilization, we quickly recognize that beasts of burden have played an important role in tilling the soil and in moving and positioning heavy objects so man could produce food and create shelter to live in safety from wild animals and the elements.

But what conceivable purpose is there for human life in the world? One thing seems clear. We know that the function we perform is not that of providing skins for clothing to a higher form of life. We also know that humans are not Sunday dinner for a Superior Intelligence. Nor do we see higher life forms tying man to a wagon or plow to exploit muscle power. If there exists a purpose for human existence, it is not to provide clothing, food or labor for a higher Intelligence. These three principal functions are performed by animals, not man.

Is there a purpose for man's existence? Or are we the result of a cosmic accident? Did an Intelligence design the vastly complex yet intricately harmonious genetic structure that perpetuates our existence from generation to generation? Or did such machinery just happen by chance? Are we a statistical bad joke, or the loving expression of Deity? There's quite a difference.

Consider this. If man's existence was not brought into being by Someone or Something, then how is it that the animals function so perfectly to meet man's needs. Why does plant life function as a food source for the animals? Viewed in its entirety, planet earth, with its seas and its atmosphere, harmoniously functions to sustain about 11 million species of life. Was it intended to function this way? Are we missing something when it comes to the purpose of human life? Is there something with respect to the presence of man on earth that transcends anything that we have thus far considered? Can it be that human life has within its fabric a distinctive imprint that goes beyond the physical existence by which animals are bound? If we are to answer these questions, it is necessary to take a step back to see things from a different perspective.

WHY DOES PHYSICAL REALITY TERMINATE IN MAN?

IN THE PRECEDING CHAPTER we noted how optimum designs exist to perform specified tasks under different physical constraints. As a result of this we also saw how certain physical functions between man and animals are performed by structures common to both animal and human bodies. When we reflect on the common functions, we realize that each of them is merely part of a list of things that are necessary for animals to survive.

We also recognized three purposes animals serve and noted that in each case, what they do is related to and necessary for the survival of human life. But do people have a purpose? If we came into existence through a cosmic accident, the answer is no; but if man is the creation of Deity, the answer is yes.

Do People Have a Purpose?

Many people today believe that life's only purpose is to have fun and games. This school of thought teaches that we should eat, drink, and be merry; for tomorrow we are going to die. That will be the end of it. They say that after death there is nothing, so we should enjoy ourselves while we can. "Look out for Number One, because no one else will. Do your thing, and do it while you can; because once you die, that's it." They believe that once you're dead and buried, you are forever gone.

Many go even further. They say life has no purpose at all; it's only a freak occurrence in which we just happen to have been caught. They go on to say that all there is is nothing; everything is just an illusion. But an interesting thing happens here. Such people, despite the beliefs they profess, nonetheless continue to eat and drink as though there were something. In other words, they continue to satisfy their appetites.

But how can people who deny that life has a purpose be truly merry? Their belief leaves them nothing to be merry about. As they approach the autumn of their life, the effort to live increases to a point of diminishing return, and eventually their life style exemplifies the living dead. But this is not true of those who have hope beyond the grave. For them, death to this world is synonymous with birth into a new world.

When a baby is born into this world, it enters the space and sunlight of a new existence while simultaneously dying to the crowded dark womb it knew for nine months. Can the same be true of physical death in this world? Do robin redbreasts and starlit skies reveal the handiwork of an eternal Intelligence who paints green pastures and majestic sunsets? Or is each newness of spring and color of autumn the result of one fortunate happenstance that created snow-laden forests and butterflies on flowers as part of the happy accident? Beliefs are the root from which sorrow and joy grow. And facts rather than philosophy ought to be the nuggets that help us decide what is true.

Is there something with respect to the presence of man on planet earth that transcends anything we have thus far considered? Can it be that human life has within its fabric a distinctive imprint that goes beyond the physical existence to which animals are in bondage? If we are to answer that kind of question, it is necessary to step back and see things from a broader perspective. We need to appraise the physical world from a reference point that allows its entire structure to come into our view. In the same way that we know of the sun's presence at night by the light reflected from the moon, in like fashion we will see that man reflects the presence of a divine image that is not directly visible. By looking at the structure of the entire physical world, we will uncover the source of the light that sparks human life, and that fans human achievement.

Organizational Ascendency

When we examine the construction of physical creation, one thing jumps out at us in terms of a universal rule. It's a law that applies to atoms, living cells, and even galaxies. In order for us to uncover this law, let's use particle physics[1] to identify a family of tiny things in the universe called fermions. These are held, so it's said, by gluelike particles known as bosons. The fermions come in two varieties, one known as quarks and the other called leptons. Likewise the bosons come in two kinds, the so-called massless particles and the very heavy particles. It's not important for us to be familiar with or understand how these particles behave or interact. What is important is that if we go to the basic constituents of the physical world we discover structure. When we examine the basic stuff of which the universe is composed, we find that even at the lowest levels, there seems to be organization.

When we study quarks,[2] we find they come in six quantum flavors, and each flavor comes in three colors. Likewise, leptons come in three varieties. The most familiar particle to some of us is the electron. The other two are called the muon and the tau particles, and each of these three varieties comes with their very own neutrinos.[3] At the most basic of levels in the universe, we find both structure and organization. And when we look at organization, we observe something very significant with respect to human life.

Consider atoms. An atom can be pictured as nothing more than an ultra-miniature solar system. Its nucleus or center is analogous to our sun, and things called electrons are whirling around the center, moving more or less in circles, as the planets do about the sun. The nucleus is typically composed of particles called protons and neutrons which themselves seem to be made up of those quarks and leptons mentioned earlier.[4]

Small-Scale Organization

Now ask yourself, who needs whom in order to exist? It's clear that the protons and neutrons at the center of the atom certainly don't need the atom to exist. They can exist all by themselves in the form of particles. The same is true of the electrons whirling about the center of the atom. They can all exist by themselves; they don't need the atom to exist. But we observe that the atom, as an entity, exists by virtue of the organization of the particles that make it up. An atom depends for its existence upon the proton, the neutron, and the electron. The particular way in which these particles are organized brings an atom into existence. It's a one-way organizational street. In this sense, we can say that the particles *function* in a way that allows atoms to exist. And this one-way street exists throughout the entire physical creation!

Consider the next step up—what we call molecules. A water molecule is made up of two hydrogen atoms and one oxygen atom. We can picture these as two small red marbles (the hydrogen atoms) and one large white marble. The hydrogen atoms don't need the water molecule to exist, any more than does the oxygen atom. In other words, the oxygen atom and hydrogen atoms can exist by themselves, regardless of whether or not a water molecule exists, but the water molecule depends for its existence upon all three. This one-way dependence of molecules on atoms (and as we saw earlier atoms on particles) is true for all molecules, no matter what their substance. It stays like this all of the way up the organizational ladder. The so-called organic molecules depend for their existence on the organization of simpler inorganic molecules. Living cells depend for their existence on the organizational properties of organic molecules.

What's truly amazing is that no matter where we may choose to stop in this ascending hierarchy of organization, we find the universal rule that *every level of organization depends for its existence on all of the organizationally simpler structures below it.* But the structures of lesser organization do not depend for their existence upon those levels above them.

Consider something as familiar as simple plant life in the sea. It doesn't need fish to exist, but the fish need it for food. Go down one level and consider the sea water itself. Sea water doesn't need plant life to exist, but the aquatic plant life, such as algae, needs the sea water.

Human Termination

Throughout the entire physical world we find a one-way organizational street. The fancy word is *anisotropy,* and it permeates the entire physical creation, continuing through plant life on land and on into the insects that exist underground. The organizational complexity continues to grow from the insects and into the simple animals, and from them through the more and more complex life forms until it abruptly terminates with man himself. *It ends with human life.* Man is at the top of the ladder. Human life depends for its existence upon the organizational properties of everything below it, but no known thing depends for its existence upon man.

Years ago I used to challenge people with the following claim: "Show me any scientific law governing the physical universe, and then assume that it doesn't exist. The consequences of it will show that human life can't exist." In the organizational hierarchy of things, everything below man has an existence apart from human life. Man depends upon everything else for his existence, but there seems to be nothing else that depends upon man.

Of course, even within these one-way streets there are many complex interactions. For instance, the oxygen that animals consume is given off by plant life, and the carbon dioxide that plant life requires is given off by the animals. Isn't it remarkable that primates have an affinity for sugar, which in a typical fruit happens to surround the indigestible pit of the fruit? Moreover, the pit passes out through the primate with nutrients conducive to good plant growth. It also happens that the plants themselves are food for animals, and that their roots stabilize the primate's habitat by preventing erosion. These and other harmonies exist throughout the vast numbers of complex structures that we find on our planet.

Man is king of the mountain. Although we know of nothing that needs man to exist, it appears that man depends for his existence on everything organizationally below him. So total and complete is this dependence that if we were to open a physics or chemistry book and hypothetically deny the existence of any natural law, we would find that the ultimate consequence of this denial would be the destruction of man himself.

Genetic Uniqueness

If everything is constructed so that we can exist, the question is why? How is it that we find ourselves in a life-support system so delicately balanced that its internal harmonies perpetuate human consciousness through time? Where did the organizational code originate that enables us to breathe and eat and reproduce and think and, yes, make moral decisions? For what reason are we in a world under circumstances of need and desire and autonomous free will?

You were conceived in a life-and-death race that ended when the fastest of 500 million sperm cells from your father's body reached an egg in your mother's womb. Is death the final outcome? Or was your birth the first of two in a master plan to deliver you to eternal life?

One thing is clear. Each level of complexity is organized in a way that calls into being the next higher level. This means that every organizational level within the world can be interpreted as having purpose in terms of the structural level just above it. But what's truly remarkable is that this organizational ascendency of patterns abruptly stops with human life.

Man alone is distinguished by an abrupt discontinuity, a chasm he presents to the organizational hierarchy below him. The human body self-evinces its own uniqueness as being the most sophisticated known object within the entire physical creation. But why?

Man alone seems to carry within the fabric of his genetic makeup informational specifications higher than anything else known. I do not mean in terms of the number of chromosomes, or in terms of the length of genes or the magnitude of genetic material within the cells. Rather, I speak in terms of the organizational complexity specifiable in an observer's overall description of the particular sequence of nucleotide bases along his DNA. In the hierarchy of organizational ascendency, the human body results from the most complex organizational specifications known to man. Where did this blueprint originate? Blind faith in unknown movements of historical chemical sequences won't do.[5] Some have said that we were planted here by a supercivilization whose home is somewhere among the stars.[6] Aside from there not being one shred of real evidence to support such an assertion, we might ask, "Where did they come from?"

Others prefer to say, "I don't know." That certainly seems more honest than pontificating that physical laws orchestrated a magic dance of lifeless particles into you and me. In this regard, all of us are free to worship whatever we wish, including warm little ponds, but we ought not confuse faith with science, particularly since there is a rational way to distinguish the two.

But does man have an attribute that separates him in absolute disunion from the animal world? Is there truly some distinctive that gives us the power to participate in a destiny inaccessible to animals, a destiny that offers the promise of eternity? If so, what is that imprint? What in man enables him to defeat the mightiest of jungle beasts despite the fact that he's physically inferior in size and strength? How is it that *man* looks into the cage at a zoo, and not the other way around? In short, what makes human life human?

We've already looked at the many common structures that exist in humans and in apes. Clearly it is not an anatomical or physiological difference that we seek, at least not on the surface.

If we can show an absolute disunion between human life and all other life forms on earth then the criterion for disunion can be used to identify the attribute responsible for human uniqueness. And once this attribute is found, we can use it to help us discover man's origin.

Sod vs. God

Were someone to attempt an overall description of a human body, its "description" by an observer would contain more information than the description of anything else in the entire universe. Furthermore, this information cannot be explained by asserting that material chaos produced it within a 30 billion light-year-wide universe that is 13 billion years old. Any attempt to understand the production of this information in terms of the physical properties of matter merely serves to push the origin of this information back to the time of the creation of the particles themselves. The evidence *does* teach that physical matter had a beginning.[7] But, to believe that the living structure of a human body gradually arose from physical properties intrinsic to nonliving matter is to believe that natural processes engaged in the systematic production of information with the passage of time. This belief is contrary to the informational loss described by the New Generalized Second Law of Thermodynamics.

Materialistic beliefs have one central thrust. They replace intelligence with randomness as the means of the production of information. This faith in physical matter sustains man as the highest authority. Were we to accept Intelligence as the source of the vast information that we have uncovered in living cells within the last twenty years or so, it would mean there exists an Authority who can dictate what man can and cannot do. Since our nature is to live without restraints, we are motivated to explain life's origin in a way that lays no claim on our behavior, and that allows us to freely express our desires. To this end materialism elevates sod that can be trodden under foot, whereas theism illuminates a God who challenges us into submission.

16

DID MAN EVOLVE
FROM APES?

ALL OVER THE world we find museums and textbooks that contain models
and pictures portraying a gradual line of development from small animals
up through monkeys to man. These very colorful displays and pictorials
are intended to show the viewer that this is how humans originated. What
young students and uninformed adults often do not consider, however, is
that the models and pictures are *fabrications* designed to reinforce the world
view of the people creating them. This world view includes the origin of
mankind and rests on a materialistic philosophy that presupposes the absence
of a divine intelligence.

At first glance, the sequence of change from small animals up through
man appears reasonable because the reconstructions are gradual, and the
changes between adjacent life forms are depicted as small. Moreover, if one
believes that nothing exists except physical matter and its motion, few alternatives remain except to suppose that humans developed in the way portrayed
in those textbooks and museums. Given materialistic philosophy, the belief
in man's gradual ascent from apes is embraced because there are no other
easy answers to how it could have happened, based upon observed similarities
in their anatomy. The conjecture seems even more reasonable when we consider that many sequences along the DNA of ape and man are similar in
appearance.

The problem, of course, is that the reconstructions are just that—*reconstructions.* They are produced by people who imagine that it must have happened
that way. But the fossil record is very incomplete, and the claim that man
came from ape actually rests upon a relatively small collection of significant
fossils germane to the question at hand. Many of the models and pictures

are based on bits and pieces of skulls and, in several instances, some bones and teeth. However, when one compares the actual data with the claims that are made, the contrast is startling.

Paleontology was founded by the French naturalist Georges Cuvier who, before his death one hundred fifty years ago, boasted that he could reconstruct an entire animal from one tooth. In February 1922 a geologist, Harold Cook, found such a tooth while digging in the bed of a quarry in Snake Creek several hundred miles west of Omaha.[1] The molar tooth soon became a pillar of human evolution known as "Nebraska Man." Henry Osborn, then head of the American Museum of Natural History in New York called it the "herald of our knowledge of anthropoid apes in America," and Grafton Smith, an expert in brain evolution at University College in London, said that the tooth was from a "primitive member of the human family." Thereafter the ape-man appeared in the scientific literature as *Hesperopithecus harold-cookii*. The genus "Hespero" put the missing link in the western world, and the new species *haroldcookii* honored the geologist who found the damaged molar (remember, that's all we've got).

The tooth was offered as proof of human evolution in the Scopes "monkey" trial in Dayton, Tennessee, and later admitted into evidence over the protests of attorney William Jennings Bryan. Bryan died in 1925, and two years later the tooth was officially acknowledged as belonging to an extinct pig.[2]

Ten years before the tooth incident, another "missing link" had appeared, called the Piltdown Man.[3] This discovery also received worldwide attention; but unlike Nebraska Man, it was an outright fraud. Yet despite the lessons learned from the 1927 fiasco, Piltdown Man continued to fool investigators for *another twenty-five years.* The deception was discovered in 1953, and the reason it took so long is *not* because the facts known at the time were inadequate to uncover the error. Instead, it was because the existence of a creature that was half ape and half man reinforced the materialistic assumptions of the world's experts who were predicting that a missing link would exist.

Java Man was another example of an alleged missing link. In 1892 a Dutch physician, Eugene Dubois, found a thigh bone in a spot not more than twenty yards from where he had discovered a skullcap a year earlier. Dubois created Java Man when he assumed that the skullcap and thigh bone belonged to each other. But this was an error, and just before his death he identified Java Man as a small, slender, longer-armed gibbon from India.[4]

A fourth example of a so-called missing link was Peking Man. The problem here was that the fossils disappeared during the Second World War, thus the primary evidence rested on models reconstructed from earlier notes and drawings. Moreover, these records show a hole in the skull, implying that Peking Man was the victim of other human hunters. I've greatly abbreviated the history of the fossil evidence, but the story is sufficiently muddled to disqualify trustworthy conclusions in the matter.[5]

There have been other alleged missing links, but they have all fallen by the wayside. In examining these incidents, one is impressed with the very real tendency of workers in this area to claim knowledge beyond what the fossils actually warrant. Moreover this tendency to say more about a fossil than one knows is true persists into the present. The old pronouncements of ape-man celebrities have been replaced by the widely accepted current scenario that man came from the chimp-gorilla line,[6] and that his "descent" * was gradual.[7] However, the comparative evidence is *so* meager that as one anthropologist put it, the entire affair is like reconstructing the narration of *War and Peace* by randomly selecting thirteen pages, and using them to fabricate the rest of the story. On those rare occasions when fairly complete fossil specimens are found, they do not show that man came from ape. Rather they teach that apes once walked the earth. This will become more clear as we proceed.

Dominant Personalities

The study of prehistoric man is known as "paleoanthropology." It's a field where beliefs and conclusions are dominated by strong personalities.[8] This is unlike the physical sciences where measurements dictate the conclusions. One such personality is Richard Leakey whose mother uncovered a skull in East Africa in 1959 and whose father discovered another skull in the 1960s. He himself found yet another skull in 1972 which became known as "Skull 1470."

Another personality who has dominated the field is Donald Johanson, who discovered the so-called Lucy Skull in northeast Ethiopia in 1974. He later discovered a number of other bones to go along with it. The reason I cite these men is to illustrate the kind of disagreement that can exist among "experts" in such matters. In this case, the reported disagreement was not only on how old the skulls were and which bones belonged to the Lucy Skull, but also on the very important question of *how many species the skulls represented.*

It's helpful to understand that when someone is called an expert in this field, that does not mean that he possesses significant knowledge regarding human origins. It only means that he knows the most about the typically sparse number of fossils he happened to stumble across. Even so, the data do not mandate definitive conclusions, and the uncertainties usually appear in very important areas. For example, the reports indicate that Johanson believed that one of his major bone collections came from a single species. Leakey concluded that the identical bones showed the existence of at least two, and possibly several different species. In addition, Johanson believed he had uncovered a human "missing link" of sorts, whereas Leakey believed

---

* Humans "descend" with the passage of time; however organizationally speaking they "ascend."

on the basis of molecular anthropology that the Lucy Skull was a late survival of an ape. Furthermore, regardless of who one believes about any of these skulls or bones, most of them seem to belong to a family of long-armed, short-legged, knuckle-walking African apes of the genus *Australopithecus*.

The Materialistic Heartbeat

But if one ignores the opinion of the dominant personalities and asks what the actual data teach regarding human fossils, the answer is that they show man existing as man for about 40 thousand years or so. The skulls and bones found in layers that are dated much older than this are *not* human, but rather belong to prehistoric creatures from whom most of the investigators presume man to have come.

Yet this presumption is demanded neither by the fossils nor from molecular phylogeny; it stems from assumptions made by people predisposed to the philosophy of materialism. If one is committed to this philosophy, then the known sequence of fossil change compels the doctrine of human descent from apes. In this case it's argued that human evolution is a fact on the basis of both these changes, and because the body of a human and an ape display similar biological structures.

It is quite common to find articles or even books publicizing the idea that people are an advanced form of animal.[9] News items in publications far removed from anthropology, but that promote the theme, "A New Ape in Our Family Tree," are not at all uncommon.[10] Also typical is the theme, "How Ape Became Man," found in reports with sweeping pronouncements that pontificate biological changes in humans over millions of years—an idea that extends well beyond the fossil data actually reported.[11] Even publicity of discoveries that give the appearance of "upsetting the apple cart" really do just the opposite, and serve to further entrench the idea that man is an advanced form of ape.

For example, researchers in Pakistan several years ago uncovered skull and jawbone fossils that were dated at 8 and 13 million years old.[12] Whereas the headlines on these reports indicated that the ancient fossil discoveries had shattered widely held notions on human origins, what the fossils in fact really did was to alter the *time* that the "man-ape evolutionary split" was alleged to have occurred. Thus, instead of the fossil discoveries forcing realignment of evolutionary claims regarding man's origin (as the headlines seemed to indicate), the publicity surrounding the discoveries actually served to underscore the idea that human beings (the hominid family) split off from the evolutionary tree of apes (the pongid family) at some distant time in the past.

The anthropological tide linking man with ape is so enormous that research has been done aimed at identifying human traits in animals. In one report, the rare pygmy chimp was heralded as being the "most human" of the apes.[13] One year later, work was published (DNA-DNA hybridization) to reinforce the idea that humans should be put with the chimps rather than the gorillas.[14] As is often the case in such matters, the scientific work itself is outstanding, but the philosophical presuppositions others bring to its interpretation force conclusions that the discoveries do *not* imply. Such presuppositions add fuel to the materialistic bandwagon that man is only his body, and that *all* that a man is evolved gradually from apes. The philosophical presuppositions permeating anthropology are *so* deep that in the conclusions of a review article citing 145 references dealing with the topic of human evolution, the principle concern was not whether or not humans came from apes, but rather whether they did so gradually or explosively.[15]

Similar Structures

The similarities between man and ape are so strong that it almost seems nonsensical to deny that the two are related. And indeed this is so. They *are* related.

But the question that needs to be raised is *how* are they related? Is our only alternative the belief that man emerged from molecular changes along the DNA of apes in a way that transposed apes to a higher plane? Or are there other options that are consistent with the data that we should consider? We now turn our attention to not only *how* the biological structures of men and apes are related, but also to the more important question: How does man *differ* from an ape?

To this end, let's proceed with the same assumptions evolutionists use to interpret hominid fossils and see their application in a transportation junkyard containing parts and fragments of airplanes and automobiles. We observe that both have tires, windows, doors, a metal body, and an engine that runs on petroleum fuel. We also observe that the shape of certain fenders gives the appearance of a transition into wings, and that the trunk hinges allow big metal lids to swing open for what may be later evolution into a rudder. In fact, we see certain cars with open trunks and note that their evolution into the tail parts of an airplane has already begun.

We also observe that the propeller in the plane can be explained in terms of some of the automobiles shedding their radiators in order to survive certain environmental conditions, thereby leaving the fan exposed to wind conditions that caused its evolution into a propeller. As nonsensical as all of this is, the logic employed to support the thesis that airplanes are an advanced species of automobiles is identical to that used to defend the belief that apes changed into men. One might counterargue that the latter is a biological system where such change is possible, but the argument is a weak one. No biological mechanism has ever been shown to *systematically* increase the complexity of a physical system through natural processes, and the New Generalized Second Law of Thermodynamics disqualifies nature's ability to produce such a mechanism.

Now extend the argument to an electronic junkyard. Here we find a television set with transistors, resistors, capacitors, inductors, a speaker, and a plug for electrical power. But we observe that radios also have these things. Furthermore, some of the radios have a glass panel in the front that contains numbers for tuning not unlike the big glass panel in the front of the television picture tube. Since both are found in cabinets with knobs that are somewhat larger on the television set, it could be said that natural processes and environmental pressures operating on small populations over extended time periods caused radios to evolve into televisions. An evolutionist could further argue that there must have been a gradual diminishing of environmental light, so that the panel had to enlarge in order for the cabinet to survive. As it did so, cross-coupling with the cabinet caused the knobs to enlarge!

These examples are not as silly as they might appear. The reasons given to defend the change of a radio into a television set are not unlike those used to support the belief that apes changed into men. The *fundamental* basis for such belief is that each displays parts that differ in their development, but yet are common to both. However, a fallacy in the evolutionary argument is the assumption that common subsystems—engines in cars and planes, or speakers in radios and television sets—logically require the evolution by natural processes of one from the other. In the examples cited, this is clearly not the case. Intelligence, not chaos, was the guiding light. Moreover, the vastly higher information content along human DNA attests to a labor of intellect rather than primeval confusion.

Biological Complexity

Some have argued that the evolution through natural processes of one species from another has been proven by data from a field of science known as "molecular phylogeny," the study of the chemical history of the amino acid sequences.[16] This false belief about molecular phylogeny comes from the failure to distinguish between the amino acid *count* along protein strands, and the information *content* resident within the actual sequence of the residues.[17]

When one considers that a typical human cell contains almost seven feet of DNA, and that its information continues to be resolvable down to distances of well under ten-millionths of an inch, one can well understand the confusion that exists regarding alleged similarities between the protein of humans and apes. For example, just to assimilate the content of this amount of information for study requires a computer whose storage capacity exceeds 10 billion bits. And were we to attempt to examine the short- and long-range interactions in and among the triplet centers throughout each of the twenty thousand DNA folds, it would require a computational capability that exceeds all of the computers that exist on earth now or that we can hope to produce in the foreseeable future.

Profound Differences

Ordinarily when we look at man and ape, the differences between the two are enormous. We see man traveling through space and apes jumping from trees. We find man sampling foods all over the world while chimps grab the closest banana they can reach. And whereas man builds thermonuclear power plants, monkeys run in fear from fire. Why is there so vast a difference? What truly divides man and ape? Is there an absolute distinction that sets human life apart from all other life? And if so, what is it? The literature of Shakespeare, the discoveries of Einstein, and the music of Beethoven have no parallel in the animal world. Did these things originate from a unique, unseen imperative? Or did they evolve from slime as the theory of evolution would have us believe?

Some say it's a mystery whose answer we may never know. Others say it is not a mystery, but a shadow of the deeper truth that the human body was actually designed, and that man was created in the image of his Designer. However, when we try to isolate the uniqueness that human accomplishment implies, we find that it is not an easy thing to identify. The reason is that many of the things that we may believe are unique to man turn out not to be. In almost all instances, the trait or characteristic that is alleged to lie exclusively in man's domain turns out also to belong to the animal world. This is why many have come to regard man as a "social animal," albeit one who lives on a higher plane of awareness and activity than do animals. Yet, if an absolute disunion exists between human life and all other life forms on earth, and if we can discover this regal distinctive, we may be able to identify the attribute responsible for human uniqueness. Once this attribute is found, we can use it to help us discover man's origin and acquire insight into the anatomical similarities he shares with apes.

Questions That Need Answers

Does man have an attribute that separates him in absolute disunion from the animal world? Is there truly a distinctive "something" that gives us the power to participate in a destiny inaccessible to animals—one that offers the promise of eternity? If so, what imprint does human life carry that uniquely separates us from all other life forms on earth? What quality is present in man that enables him to defeat the mightiest of jungle beasts, despite the fact that he is inferior in size and in strength? How is it that at a zoo, man enjoys the privileged position of looking into the cage as a visitor, and not the other way around? What makes human life "human" and what makes animal life "animal"?

WHAT DO ANIMALS AND PEOPLE HAVE IN COMMON?

WE'VE ALREADY LOOKED at the many common structures that exist in an ape's body and a human's. Clearly, it is not an anatomical or physiological difference that makes man "man," and distinguishes him from an animal— at least, not on the surface. Although there are certain anatomical differences, basically they are quite similar.

The many similarities between the body of a man and an ape have led many to falsely believe that human life is simply an extension of the animal kingdom. These beliefs arise from three basic assumptions: (1) Man is only his fossil; (2) fossils show all that's different; (3) nature produces change.

But the fossil record demonstrates *difference*—not change. Although no one knows how dissimilar biological structures arose, the present belief that one species issued from another is a working hypothesis that offers a basis for asking questions. In like manner, astronomy was fueled by the belief that the earth was at the center of the world. This was the basis for asking questions for over fourteen hundred years until Copernicus showed it false in 1543. The evolution of species is a working hypothesis that is unproven, and different fossils with common features can be understood in terms of common descent or common design. In the case of man, the situation is more complicated because the fossil skulls are a physical shadow of a deeper behavioral dimension.

Of course, all of us acknowledge that the behavior of people differs from that of animals; but the differences are regarded as a separation in *degree*, not in *kind*. In other words, human life and animal life are seen to be separated in terms of gradual differences, but not in terms of an absolute disunion.

In this school of thought, man is regarded as a social animal living at a higher level of existence than other animals. Thus, in the last analysis, this outlook considers man to *be* an animal. Furthermore, when attempts are made to find *fundamental* differences between humans and animals, they seem to fail. This doesn't mean that differences can't be found, but rather that when they are found, they prove to be differences that are not *fundamental.* Let's look at some examples.

Expectation

There are those who have held that the real difference between man and animal lies in man's capacity to have hope, to look forward to better times and more favorable circumstances with expectation. But surely this can't be the fundamental thing that separates man from animals. For example, were we to sit on a park bench, would not a pigeon come along expecting (in other words, hoping) to be fed? After all, is not hope simply an expectation of sorts? Ducks expect food near the lake in a park. Likewise, seals expect food in a zoo.

Many animals exhibit clear expectation in matters of aggression, and the owners of dogs and cats will testify that their pets display hope of special favors under situations of training and reward. Years ago I had a dog named Coco that was tied nearly 150 feet from the rear door of our home. When I went out the door carrying his food, Coco couldn't see what I was carrying; but my mere presence near the back door gave him hope. He would jump up and down, wagging his tail, fully expecting to be fed—even though he was easily 150 feet from me. That dog had hope. On other occasions, Coco would be in the house when a female dog in the neighborhood came into season. He would stay at the back door with his tongue hanging out and his tail frantically wagging, his eyes pleading for me to open the door. That dog expressed anticipation.

Consider cats. When a female and a male cat are together, and an unfamiliar male cat comes on the scene, you'll see the female cat walk to one side and the two male cats square off in an obvious expectation of a fight. The point is, whereas it's true that man has expectation, we find a similar trait exhibited by animals. To be sure, it's not the same kind of expectation to which man can aspire. Nonetheless, it *is* expectation and, therefore, hope. Although the hope or expectation found in animals differs in *degree* from that of which human life is capable, *it does not differ in kind.*

Yet if man carries an imprint that separates him from the animal kingdom, it must be a total separation; it must be a regal distinction, a division that detaches man from animals, not in degree or graduation, but in kind. The distinction we seek is something that separates man from animals in total disunion. If we are to find such a distinction, we must look beyond the experience of expectation because this is something common to much of the animal kingdom.

Reasoning

At this point many focus on man's superior mind as the basis of his separation from the animal world. They say, "It's obvious what separates man from the animal kingdom. It's man's ability to think!" But are they right? At first glance we might say yes. We all know that animals can't think the way humans can. Thus it seems evident that man's mental faculty is truly the distinguishing mark that sets him apart. At first this might sound reasonable, but when we take a closer look, it begins to lose its appeal.

For instance, in an experiment done many years ago a chimp was put inside a cage and not fed anything for several days. Then bananas were placed outside the chimp's cage, just beyond his reach. Try as hard as he would, the chimp just could not reach those bananas. Then he was given two poles, neither of which was long enough to reach the food, but which were designed to be put together to make an extended pole long enough to reach the food. After several hours, the chimp used his mind to put the two sticks together and then used the one long pole to reach the bananas. Later, the experiment was repeated, but this time with the food further from the cage so that three poles were needed to get the food. He soon figured out how to put the poles together in order to make one very long pole to get the food. This experiment confirmed what we know in several other ways, namely, that animals do think. To be sure, they don't think at the level we do; nonetheless, they do think.

Mice, for example, have been routinely trained to reason their way through very complex mazes, and many years ago the Russians taught birds to peck at certain colored lights in orbiting space ships. Several years ago I learned of work done where birds were trained to reliably differentiate between pills of different shapes and to remove one shape from a small production line. Also, I came across a report of birds being trained to align the cross hairs in the bomb release bay of an airplane. The point behind all of this is that there are experiments galore which demonstrate that animals have the capacity to think. Again, I stress that the thought activity of these animals is pale and primitive compared with human standards of thinking. The degree to which animals can think is extremely shallow when compared to the thought processes within a human being. But even so, animals *can* think. Therefore, the ability to think is not the fundamental thing separating human life from the animal kingdom. Although there is a difference in the *degree* to which animals can think, that difference is not a difference in *kind*.

Communication

Some have said that the basic difference between man and the animals lies in the fact that humans communicate with one another. But of course, we know today that animals do likewise. In every forest of the world we find birds festively singing, and in all the jungles chimps are squawking at one another. Mice squeak to each other in the grass of the fields, and dolphins do likewise as they chirp to their own kind in the depths of the sea. Thus, animals *do* communicate with one another.

However, here we need to make an important and unusual observation. Although animals can communicate with one another, the number of distinct signals available to them when they do so is severely limited. The last time I inquired into this, I learned that the maximum number of distinct signals was only thirty-seven. This was with the rhesus monkey species. The number may be larger now, but if it is larger, it is still going to be pitifully small in comparison to human communication. In fact, it's going to be so small in relation to human language as to provide no logical basis for comparison.

Genetic Control

There's a very simple reason why this is so. In the absence of activity by a human intelligence, *all animal communication is genetically preprogrammed.* Some researchers believe that animal capabilities are much more limited than this, and that their intelligence level when compared to humans is *so* low as to imply that animals may not even be "conscious" nor have "intentions" in the sense that we use these terms. It is even said that animal behavior can be fully explained in terms of cause and effect mechanisms.[*] While this may be an oversimplified view of animal behavior, it illustrates the low degree to which animal capabilities have been regarded. This does not mean that there cannot be environmental inputs and even learning experiences that influence the sounds that animals utter, but it does mean that if such factors are present, in the absence of human intelligence they operate in a genetically prescribed manner. This is true of the sounds made by elephants, the songs sung by birds, and even the so-called "waggle dance" performed by honeybees.

The Song and Dance of Life

Studies have been reported in which birds were brought into the laboratory at an age of between two and ten days and trained for about forty days, using song syllables characteristic of that species of bird.[2] It was discovered that the songs sung by untrained birds of the same species (but raised from the time they hatched) had song syllables very similar in structure to those of the trained birds of that species. Furthermore, it was learned that the trained birds had a memory that was predisposed to retain the song material characteristic of the particular species. In other words, songs that were characteristic of the species and that had been taught the birds during their first two months of life were sung by the birds eight months later, with no rehearsal in between. Thus, the birds were not only predisposed to easily learn songs with syllables common to the species, but furthermore, the structures of

---

[*] Some work has been done which suggests that animal behavior is mechanistically explainable in terms of stimulus-response theory.[1]

the syllables themselves were known even by the birds of that same species without any training.

Whales also "sing," and computer analysis of their songs shows that all whales sing one "song"—but with "dialects" that differ, depending on their location.[3] Although the musical content of their songs can be quite varied, a genetically preprogrammed set of laws in humpback whales dictates the same structural pattern all over the world, regardless of their location. Thus, whether it's a bird or a whale, the song is under the control of genes. Moreover, any later learning that may modify the content of these songs is likewise done under the control of these genes.

Likewise, the honeybee is genetically able to perform rapid movements known as the "waggle dance" within a beehive. A scout bee finds food outside the hive and returns and communicates the location of the food to all of the other bees in the hive. It does this by moving in a circle if the food is less than three hundred feet from the hive, or moving in a figure eight if the food is more than approximately three hundred feet away. The faster the bee moves, the farther is the food. Also, the direction of the scout bee's body with respect to gravity inside the hive reveals the direction that the bees must fly outside the hive with respect to sunlight. If the scout bee's body is pointed up, the bees fly toward the sun; if its body points down, they are to fly away from the sun. The communication system is so elaborate that on cloudy days the bees have a backup mechanism based on their memory of the sun's previous diurnal course in relation to landmarks that are local to the hive.[4] Thus the shape of the pattern traced out in the dance, together with the speed of the bee and the orientation of its body with respect to gravity inside the hive, all serve to communicate information to the other bees as to the distance and direction of the flight they must take to reach the food.

The important thing to realize is that when a scout bee stumbles across flowers, the waggle dance is not something that it logically reasons out. A bee's eye has over eight thousand individual lenses through which it sees in virtually all directions. If a scout bee comes across a sugar-laden flower, it doesn't carefully think through how to tell the other bees about the flower, but instinctively flies back to the hive where it automatically does the waggle dance. Despite the many complexities of this kind of motion as a means of communicating information, the scout bee proceeds to "do its thing," because all of its actions are under the control of instructions genetically preprogrammed at birth along the DNA within its body.

Another thing to consider is that the scout bee must accurately communicate the location of the food to every other bee before they dare leave the hive. Otherwise they will die if they don't find the flower because when bees leave a hive in search of food, they take with them only enough sugar to reach the flower. The only way the bees are able to return to the hive is by using the sugar found in the flower. If you see a bee limping along in grass near some flowers, you're looking at a creature that didn't properly receive the message, and who is doomed unless it can reach a flower.

Despite all of its intricacies, the instructions that control the waggle dance exist in a small part of the bee's genes. If we take a very young bee, raise it outside the hive and then place it inside the hive, it knows how to interpret the waggle dance. Although this dance is the most sophisticated of all the known forms of animal communication, it nonetheless consists of a very low number of signals. There is an interesting parallel between the scout bee's message and Christ's gospel which is discussed in Appendix 7.

Instinct

The number of distinct signals available to an animal for communication is very, very small. In stark contrast, even a tiny child has the ability both to create and to understand sentences using numerous combinations of words and symbols. Furthermore, without any idea whatever of grammatical rules, the child can generate an *indeterminate* number of sentences. The reason for this is that mental activity within human life is not enslaved to genetic instruction. To be sure, there are instincts which are present, but man is not under compulsion of the flesh to obey them. For example, although a person may be hungry, he or she is still free to give his food to another human being. But in the absence of human intelligence, if we put two hungry animals together with only one serving of food, we know what will happen. Both in behavior and communication, animals live under the tyranny of their instincts. For the most part, man is free of these things; this freedom is the sword that divides human and animal life, and the root that grows a stairway to the stars.

18

DOES MAN REFLECT A SUPERNATURAL IMAGE?

THE TERM *instinct* is used by scientists to mean an unlearned pattern of animal habit. It does not involve intelligence, nor does it embrace thought or learning or even memory. For example, when the temperature in a beehive rises 3 percent above 94 degrees, the bees position themselves throughout the hive and move their wings in harmony to produce acoustic waves that lower the temperature. Conversely, when the hive is too cold they create heat by metabolizing extra sugar above and beyond their normal diet.* The bees do not reason this out. All of the needed information resides in their genetic structure.

We marvel at the discipline displayed by ants when we see their armies march in columns with military precision. We're in awe at the engineering skill evidenced in the complicated underground passages and chambers they build. Moreover, who of us isn't impressed with how they grow fungus for food, how they milk aphids for honeydew and enslave other ants to do the numerous tasks needed for their survival? Yet, as astounding as these things may appear, the most amazing thing of all is that the ants do not reason these things out.

Although it may seem that such activities are directed by highly intelligent creatures, what's really true is that the ants are doing exactly what their ancestors did before them with no thought whatever as to why.[2] These tiny

---

* The bees also regulate swarm mantle and core temperatures by adjusting the percentage of swarm space they occupy, thereby controlling convective heat loss from the swarm interior, and the porosity and swarm surface area associated with passive loss from the exterior.[1]

creatures are driven by a genetic program rather than an act of will, and the patterns of behavior defined by their DNA nucleotide sequences create habits that are energized at birth and which continue until they die.

Although the ants may appear to be intelligent, it is more accurate to regard them as tiny, preprogrammed, organic machines that function and communicate in ways not unlike the satellites and space probes we send to explore distant planets. In ways surprisingly similar to animal life, these space probes "see" radiation and "hear" magnetic fields, store the information in memory banks, and then communicate what they've found to others, namely us. Animals do likewise. They see and hear, remember what they've found and then communicate it to other animals with similar genes.

Insects "see" ultraviolet landing patterns on flower leaves; bats avoid obstacles by detecting sound waves transmitted by their sonar system; bees, birds, and bacteria all have magnetic fields in their navigational repertoire.[3] The animals and space probes share something in common. Both operate under instructions from the intelligence that created and programmed them, and neither has a will of its own in the sense of decision-making that parallels human thought.

When our spaceships "see" and "hear" the radiation and magnetic fields in their outer space environment, they store and then manipulate the data under preprogrammed instructions designed to facilitate its transmission to earth. The operation of these interplanetary probes is not unlike that performed by a scout bee that locates food and communicates the information to the other bees in the hive. Like the space probe, the bee functions in alignment with preprogrammed instructions. These genetic instructions exist throughout the animal kingdom and are responsible for the migration patterns of birds, mammals, fish, reptiles, and even invertebrates.[4] The control exercised by the genes of particular species is so strong that in some cases the animals die following them. For example, hundreds of whales and dolphins have succumbed on beaches at locations where they followed the magnetic field of certain rocks, mistaking that attraction for the earth's natural magnetic field, which is weaker in those regions.[5]

These considerations lead us to the startling conclusion that in the absence of human intelligence, all animal communication is the result of a genetic program the animal acquires at birth. This means that in the absence of human intelligence, all animal communication appears to have been preprogrammed.

Universal Rules

As best as can be determined, every species of animal life communicates with members of like kind under instructions contained in the genes it receives at conception. The communication occurs in the form of genetically-preprogrammed signals that are unique to the species, and which involve the transmission of physical energy between two or more of them. This energy will be in the form of light,[6] sound,[7] or chemicals.[8] These signals are automatically generated inside the animal, either in response to something in its environment or because a biological change takes place in its body. What's truly astounding is that despite the intricate details and complexity of the various kinds of communication animals employ throughout the world, *all* of their communication appears to lie in only three areas: mating, aggression, and food.

In the case of mating, chemicals of differing kinds may be involuntarily dispersed that are unique to a particular species. Moths, for example, do this, but it happens automatically and without any conscious act or decision on the part of the moth.[9] At the appropriate season and time of year, chemicals are released and the moth has no say-so whatever in the matter. This is true for *all* insects, as well as animals, birds, and fish. Communication regarding mating is a phenomenon that lies outside the control of the members of the animal kingdom. This is so not only for chemicals, but also for other forms of energy as well.

Crickets for example, employ sound energy to sing a song whose frequencies and pitch are genetically preprogrammed by the central nervous system.[10] Likewise, light energy allows the change in colors along each side of the cuttlefish to be communicated to another cuttlefish of opposite gender to lure it for the purpose of mating at the appropriate time. Even deep-swimming fish are equipped with sensitive light detectors.[11] The fish has nothing whatever to say about the romance. This lack of say-so as regards mating is a "romantic assent" that is imposed throughout the animal kingdom. It is a universal constraint for which there is no known exception. Succinctly put, if you're an animal, you must do your thing. In fact, were there an exception, given enough time the species would become extinct. However, unlike in the animal kingdom, this rule does not apply to man. When it comes to mating, people are free to say no. In the animal kingdom, once the chemicals are dispersed or the song sung or the light lit, the insect or animal or bird or fish must respond and eventually copulate. They are in bondage to their instincts and for them no alternative course of action is possible. *They do what they do because of what they are.*

The second form of communication lies in the area of aggression. This too operates under a universal rule. In this case, all animal communication is genetically preprogrammed to produce behavioral changes that create the temporary illusion that the animal is larger than its actual size. Examples include ruffled feathers, extended fins, raised crests, open mouths, and bobbing heads. The charade is effective because the adversary is bound by a similar genetic program that corroborates the imposter's buffoonery. Humans need not be as easily impressed with such antics because humans are free to override their instinct by exercising will.

For instance, when confronted by an ape beating its chest in a jungle, man can decide to stand his ground, aim his gun and shoot it. This is not true for animals. Their genes either compel them to fight in fury or run in fear. Moreover, the *way* they fight or run is likewise genetically prescribed to them. Humans, on the other hand, are free to decide *how* to fight. In the movies, for example, heroes fight "clean" whereas the bad guys fight "dirty." Animals are denied such choice. As regards behavior they are neither "clean" nor "dirty"; they are animals.

The third area of animal communication concerns food. Here, the universal rule is that the more intense the signal and the longer its duration, the greater is the distance one must travel to find the food. This is true of zebras, of butterflies, and of fish. Ants are bound by this rule as well as elephants. The genetic program dictating the edict is common to each, and it shows no favor. We might expect that this would not be the case had the rule evolved in accord with the modern synthesis. Wouldn't it seem more natural to have differing selection rules for food in an anthill than on an African plain? Why should the environment of birds perched in trees produce the same rules as for fish swimming in the depth of the sea? Clearly, something else is at play here, something that has given animals, fish, and birds alike a universal rule to which they must all adhere, and from which they cannot depart.

So we see that throughout the animal kingdom there is communication,[12] but it's all genetically confined to these three areas. These universal laws of communication not only mandate *how* the transmitted signals are to be interpreted within the animal kingdom, but *what* categories of dialectical intercourse are permissible. Animals don't discuss great works of art, nor do they decide which musical concert to attend. They don't plan recipes for the week's meals, and they don't argue over which religion is right. Instead, they have one goal in life—to survive. In order to achieve that goal, there are only three things of concern to them: mating, aggression, and food.

Language

We now have a glimpse of the divine imprint that impregnates human life and separates man from every creature within the animal kingdom. Why is it that man lands on the moon while monkeys land on trees? The answer is that man alone has the capacity to distill into his mind the collective experience and knowledge of thousands of years of prior generations, enlarge upon it, and then transmit all of it to a future generation. But *how* is he able to do this?

The answer is that out of the 11 million species of life on earth, *only man* has the capacity of the "word," the ability to crystallize coherence out of chaos by creating within the mind ordered composites of mentally synthesized abstract elements which he then translates into various physical forms suitable for communication to other human life. Animals cannot do this. Every animal that's ever been born must survive with the same information that was available to its ancestors, and that will be available to its offspring. All the generations of animals are similar; none carries with it any advantage unavailable to its forefathers or its progeny. The reason for this is that an animal's actions are controlled by the instincts it obtains from the genes of its parents. In the absence of human intelligence, all inputs derive from the time period of the birth and life of the animal, and all the information available to the animal is confined to events that occur in the space and time of its physical environment.

This is not so with human beings. A parent can deliver to a child knowledge of events that transpired in the space and time of another age. Whereas animals are in bondage to the time period into which they are born, man is free from such constraint and is able to lift himself up and outside the space and time of his physical existence. Of all God's creatures, man alone has the capacity to receive, supply and transmit information through time. This is significant because *it provides a basis for human accountability beyond the space and time of any one generation of human life.*

Morality

In the last analysis, all morality is based upon the ability of humankind to receive an absolute code of moral dos and don'ts through time. For example, the Ten Commandments that laid claim on the behavior of human beings living thousands of years ago likewise impose moral bounds on the behavior of people today. This isn't to say that everyone living today acknowledges these commandments as morally binding; but the commandments haven't changed in thousands of years. The Bible's explanation for this state of affairs is that the commandments come from a settled Mind that is *absolute* in its pronouncements.[13] Since truth doesn't change, but circumstances and feeling do, one would think that after three thousand five hundred years a fickle mind would have offered an Eleventh Commandment—or at least improved upon one of the ten. But this hasn't happened. The Ten Commandments stand today as they were originally given, and they illuminate a standard of human behavior that would usher in Utopia itself were we just willing and able to do what they say. (For further discussion of Christian doctrine on this point, see Appendix 8, "Reprogramming Humanity.")

However, there is another kind of moral standard which is not absolute, but *relative*. It goes under a variety of names, but the one that's perhaps most descriptive is "situational ethics." Among other things, this belief asserts that ethical behavior does not depend upon a code, but a situation. Thus what is moral is relative to the situation in question, so that the same behavior can be morally right in one situation, yet morally wrong in another. The concept of relative versus absolute values is old; people have traditionally found a relative standard attractive because it gives one the freedom to interpret situations in ways that permit self-serving behavior to appear morally right.

But consider what it means to submit oneself to a *relative* code of dos and don'ts. In doing so, do we not accept as a basis for right and wrong only the events that transpire in the space and time to which animals are in bondage? And do we not abandon as a standard for morality the transmission through time of rights and wrongs that transcend the instincts and impulses of any one generation?

Of all God's creatures, only human life can receive and understand moral instructions through time. But if we ignore the demands or refuse to obey, then we are so much as saying that we are the highest authority and that all morality is consigned to culture rather than creation. In this case man is accountable to no one but himself. Thus the distinction between what's moral and what's honorable disappears, and behavior that's civil is soon accepted as moral. The restraint on man's self-serving nature disappears, and changing laws liberalize existing mores into license for free expression of human desire. Morality as a restraint imposed by accountability to a higher Authority is thus redefined, in effect, to permit free expression of the flesh.

The conclusion, then, is that true morality is based upon the transmission through time of an absolute moral code of rights and wrongs that transcend the instincts and impulses of any one generation. Were it otherwise, morality would cease to be a constraint external to man's self-serving nature. Nor is morality the social expression of man's collective desire. Moral law isn't social law. Morality imposes restraints on human passions and appetites whereas society displays indifference to all indulgences that do not endanger its members.

Uniqueness

Of all God's creatures, man alone is a moral being. But when we abandon absolute morality in favor of rights and wrongs relative to the time frame of our generation, we foolishly elect, as a basis for determining what is right and wrong, the circumstances and environment to which animals are in bondage. This means that we are voluntarily constraining ourselves to instincts and impulses whose central thrust is instant gratification. Moreover, to abrogate an absolute code of dos and don'ts that has instructed thousands of years of human life is to elect as moral a set of standards relative to the time period in which we live. In this regard, how do the basic environmental inputs that guide human life differ from those that guide animals? Does not human uniqueness come from man's capacity to lift himself outside the time constraint into which he's been born?

Unlike animals, we are able to free ourselves from the limited experience and knowledge of only one lifetime by receiving and acting upon time-tested information. *The moral basis for human behavior is a set of instructions whose intrinsic wisdom transcends the instincts and impulses of any one generation.* To this end, the Ten Commandments constitute an absolute code of moral precepts that embraces the essence of man's stature as a moral being. But whenever man succumbs to the impulse of a particular lifetime and abandons this absolute morality in favor of a contemporary ethic, he lowers himself into the animal kingdom. This will happen whenever the impulse of man's lust dominates the sanity of his mind. Here he will vent the bias in his heart toward a moral code that allows him to do what he wants to do because it satisfies his fleshly appetites—cravings not unlike the animal world.

We noted earlier in this chapter that all animal communication lies in three areas—mating, aggression, and food—needs common to both animal and human flesh. However, human aggression presupposes personal rights that, when violated, lead to anger. In the animal world these rights are confined to one's mate, territory, and food. But human flesh is predisposed toward lust, pride, and greed, which respectively distort his perceived rights into cravings for sex, dominance, and wealth. Lust pants for the body, pride finds reason to scorn, and greed envies another's good fortune. These encourage aggression, not because legitimate rights have been violated, but because selfish goals have nurtured indifference to the rights of others. This aggression is unique to man because it's rooted in human desire instead of need. And it is seductive because it stems from a pliant ethic that responds to self-serving beliefs. History bears witness to uninterrupted evil on earth because each generation disregards the timeless moral code that would bridle its desires.

In God's Image

Thus, it is the capacity of human life to receive, supply and transmit the "word," as recorded through the generations, that separates us from all other known life forms and gives us dominion over the planet earth. It's fascinating that the divine imprint of this ability was foreshadowed thousands of years ago in the opening chapter of the Bible. Genesis chapter 1, verse 26, declares that man is made in the image of God; verse 1 of the first chapter of John's Gospel states that the Word *was* God and became incarnate in the person of Christ. Thus we find man's unique image, namely, the "word," identified by the Bible with the Creator. Furthermore, the same Bible verse that says man is made in God's image also teaches that man will have dominion over planet earth. What unique distinction gives man his commanding position over all other life forms? Is it not his capacity to transmit information through time and receive the distillation of thousands of years of prior knowledge into the present?

This means that the very attribute identified by John's Gospel with God, namely the Word, is found to be possessed by man as the very attribute separating human life from the animal kingdom.

Eternity

Thus man's regal distinction, the unique human quality that positions us in absolute disunion from all other known forms of life, is a divine imprint, a consecration, as it were, with eternity in view by virtue of an absolute code of moral rules that self-evince Authority over human behavior under the penalty of eternal judgment. Such hope is inaccessible to animals. It is available only to a life form capable of receiving and transmitting absolute truth through generations of its existence. *We* are this life form. (Readers interested in the origin of these rules as well as the Person who fulfilled them will find Appendix 9, "The Moral Code," of value.)

So whereas man can refuse moral precepts, animals are denied the choice. They live and die under instincts that are genetically propagated through reproduction, and that regulate their survival while on earth. Human beings do not wear a genetic strait jacket; therefore instincts do not bind human choice. The freedom of human life to accept or reject moral commands that propagate through time identifies that life as moral, and certifies man as a moral agent who is accountable for his actions.

WHAT DID CLEVER HANS
TEACH MEN ABOUT APES?

WE'VE SAID THAT the capacity of human life to receive, supply and transmit the written word is unique to man, and that it has been with us for thousands of years.[1] For example, we find evidence of many distinctive human motifs on temple walls in the form of hieroglyphics,[2] drawings enunciated in artistic displays along parapets in caves,[3] and lunar calendars engraved on prehistoric bones.[4] In each and every case we find that humans have mentally synthesized abstract elements into ordered composites and then translated these complex patterns into written records that both contain and communicate information that would otherwise be unavailable.

But if this capacity to lift ourselves up and outside of the time frame of our birth is unique to man and inaccessible to animals, how is it that we read from time to time of experiments indicating that animals are capable of language,[5] mathematical concepts,[6] and of even understanding and forming simple sentences?[7] Papers have been published, for example, saying that dolphins are capable of language,[8] and that chimps have been trained to communicate with their trainers by making simple sentences using plastic symbols[9] or computer-generated tokens.[10] If the "word" is unique to man, how can animals also possess it?

The capacity to assimilate and to communicate information outside of the time period of one's birth is an attribute absolutely unique to human life, a quality that is nonexistent in the animal kingdom. Yet a number of people, particularly in recent years, have made impressive-sounding claims regarding animal speech and animal language.[11] One expressed the extreme thought that "even orangutans are all too human,"[12] which seems to imply that were we to give apes the benefit of human culture and education, they would begin to take on human qualities. An ape named Lana, for example, allegedly did this in the context of language.[13] Back in the early 1970s a computer-based language was developed; its purpose was to see whether an ape could use language. In the computer system that was developed, messages could be typed onto a keyboard and then read using a visual display. The early conclusion from this work, which was widely believed as recently as 1980, was that Lana was capable of using symbols in language.[14]

In earlier work with different trainers, a chimp named Sarah also was believed to have the ability to use language.[15] In the case of Sarah, plastic symbols were used, rather than a computer. In the late 1960s much publicity gave the impression that Sarah could create sentences out of the plastic symbols. Furthermore, it was reported that Sarah had a reading and writing vocabulary of about one hundred thirty words, and that her understanding included concepts of actual sentence structure.

It was said that the chimp understood the use of verbs, adjectives, conditionals, and even compound sentences. Until the 1980s, these beliefs were widely accepted as valid. But their acceptance was premature, and today we know that apes are *not* capable of language. To see why this is so, let's contrast their so-called language with the waggle dance done by the scout bee discussed in an earlier chapter. In doing so we will acquire insight into the true state of the matter.

Animal Communication

When a scout bee does the waggle dance to tell other bees in a hive the direction to fly in search of food, it executes a number of sophisticated maneuvers that communicate an impressive amount of information.[16] Not only does it deliver navigational inputs such as target distance, solar direction, and angle of flight, but it actually compensates for the sun's movement in the sky by time-averaging the orientation of its body as it traces out the figure eight.[17] From where does such sophistication come? The answer is from the "software" along the genetic material which the bee receives at birth.

Human Trainers

Throughout the animal kingdom—regardless of whether bird, fish, animal or scout bee—communication is executed among members of the same species *without any interference* whatever by human intelligence.[18] In the case of the apes, however, a new ingredient is added, viz., human beings. In this instance animal trainers deploy their human intelligence to see whether animals are capable of using language. Moreover the studies are done in ways that, of necessity, force the apes to intimately interact over extended time periods with human intelligence and expectations.[19] In other words, whereas the scout bee tells other bees in the hive where food is located through genetically controlled chemical odors [20] in conjunction with instinctive body movements, in the language experiments *human intelligence* attempts to teach apes the use of language by means of "words" created either as tokens on a computer or in the form of plastic symbols. But consider what it means if you and I engage in such activity, and are successful in teaching these animals language. The ramifications and implications are profound.

Animal Implications

For example, one thing it means is that human intelligence has succeeded in freeing animals from some of the instincts they receive at birth. It also implies that with sufficient training and environmental input, their linguistic ability could improve to the point where animals might converse with one another. Given enough time, their improved language ability could be imagined to resemble that of humans. Moreover, once dialogue occurred it might generate insights showing that their present state of affairs is the result of "adverse" evolutionary circumstances. If animal conversation became common, laws against discrimination and for equal opportunity could be developed to protect animals from the environmental factors that victimized them into a disadvantaged position relative to humans.

Indeed, one writer went so far as to suggest that although humans differ profoundly from animals, it's easy for people to be blind to special circumstances which, according to this idea, brought about the "seemingly God-given division" that separates man and animal.[21] He also alleged that, except for human culture and education, man's mind "is not so different from an ape's." He then expressed the corollary that were people to expose an ape's mind to human culture, then apes might acquire human qualities. Furthermore, were humans to speak to apes "in the right way," they might also speak back.

Are these informed opinions? Or do they show undiscerning acceptance of the rubbish that has passed for science in the area of animal language? These views have so little factual content, yet they provide perhaps the strongest evidence thus far for the common ground that is thought possible between a human and ape mind. Yet even here the apparently small distance between the two is by human choice and not necessity. In light of the recent indisputable evidence now available on this subject,[22] it is no longer tenable to believe that natural circumstances can decrease the infinity that exists between the human and the ape mind. Monkeys land on trees while man lands on the moon, and to believe that special circumstances produced the difference is to invent past events that are unknown and unexplained, and that contradict present evidence.

Historical Perspective

The question is, of course, are apes really capable of using language? Up to about 1980, the answer was believed to be yes, and by a large number of investigators.[23] Many experiments had been done. Apes named Austin and Sherman, as well as Lana, were taught to label different foods and tools.[24] The chimp, Sarah, then fourteen years old, was even said to be able to infer the nature of problems and to recognize potential solutions to them.[25] Furthermore, six wild-born chimpanzees, five to seven years of age, were reported to be capable of humanlike spatial memory organization.[26] Paper-marking tests were devised for chimpanzees [27] three years after "social conditions" were believed to determine the rates at which the chimps approached "hidden, distant goals." [28] This was a time period when it was thought that language in children and chimpanzees could be compared.[29]

But as with all questions, it's often quite helpful to establish a perspective. In this case we need an historical perspective. How new are these claims that allege that animals are capable of using language? The answer is not very new at all. In fact, in 1661 Samuel Pepys wrote that it was his opinion that apes might be taught to speak,[30] an impression obtained when he met a baboon for the first time. Somewhat more recently, in 1885, Sir John Lubbock wrote that rather than trying to teach animals our ideas, it might be better to devise a code of signals so that the animal could communicate its ideas to us.[31] Twenty years later, and colored by the alleged academic antics of a horse named Clever Hans, a psychiatrist said that an animal can think in human ways and express human ideas in human language.[32]

Notwithstanding asinine views of animal efficacy, the observable facts show that animals are organic machines energized by instincts. In the absence of human intelligence, animal behavior expresses itself under a dictatorial genetic system that imposes common controls from generation to generation. This is why the language experiments with apes required training so structured as to be logically equivalent to teaching a child to swing through trees while supporting him with cables, harnesses, and nets.[33] In fact, the training of animals to perform longer and longer sequences of signs for rewards is not at all new or even novel. It has been done with pigeons [34] and even with worms.[35] It certainly does not imply the use of language. Furthermore, all such sign behavior on the part of animals is mechanistic in that it can be essentially duplicated on a computer.[36] The alleged "language" of the chimp Lana has been reported attributable to only two basic processes called paired associate learning and conditional discrimination learning.[37] This means that, as a practical matter, a computer can be programmed to simulate the alleged language behavior of the chimp, a result that underscores the machine-like character of animal behavior.

Clever Hans

This raises an important question. Why have some intelligent people wrongly believed (some still do) that apes have the ability to use these signs in ways that are characteristic of true language? How were they fooled into accepting the idea that animals could do things that they really can't do? The answer lies in an ability that animals *do* have, an ability that is relatively unknown but which played a major part in the hoax apes have unknowingly perpetrated on their trainers. Although trainers have been fooled by this ability in many varied situations, over a good number of years, the effect is best illustrated in the story of the trotting horse, Clever Hans, from the early 1900s.[38]

Clever Hans was not your ordinary horse. His owner was so captivated by the extreme degree of intelligence the horse appeared to possess that he exposed the horse to the equivalent of several years' high-school education. People traveled for miles to see the horse, and to view first hand the near miraculous intellectual wonders that it ostensibly performed. Clever Hans astounded audiences with his ability to solve very complex math problems. He could also answer nonmathematical questions as well.

When asked a question involving numbers, the horse would answer by pawing the ground with his hoof. Questions that demanded a yes or no response were answered by shaking his head up and down or left and right. Furthermore, the horse could also name colors. This was done by picking up colored rags. The horse drew worldwide attention, and large numbers of people—including medical doctors, animal experts and even circus trainers—attempted to discover how he could be so smart. They studied the horse, investigated its owner, and questioned the people who asked questions of the horse. All attempts at discovering the source of the intelligence the horse displayed failed. Cavalry officers, psychologists, and well-known scholars got into the act, but none was able to learn why the horse was so bright.

One day, when it seemed there was nothing left but accept the seemingly scholarly horse at face value, the mystery was abruptly solved. Someone thought to ask the horse a question whose answer was not known by either the questioner nor anyone else physically close to the horse. Suddenly the horse became dumb. Not only did it not know the answer [38] to the question, it became obvious that it had not known the answer to any question *ever* asked of it.

Years of intimate familiarity between the horse and its trainer during many teaching sessions had enabled the horse to interpret extremely small movements of his trainer's head and body. At each demonstration, when the horse reached the correct answer, it had been able to detect an ever-so-slight unconscious movement of his trainer's body. For example, the horse answered number problems by pawing the ground with its hoof. While it did so, the trainer habitually leaned forward ever so slightly until the paw strokes equalled the correct answer; then, imperceptibly, he would relax somewhat. This small movement was an unconscious thing on the part of the trainer, and although unseen by humans, it proved a clear signal to Clever Hans.

Likewise with head movements to yes and no questions. When the horse started to answer by moving its head in the wrong direction, a slight twitch of discomfort by its trainer was a signal for it to reverse the direction of its head movements.

Animals make exquisite observers, and over the course of many training sessions Clever Hans had acquired such familiarity with his owner that he could decisively distinguish human head movements *well under one hundreth of an inch.* [38] Thus, for example, when the horse's nose passed over the correct colored rag, the inadvertent expectation of its owner produced more than enough motion for the horse to detect.

Despite the discovery that Clever Hans wasn't clever, a profusion of pet owners seemed to come out of the woodwork, making all kinds of claims on behalf of their four-legged companions. Cats, dogs, and other domestic animals suddenly had become instant oracles of wisdom as their owners vouched for their IQ. In the next thirty years over seventy animals that were alleged to "think" made their appearance with their two-legged counterparts in hope of stardom.[39] But all were doomed to failure. The energizing agent behind the performance of each animal proved to be the intelligence of its master. To eliminate the newly discovered effect in scientific studies, European psychologists demanded that all contact between the experimenter and the animal be eliminated.[40]

This precaution was voiced at least twenty years before serious language experiments with animals had begun, and yet it was not heeded. As a result, the animals' ultrasensitive and unseen perception of human expressions and mannerisms became the dominant mechanism behind ill-founded language claims that followed. An animal's discernment of its trainer's expectations coupled with its superior sensory organization explains what has been happening for years in the language experiments with apes.[41]

Video Exposure

Only recently has it been realized that apes do not display linguistic ability.[42] Rather, like Clever Hans, they mirror the human intelligence of their trainers.[43] Indeed, so subtle is the effect of this mirroring with apes that it was discovered only after many hours of careful study of videotapes by an able researcher whose mind was open to learning the truth about the matter.[44] The breakthrough came when a young chimp named Nim [45] was trained with sign language.[46] Initially the chimp appeared to use signs in ways characteristic of true language, much as humans do. But later, when videotapes of the results were carefully and repeatedly studied, it was discovered that the chimp used the signs only when prompted by the trainer. Moreover, when the chimp did this, it repeated the trainer's signs without adding any new ones of its own. This occurred as much as 40 percent of the time.

Furthermore, when new signs were added, they were found to contain no new information. The data reported in this work [47] show that the chimp's use of signs was merely the result of cues it obtained from its trainer.[48] When the researcher studied films of the other apes that were supposedly capable of using language, he discovered the same thing, viz., that apes were responding to the motions and gestures of their trainers. These experiments underscored something that has been known since Clever Hans. Having sensory ability vastly superior to humans, animals make excellent observers and often are extremely skillful at interpreting human expression.

These recent analyses are sobering and show that the conclusions that apes have linguistic ability are without substantive evidence; they are, in fact, *wrong*. [49] This isn't true of only Lana and Sarah. Another category of investigators has been at work raising both chimps and gorillas in a highly social, family-type environment in which the trainers attempt to teach the animals sign language as mentioned earlier.[50] The first chimp, allegedly proficient in producing sounds of this kind, was Washoe. What may not be so widely known is that about *sixty people* were involved in attempting to train this chimp, although a core of about eight did most of the work.

In the early 1970s a female gorilla named Koko was also trained at doing the same thing.[51] In this case forty people were involved, with an estimated core group of about six. That's quite a "teacher-to-student" ratio. Can you imagine what the linguistic ability of an ordinary child would be with such educational blessing? It's interesting that when the same techniques used to teach apes language were applied to mentally retarded patients at the Georgia State Retardation Center,[52] the *retarded patients were much easier to teach than the chimps,* despite all of the problems these patients had, including extremely low IQs of between 20 and 40.

Other Language Experiments

Thus, beginning in 1661 with Samuel Pepys's first encounter with a baboon, and extending all the way into the twentieth century with much serious work beginning in the 1960s and continuing through the late 1970s, it was almost unanimously (if erroneously) agreed upon that apes are actually capable of using language in much the same way as man. A number of factors contributed to the misleading of the investigators. For example, after the chimps had been taught to communicate with each other there were times when their success rate reached 95 percent. But these experiments used word symbols generated by a computer. When it was turned off, communication dropped to about 10 percent, thereby indicating that apes do not have the capacity of abstract cognition. When they communicate, they do so by using a computer or plastic symbols, i.e., things supplied by human intelligence. Moreover, the linguistic ability they display does not reflect language ability. Instead, it is the ape's response to miniscule motions by its trainer whose linguistic expectations are then mirrored as "language."

In the early 1960s, dolphins were reported to be capable of language.[53] At that time people foolishly speculated that since dolphins had larger brains than any other mammal, they might even be *more* intelligent than man. Sober inquiry, however, has shown that this is not the case.[54] This dolphin mystique was elevated to a cultlike fanaticism, having nothing whatever to do with reality.[55] Today it is recognized as complete nonsense.

Since apes were thought to be intelligent and capable of language, one wonders why no one thought to train them at least to clean their own cages? No one has ever succeeded in getting even one of the thousands of apes in zoos all over the world to prepare its own food or clean up after itself. One may argue that apes have no interest in such work. If so, then we are forced to conclude that neither apes, nor dolphins, nor any of these animals seem to show interest in anything that humans find worthwhile. Where then does their intelligence lie? Humans are the ones who prepare the food and clean the cages and do all kinds of other work. Animals work only when they are forced to.

Abstract Cognition

Humans are *able* to force animals to work because man has dominion over planet earth by virtue of his ability to receive and transmit information through time. This ability is unique to human life and it gives each of us the capacity to comprehend the message that perpetuates through time, promising eternal life to those who will trust it. The message is briefly discussed in Appendix 10.

Whereas you or I can close our eyes and mentally reconstruct abstract representations of reality, an animal seems incapable of doing this. For example, we can close our eyes and yet, in our mind's eye, visualize Christ hanging on a cross as a sin payment for our failure to do all that God requires. Furthermore, we each have the power to understand that event as a passport into eternal life, and to make a decision apart from instinct regarding whether or not to take advantage of it. Irrespective of one's response to this example, the point is that an animal is *incapable of the visualization, the understanding, and even of the decision.* Man alone, of all the known species within the universe, has this distinctive attribute—the capacity of the "word."

The Word

Why should man, of all the known life forms, possess this incredible capacity to receive and comprehend information from a time period in the past, and to assimilate and transmit that information into the future? Stated differently, why does only human life have the capacity of the "word"? Why is there absolute disunion between us and all other known species on our planet? In five thousand years of human record, the Bible is the only writing that clearly answers the question. Its answer is that human life is made in the image of the Supreme Intelligence who designed and brought it into existence. It's clear from the empirical facts that human life, as a species, is indeed distinct and different from all of the other known species in the world.

Is there any evidence that relates this distinctive attribute of human life with the creation of human beings? Is there evidence that correlates man's capacity to manage information outside the time frame of his existence, and the unique informational specification we now know resides within the particular sequence of nucleotide bases along the DNA strand of his body? The answer appears to be yes. Data were obtained from six adult patients who needed to undergo surgery in the left hemisphere of their brains. By studying electrical impulses within the brain, scientists were able to establish that the neurological and physiological correlations unique to human language are "specific" to the language cortex in the left hemisphere of the human brain.[56]

In that same year, computer experts in artificial intelligence recognized that human beings assign meaning to verbal utterances—meaning that depends not only on the words but also on the state of mind and knowledge of those deploying language.[57] This inescapable intimacy between language and mind was anticipated ten years earlier. One of the greatest thinkers of our time in the field of human language identified a unique feature of the human mind. He found that a child seems to possess at birth an innate structure that enables a natural understanding of the spoken word.[58] What this means is that the capacity of the "word," the unique distinction that gives man the faculty of human language, is itself genetically traceable to the informational specification along the DNA strand which encodes human life and which, therefore, came into existence at the time human life was created.

This aligns with the biblical doctrine that portrays the Creator as the Word, and man as his image. If the divine attribute of man's Creator is the Word, then the human capacity to perpetuate an absolute moral code through time is itself an ever-present shadow of the moral image overlaying all generations of human life. Man is thus illuminated as life's singular moral species with access to eternity. This "passport" is embodied in a Creator's timeless message that only man can receive. Although man is free to disregard it, the message contains assurances that the purpose for which it was sent will nonetheless succeed. This means that failure to accept one's destiny cannot be the fault of the message,[59] but rather lies in its rejection.

20

IS THERE A WAY TO LIVE FOREVER?

MAN *is* a moral creature by virtue of transcendent wisdom intrinsic to a moral code that is immune to the instincts and impulses of any one generation—instincts that hold animals captive, but from which man is free to escape. However, when humans abandon absolute morality in favor of the rights and wrongs relative to their own time period, they voluntarily constrain themselves to the instincts and impulses of one generation. They thus partake of the same circumstantial basis to which animals are in bondage and, in so doing, conjoin themselves to animals, i.e., to a form of life that is incapable of moral behavior. As we have seen, animals are incapable of moral behavior in an absolute sense. They have knowledge provided only by their immediate environment; and in the absence of human intelligence, as they store, retrieve, and process this knowledge, they do so with an intent and expectancy whose only thrust is *immediate gratification.*

People, however, are able to defer their gratification, and practice self-denial. Imagine the chaos that would occur in a future eternal life if all of us freely expressed ourselves without obeying any laws. The only way to avoid the conflicts that would arise would be to subjugate our desires to the wisdom of an all-knowing governing Authority. The exclusively human trait of self-denial that this would require is practiced each time we stop at a traffic light, pay a bill, or use a court of law when wronged. Except for man, no other known species of life is capable of choosing self-denial for the benefit of another. Only man refuses food in times of hunger, elects pain when offered relief and abandons desire when invited to fulfill it. Animals do exhibit self-denial for their offspring; however, this is not by choice but by genetic mandate. Man's self-denial for his neighbor is a moral decision to which conscience speaks.

Self-taking leads to a pit of despair that communes with the animals; but self-giving aligns with hope for eternal life. And whereas self-denial builds character for eternal living, instant gratification digs mudholes that nurture progressive filth. Animals have no choice. For them, mudholes are the only alternative possible, and so their "filth" remains physical. But humans are capable of moral decisions that impose "mudhole" accountability to which the Bible imputes eternal consequences. Yet, is the Bible's message one of deliverance or one of judgment? The answer is both! It foreshadows life or death, hope or doom, joy or despair, and it says the choice is ours. It puts paradise on one side of the balance and eternal destruction on the other. With regard to which way the scale will tip, it makes quite clear that the love of God can never embrace what his holiness must condemn.

The Question of Context

Many people have an opinion of the Bible that is based upon what others understand it to say; but few ever take the time to read what it says first-hand. Were we to do this, difficulties could arise. One problem is that a special "lamp" is disclosed by its author as necessary to understand the Bible.[1] Another serious problem is that the human writers who penned the manuscripts are not the Intellect who authored its content.[2]

The picture here is that of an orchestra with each book of the Bible an instrument. The book of Genesis doesn't read the same as the Psalms, and they in turn read differently from the Minor Prophets. Likewise, neither does a trumpet sound the same as a violin, or a violin the same as a piano. Yet they are all playing one song written by one author. An accurate understanding of any one verse of Scripture requires that the entire Bible be kept in view. When this is not done, context is destroyed and verses can be chosen to say anything that one desires. For example, consider the following quotes from Scripture: (1) "Judas went and hung himself." (2) "Go thou and do likewise." (3) "Whatever thou doest, do quickly."

In this example, Scripture is quoted, but the context is mutilated. In the paragraphs that follow, we give a sweeping overview of what the Bible reveals concerning our plight on earth and God's provision for escape. Although these truths have been expressed in terms of contemporary usage, I have sought to preserve the Bible's context. This will allow the message these truths contain to be easily understood by a casual reader.

I have tried to explain doctrine regarding mankind's dilemma and an individual's decision for deliverance from death in a way that is true to all of God's Word. To the serious Bible student, let me say that he or she will want to be careful to distinguish actual Bible teaching from one's cherished traditions or hidden agendas. To this end, the perspective here presented may be new, but its truths are entirely biblical.

What's in the Bible?

By way of overview, the Bible can be divided into three parts: the Old Testament (thirty-nine books) says that man's in trouble, but that God's sending a life raft. The four Gospels say that he has arrived and his name is Jesus Christ. The Epistles (twenty-three remaining books) say that he is coming again. From cover to cover, the Bible is a record of God's revelation to man concerning a God-anointed end-time King who will deliver man by judging the evil that afflicts him. The central Old Testament message is that the Messiah is the actual saving presence of God on earth, whereas that of the New Testament (Gospels plus Epistles) is that the words and the deeds of Jesus *are* the words and deeds of God. With that summary introduction, let's rerun the script under a magnifying glass.

If we go back to the beginning, the Bible teaches that human intelligence is the object of conflict between a Supreme Intelligence who is the Designer and Creator of all that we see, and a perverse intelligence who is in rebellion against his maker. The Supreme Intelligence is described as a Being of love warning mankind of impending disaster and announcing his provision for escape. The perverse intelligence is revealed to be actively at work to discredit the message as part of a plan to subjugate mankind. People are portrayed as living agents who communicate with one another through oxygen-burning organic machines called human bodies, and physical death is disclosed as entrance of the living agent into a new world in the form of a spirit that separates from a body when it ceases to function.

The Bible depicts man's spirit as the kernel about which a new "resurrected" body is to be later placed. The need for a future perfect body is justified in terms of incurable defects now present in all flesh, defects that were genetically propagated from mankind's earliest parents at the time the perverse intelligence engineered their fall.

Thus, the biblical diagnosis of man's problems is that he has a fallen nature that was produced when the flesh,* originally designed by the Supreme Intelligence as a container to mold self-*giving* spirits, became altered to produce self-*taking* agents with a propensity to satisfy their desire while experiencing the least possible pain. Evidence has been published indicating that the genetic "triplet" code responsible for the assembly of flesh in every living creature came into being by a transition from a far more primitive "doublet" code of much greater information content.[3] This is a discovery that is consistent with the biblical narrative.

Thus, the picture painted by the Bible is that the living agent (man) is a

---

* As used here, "flesh" primarily means the gray matter of man's brain. All other parts of his body only function to preserve this gray matter.

degenerate spirit (programmer) in degenerate flesh (hardware). To correct the problem, the Supreme Intelligence entered space-time to die in virgin-born flesh free of these defects for the purpose of both legally settling man's debt, and of releasing a perfect spiritual template suitable to regenerate (reprogram) human life. The Bible teaches that Christ returned bodily in full view from the grave as a public demonstration that eternal life is available to humans; but it also teaches that spiritual rebirth is necessary to receive that life. The reason is that God will not entrust a super computer (resurrection body) to a degenerate programmer (unregenerated person).

The Fall of Man

The biblical account of how man's nature became altered is that before the fall, Adam lived in a garden whose produce met all his needs. He was allowed to eat of every tree in the garden except the "tree of the knowledge of good and evil." The command given to Adam was: "Of every tree of the garden you may freely eat; but of the tree of the knowledge of good and evil you shall not eat, for in the day that you eat of it you shall surely die" (Genesis 2:16, 17, *New King James Version*).

The forbidden tree was in the middle of the garden beside another tree called the "tree of life." [4] Since both trees were in the garden, before the fall Adam was allowed to eat of the tree of life—an act the Bible identifies as synonymous with eternal life. [5] Genesis 3 teaches that, after the fall, Adam and Eve were expelled from the garden without eternal life. Since physical death attends spiritual death, this change from life without an end, to life without ease until death, implies that, at the very least, the physical part of man's nature was altered at the time of the fall. This physical part being man's body,[6] it means that the informational specifications along his DNA must have undergone a change. Other Bible texts dealing with sin confirm that Adam's flesh underwent a change at the time of the fall. These texts teach that man's flesh is an ally and vehicle of sin,[7] that this was not the case before the fall,[8] and that the change occurred at the time of the fall.[9]

Can Man Really Choose Right from Wrong?

Flesh by itself is nothing more than three-dimensional polypeptide chains described by high polymer chemistry, whereas sin is willful disobedience of God's laws. Therefore, sin is a matter of the spirit, because it involves an act of the mind.[10] The alteration of man's physical nature into a vehicle of sin thus implies that man's present spiritual weakness traces to Adam's altered flesh. Genetically transmitted destructive defects appeared after the fall in the organic structure of man's brain that permanently altered his spiritual nature.

The absence of conflict between the flesh and the mind before the fall, and the waging of war afterward against rightly ordered affections within the mind,[11] shows that the fall of man must have involved a change in the organic structure of his brain. This implies that spirits are molded or shaped on earth by flesh, and not vice versa.[12] Since ants and elephants differ only in their information specification along the DNA, it is not surprising that man was changed when the specification along Adam's DNA was altered in the fall. Adam was able to obey God's command,[13] but yet chose to eat from the forbidden tree.[14] Therefore, Adam was free to choose wrongly but was not under compulsion of the flesh to do so. However, the Bible teaches that after the fall everyone chooses wrongly,[15] and it explains that problem by revealing that the entire human race inherited defective flesh.[16] The reason is that all people were procreated from genetically defective organic machines.[17]

As a boy, I recall asking how it was fair that God blamed me for something Adam did. In my youth though, I totally missed the biblical answer that my flesh traces directly back to Adam's body, and my behavior for which I'm responsible comes from a mind shaped by that flesh. Therefore, the only lasting solution to wrong behavior is a new mind.[18]

Only a self-sufficient being is able to make objective judgments of good and evil that harmonize with his entire spiritual and physical creation. Such judgments by a finite being such as man will always be from a self-serving posture that is limited by incomplete understanding. The result is a series of unforeseen consequences that are detrimental to the welfare of others. This is why we find the tree of life beside the tree of the knowledge of good and evil. It teaches that only an eternally existing Intelligence is able to decide what is right and wrong. When Adam disobeyed, he assumed control of his life and took upon himself the divine prerogative of determining good and evil. The result was an altered nature whose physical part eventually ceased to function.[19] The Bible attributes the deception that eventually produced such death to a perverse intelligence named Satan—a created cherub sent into the garden to protect man,[20] but who rebelled because he had a jealous desire to become like God.

How Can Fruit Change Flesh?

The Bible unambiguously teaches that the nature of every human being on earth was altered at the time of the fall [21] when mankind's earliest parents ate the fruit of a certain tree. However, many people find it difficult to understand how the act of eating vegetation can permanently alter human nature.[22] In this regard, we note that certain Bible texts [23] suggest that the "trees" in the garden may not be intended as literal vegetation, but instead are a metaphor to communicate literal truths of past events whose context lies outside human experience. Jesus Christ himself confirmed that it was not the eating by Adam of the literal produce that produced the change because Jesus taught that nothing a man eats can defile him since it doesn't enter his "heart," but rather his stomach and is thus passed on.[24] The fruit described in Genesis defiled not only a man but the entire human race. Therefore, the only logical conclusion possible is that the fruit was *not* something that went into Adam's stomach.

Since flesh is the container by which the "spirit" is molded, the altered informational specifications along Adam's DNA produced a self-taking human nature bent on satisfying its desires with the least possible pain. Six elements common to the nature of all mankind emerged: hatred, envy, lust, pride, anger, and selfishness. Although these elements are with us today, they are masked by the contrived veneer of secular humanism—a religion promulgated in societies materially able to satisfy the physical appetites of its members. However, when these appetites go unfilled, man reverts to the self-taking behavior of his maligned nature. Since no human society can satisfy the appetites of all of its members all of the time, human conduct is ultimately controlled by social deterrents that inflict pain on unacceptable behavior.

Why Is Secular Humanism Untrue?

Secular humanism postulates the inevitable evolution of man's goodness and, thus, the demise of such deterrents. There is no historical warrant for this assumption, however. As seen from the perspective of Scripture, neither can there be any rational hope of its future fulfillment because the goals of humanism are incompatible with the nature of man. Examples include the willingness of college-trained people to design Hitler's ovens, the slaughter of well over 100 million people in plans engineered by communist governments, and a nuclear holocaust that possibly awaits * mankind due to decisions by alleged brilliant minds.

The good news is that hope actually exists for mankind. But the irony is that it lies in a book hardly anyone ever reads, a book ridiculed by each generation but thereafter vindicated by the knowledge of a later generation. Today, millions of people regard the Bible as a poor history book sprinkled with fantasy and myth. This mindset employs Christianity as an ethical standard for young children, sees faith as the activity of fools, and explains biblical promises as a psychological crutch. Love is consigned to the action of lust, and historic truths are deemed intellectually unacceptable. It's said that the historical Christ is unknowable and that the history of his mission cannot be written.

God is regarded as the residue of a dark past, and spiritual truths are dispersed throughout a pietistic amalgam laced with the humanistic creed: All there is—is matter and matter in motion. But we have seen that such thought is not supported by twentieth-century science. Modern knowledge has not shown the Bible to be false. Appendix 11, "The Rise of Humanism," outlines how this erroneous belief developed.

Humanistic doctrines thrive because they are justified by the use of philoso-

---

* Man has never made a weapon he hasn't used.

phies that impersonate science. As modern science uncovers physical truths, secular humanism colors them with philosophical innuendos. The influence of humanism can be seen in the way it has shaped widely held ideas about scientific discoveries. For example, in the public's mind, life came from slime, has been created in a test tube, and can be found in outer space. Yet not one shred of data exists to support these beliefs. The popular notion that speciation is explainable through natural processes is likewise without empirical warrant. The fact of change in the fossil record is not at issue. What's in question is the blind, humanistic conjecture that living structures of ever increasing complexity were systematically assembled entirely by natural processes. The Bible says that this is not so, and the New Generalized Second Law of Thermodynamics appears to confirm it.

Has the Bible Been Ahead of Us?

Modern knowledge is vindicating the Bible archeologically, biologically, and anthropologically. Nuclear ruin, global famine, and human despair are knocking at our door, yet we continue to look to ourselves for salvation. This is not happening because the evidence supports such a view, but rather because most deem the alternative described in the Bible unacceptable.

We swim in a sea of providence while demanding proof that there's water; and we point our telescopes toward the fringe of our four-dimensional, space-time guppy bowl only to see our anthropic reflection illuminate an exterior design. Indeed, the creation is *so* overwhelming that it incapacitates our faculties to rationally comprehend it. It testifies to a way of escape against the din of those who say: "There is no God." One can jump off a high building and all the way down shout that there's no such thing as gravity, but eventually the bottom must come, and with it the price of such folly. Physical and spiritual laws really differ in only one respect: The latter have deferred consequences. Therefore, in the last analysis, it is not so much that we break God's laws as it is that they break us.

How Does One Have Eternal Life?

The Bible teaches that eternal life is coterminous with the Supreme Intelligence who created all that we see and are, and that the loving nature of this Intelligence is expressed when we cease to resist his initiative to overlay his life upon ours.[25] But the "love relationship" he offers requires the voluntary surrender of one's self into his loving care—and this in turn requires an act of will.

How does this happen? First we are exposed to the truth. Then we give intellectual assent that what we have been exposed to is true. But the interchange of life occurs when we take the third step and make a personal commitment *to* that truth.[26] To this end man is given freedom to choose in a world free from interference, due to certain limitations imposed by the Supreme Intelligence upon himself. These self-imposed limitations God has instituted are not unlike those we place on ourselves when we agree to adopt an orphan child. Although we are still sovereign in our home, we have nonetheless voluntarily obligated ourselves to guarantee the child's welfare, and to limit our activity in the home by subjugating portions of it to the needs of the child.

The Bible describes God limiting himself in a contract called the "second covenant" (New Testament). The agreement offered is this: In return for our love and submission to him, he promises to love and deliver us from a judgment with everlasting consequences that will otherwise follow our physical death. The Bible identifies these consequences with an eternal horror wrought by the perverse intelligence, but teaches that the Supreme Intelligence so loved man that he entered human flesh and died to pave the way for man to escape. Thus, the gospel becomes a message of hope, the Bible a "roadmap to eternal life," and Christ, God's "provision for the escape."

The escape route is appropriated by the mechanism of faith [27] which can be thought of as the tube in a blood transfusion with Christ the life that flows through it. Faith requires that a person believe that God exists,[28] accept his plan for deliverance,[29] and trust that he is able to perform it.[30] This means that a person must be willing to accept God's initiative to love and save him [31]—an act in which *human free choice enables God to express his love*. In other words, the Bible teaches that man was given freedom to choose so that God could express his love, and that God's giving humans the capacity of moral choice was for the purpose of our choosing him. However, not only are we free to choose otherwise; the Bible teaches that most do so.[32] Some argue that if God is so loving, why does he allow evil. The Bible has an answer. Let's see what it is.

Why Does Evil Exist?

The Bible clearly explains the origin of evil: *All evil results from the misuse of free will.*

There are three kinds of evil: natural, biological, and spiritual. The Bible implies that natural disorders such as earthquakes, floods, tidal waves, volcanic eruptions and the like, are the residue of Satan's misuse of free will on a cosmological plain. Spiritual disorders such as plunder, injustice, poverty, fear, wars, and famine are explained in terms of the misuse of man's free will. For example, consider famine. There are about 500 thousand species of known plant life on earth, of which at least 10 percent (50,000) are edible. Of these, only three hundred have been commercially cultivated; a mere thirty provide 95 percent of all human calories and protein.[33] Thus, we need to ask: Do people starve because of lack of food, or because of our misuse of resources?

Biological disorders include cystic fibrosis, enzyme disorders, brain malfunctions, heart disease, allergies, muscular dystrophy and sclerosis, various kinds of cancer, diabetes, and so forth. More than two thousand five hundred diseases have been traced to flaws in our DNA.[34] The Bible reveals that they originated in the degenerate flesh that materialized through the misuse of free will. Human cells contain twenty-three pairs of chromosomes, each with over three thousand microscopic genes of which about six are defective in every person alive. They do not affect most of us because they are masked by normal genes.

Thus, thousands of people, although free of the symptoms, are carrying such genetic disorders as hemophilia, Huntington's disease, and sickle-cell anemia. Since the Bible teaches that death entered the human race at the time of the fall, it comes as no surprise that progeria—a syndrome of accelerated aging in which children become bald at age three, wrinkle by age ten, and die of "old age" at sixteen—has been genetically implicated. When certain vitamins (antioxidants) are advocated to promote health (by reducing free radicals), some of us choose not to accept them on the basis that taking pills is not natural. This attitude illustrates ignorance of the basic Bible teaching that mankind was natural prior to the fall, and that health afterward is simply the state of compensating for our defects—not only the physical things listed above, but also the spiritual shortcomings we see all about us.

Criminologists, for example, estimate that a male baby born with an extra Y chromosome is ten times more likely to end up in a maximum security prison than other males. This is due in part to a tendency toward extreme violence conjoined to a low IQ. Similar aggressive behavior in both males and females has been shown due to hormone levels during gestation.[35] Although linked to prenatal exposure of synthetic progestins, gene-related hormone variations before birth, the data indicates, help determine aggressive tendencies in people.

The role of hormones in such behavior is seen, for example, in a study of university wrestlers. It showed that, after a match, winners had greater percentages of testosterone increase than losers even though both had the same level before the match. Several studies both in the U.S. and abroad indicate violent parents beget violent children, even when the youngsters are raised in nonviolent foster homes. Such genetic leanings do not excuse bad behavior, but they do help explain why the history of each generation of mankind is marred with prisons, wars, and bloodshed. It is not so much that man is bad, as it is that he is *bad off*. Thus, the biblical diagnosis of man's problems is not his political, social, or economic system, but rather it is *man himself.* [36]

Summary Overview

Sand and stars are before us, and the choice is ours. We can feed upon the scum of fleshly appetites, or we can enter the life outside of time designed by him who caused us to be. Shall we reach beyond the visible horizon to fulfill the destiny for which the universe was created? Or shall we slide into a mudhole from which we really did not come? All of life can look back to "origin," but only man can lay claim to "destiny." The choice is ours, the time is now, and the stakes are real. Life and death have cast their vote; the vote we cast will break the tie. Whatever you choose will be your choice forever; and if you abstain, then death will cast the vote for you. When all is said and done, we find ourselves at a fork between two paths: one that entices us into decadence, and the other that beckons us unto destiny. What will eternity show your vote to have been?

Appendix 1.   The New Inflationary Theory of the Universe

To explain how the universe came into being, any sensible mathematical theory of origins must address the widely held conviction among scientists that the space-time fabric of the present universe is very flat—a situation that corresponds to extremely high mixing and, therefore, large homogeneity and entropy. (The entropy is greater than 10^{87}.) Yet, at the same time, telescopes reveal that stars collect into galaxies, which in turn gather into clusters, and that some of the clusters even collect into superclusters.[1] Any mathematical theory of the universe must, therefore, explain at least two things: (1) The present homogeneous smoothness over large (long-range) distances, and (2) the gathering of stars into galaxies and clusters over small (short-range) distances.

Astrophysicists have explained this state of affairs through the New Inflationary Theory. This can be viewed as a refined version of the older Big Bang Theory. It is highly mathematical, and teaches that the universe underwent a rapid exponential expansion in its very early moments. During the rapid expansion, causality produced long-range homogeneous mixing *and* localized inhomogeneous seeds that later coalesced the galaxies and clusters. This mathematical description of our universe also explains the absence at the present time of certain large particles known as magnetic monopoles, and the huge entropy due to the mixing mentioned earlier.

It is significant that the New Inflationary Theory has been so successful. The reason is that it essentially stands alone in explaining the absence of the large massive monopoles that are missing from the present universe. These large particles are predicted by virtually every elementary particle theory through symmetry reduction to a direct product with a U(1) group, and, as such, it was thought their presence would be necessary to any successful theory. In addition, the high mixing and entropy are very nicely explained by assuming that the universe expands in certain ways allowed by the New Inflationary Theory, supercooling over an extended time period followed by the release of latent heat through a first-order phase transition into a metastable state. However, when we use the New Inflationary Theory to examine the earlier idea that a quantum fluctuation may have produced the universe out of nothing, we find that quantum fluctuations are not a "free lunch" from nature—a conclusion that we can hold with reasonable confidence in view of the many successes of the New Inflationary Theory.

The Final Straw: "Causality"

Suppose, for the sake of argument, that despite all of what has been considered, we choose to defend the belief that the universe arose through a natural event. On the surface it would seem all we need to do is reject the New Inflationary Theory that disqualified a quantum fluctuation from making a universe. Then we could say that the universe *did not* expand in the way described. Furthermore, we could even attempt to justify our belief by noting that energy positivity is not satisfied in the Hawking-Penrose singularity theorems.[2] Moreover, we can claim that the large-scale mixing (flatness and high entropy) throughout the universe is due either to black holes evaporating or to internal rearrangements within the universe. The former can be thought of as cosmic vacuum cleaners disappearing from outer space, and the latter as high-heat production from homogenizing the initial chaos. But if we elect to go this route, and abandon the rapid expansion taught by the New Inflationary

Theory, we are left with the following question that would appear to be insuperable: How do regions of the early universe that are causally disconnected become so uniform in their later history?

Thus far, the only good answer is that this later history somehow preexisted in the *initial condition* that gave it birth. If so, then the present large-scale mixing (huge entropy) means that the universe originated from an initial state that was so "ordered" (virtually zero gravitational entropy) that its existence through natural means strains the bounds of credulity. Stated differently, for our universe to have survived more than a Planck time (10^{-43} seconds), it must have been tuned to better than fifty decimal places.

It further means that indescribable upheaval identifiable with extreme disequilibrium processes attended the early growth of the universe. If so, it would be virtually impossible for the initial condition to causally influence its later history in any direct way. Thus far the only logical solution out of these problems is to suppose that the universe underwent a rapid early expansion, as described by the New Inflationary Theory.

Appendix 2.   Entropy and Disorder

In 1914 Max Planck (based on Constantin Carathe'dory's 1909 solutions to the Pfaff equation) [1] realized that entropy represented the number of internal configurations possible for a system. These configurations represent the number of microscopically distinct ways a macrostate (classical description) can be realized for a specified energy. The notion of heat exchange followed as a result of this.[2]

The application of information theory [3] to classical statistical mechanics [4] unified the older thermodynamics into quantum statistical mechanics [5] and paved the way to our modern understanding [6] of entropy.

We noted earlier that entropy can be correlated—but not identified—with disorder. And we said, moreover, that this correlation is valid in only three cases—ideal gases, isotope mixtures, and crystals near zero degrees Kelvin. The truth of the matter is illustrated by considering the two chemically inert gases, helium, and argon.[7] In our mind's eye we imagine two balloons, one filled with helium and the other with argon. First, we lower the temperature of both balloons to zero degrees Kelvin. This makes all the gas molecules stop moving in either balloon. Next, we get the molecules moving by heating both balloons to 300 degrees Kelvin (room temperature). Were we to mathematically calculate the increase in entropy, we would find that it was 20 percent higher in the argon balloon than in the helium balloon (154 v. 127 joules per mole per degree Kelvin). But since helium molecules are ten times lighter than argon molecules, they are moving three times faster and thus are more disordered. Here, then, is an example where higher entropy is accompanied by lower disorder, thereby demonstrating that we cannot identify one with the other. In the particular example cited, the greater argon entropy comes from the closer quantum translational energy levels identified with its greater molecular mass as described by the Sackŭr-Tetrode equation.

Let's look at another example. Were we to continue dissolving salt in an isolated glass of water, we'd reach supersaturation, a point where the water could not dissolve any more salt. Under certain conditions, the dissolved salt can be made to separate from the water. When crystallization happens the entropy always increases. However, the temperature can go up or down, depending on the kind of salt used and the thermochemistry of the solution.[8] This means that the motion of the molecules, and therefore the disorder, can go up or down, whereas the entropy always goes up. A less obvious example is the spontaneous freezing of supercooled water.[9] Again we see that the entropy must increase, whereas the disorder can go up or down.

Having shown that entropy cannot be identified with disorder, we might ask: What has uncertainty to do with the Second Law? To answer that, we need first to realize that the older ways of stating the Second Law were special cases of the more generalized modern version. For example, the older renderings were only valid for thermodynamic variables, such as measurements of temperature or pressure. However, the new, generalized version is true for any observable whatsoever. Also, the older laws could only be used under equilibrium conditions when things were quiet and at rest. But the New Generalized Second Law is free from this requirement and is valid in nonequilibrium situations as well. But this still doesn't answer the question: How does uncertainty relate to the Second Law?

Suppose we want to measure the location and speed of one or more of the water molecules mentioned earlier. How could we do it? When we think about that question for a while, it becomes obvious that we must use energy of some kind in order to measure what the molecule is doing. The energy might be in the form of a light beam or an atomic particle or whatever—this part of the question is unimportant for our purpose here. What is important is the fact that an observer or an intelligence must spend energy to acquire information.[10]

The act of using this energy to learn the water molecule's location and speed *changes its location and speed.* In fact, the more energy we have to use, the more we affect the result that we want to learn. Thus, the goal in such measurements is to use as little energy as possible in order to affect the result as little as possible. However, regardless of how small the energy used, the molecules *are* affected.

These considerations impact the New Generalized Second Law of Thermodynamics, which teaches an important and fundamental truth about the physical world. In all such measurements the act of looking at the molecules causes them to move and locate in such a fashion that the observer's uncertainty as to their whereabouts is as high as nature can possibly make it.[11] This means that the actual physical location and speed of these molecules in space and time are mysteriously coupled to the knowledge that a living intelligence has regarding their whereabouts.

Technical people who have been trained to think of entropy in terms of heat exchange can have a difficult time believing that the older ideas are a shadow of reality's invisible embrace of the observer. The notion of identifying a *decrease* of entropy with "information" is hardly obvious and so *un*intuitive that even those who have spent a lifetime on the subject receive it with reluctance and resistance.

Jaynes, for example, recalls a professor at Stanford who gave a widely acclaimed course of Statistical Mechanics and who, despite many luncheon conversations following the lectures, "adamantly rejected all suggestions that there is any connection between entropy and information." [12] The question he raised was "*whose* information?" The reason for the question is that whereas different people have different degrees of uncertainty, entropy has a very definite physical magnitude. The answer, of course, lies in understanding that the entropy of any system is the uncertainty of *that* observer whose only knowledge of its (small scale) inner workings came from observing its (large scale) external indicators.[13]

For example, consider the hands and numbers on the face of a windup wristwatch. Loosely speaking, the entropy of the wristwatch is my ignorance (uncertainty) of its inner workings when all I have to go on is information from the numbers and hands on its face. Sound obscure? Well, if you don't fully understand it you're in good company, because neither did the professor. As a result, Jaynes spent another five years clarifying the issue.[14] About ten years later, Hobson, Zubarev, and others combined these concepts with quantum mechanics to give mankind a powerful universal tool with which to probe physical reality.[15]

One thing taught by this New Generalized Second Law is that the mere act of our looking at something forces a rearrangement that maximizes our uncertainty of its changed state. In some quarters, scientists are seriously pondering whether or not thinking alters physical matter.[16] Quantum physics has deeper mysteries than this,[17] and Bohr has been quoted as saying: "Anyone who is not shocked by quantum theory has not understood it." One reason this is true is that *quantum laws do not describe objects with an independent existence. Instead, they describe statistical relations among observations.*

The principal message here is that the observer is central, because in the final analysis physical reality is what *we* observe it to be. It exists because we say that it does, and apart from us its existence cannot be rationally defended. In this sense, it *has* no existence except for the description to which we bear witness. Were we to believe that "something is there" without someone to observe that it is there, how can we demonstrate that what we *believe* is there is real if there is no one to observe that it is there?

What we *do* know is that there is a mysterious correspondence between the pattern of physical laws in the world and the pattern of logical relations in our mind. This is why we can first calculate on paper the rockets we later build, and then see them successfully launched to the moon. But the Bible claims that reality extends beyond the moon and into realms that make the stars seem near. Is this true? Perhaps a better question is: Who of us can say it's not? The Bible declares that not only is it true, but that our destiny resides there.

Appendix 3.   Generalized Entropy

Time can be divided into two parts: the first in which observations could have occurred, and the second where they could *not* occur. We ordinarily call the first past, and the second future. This division of time into information gathering and predictive periods is the fundamental basis of irreversibility and the New Generalized Second Law which can be stated in the following way. The entropy of any physical system at time "t" is:

$$S(t) = -k \int \tilde{w} \ln (X\tilde{w}) \, dZ$$

where "k" is Boltzman's constant ($1.38 \ 10^{-23}$ joule/°K) and:

$$X = h^{3n} \prod_{i=1}^{r} (n!)_i$$

In this latter expression, "h" is Planck's constant ($6.6 \ 10^{-34}$ joule-sec), and "r" is the number of distinct groups of indistinguishable particles "n" in the system. If r = 1, then the right product reduces to "n!" And if all particles are distinguishable, it reduces to "1."

For a system with "n" particles, the phase point is:

$$Z = (q_1, q_2, q_j \ldots, q_n, p_1, p_2, p_j \ldots, p_n)$$

where q_j, p_j are *vectors* that represent, respectively, the location and momentum of the jth particle.

The probability density "w" is:

$$w = w(Z,t)$$

and $\tilde{w}$ is that distribution which maximizes the observer's uncertainty S(t) subject to the predicted values of the observables at time "t." What this means is that if at time t = 0 an observer acquires data regarding w(Z,0) by measuring certain observables, and if predictions are later made at time "t" about these observables, then the distribution $\tilde{w}(Z,t)$ most likely to occur within the system is that which maximizes the observer's uncertainty over "Z" subject to the predicted values. Since an observer's predictions at time "t" contain less information about Z than the data at t = 0, an observer who manipulates the constraints in a closed system can never gain information, but instead will lose it with the passage of time. S(t) is a generalization of the equilibrium entropy that depends only on the values of the observable quantities and has macroscopic experimental significance.

For example, the entropy increase attending the free expansion of a gas results from the increased uncertainty of the location of the molecules. Likewise, the entropy increase associated with the final adiabatic mixture of two gases with dissimilar temperatures arises from the increased uncertainty of the molecular velocities.

The failure to recognize entropy as the observer's uncertainty arises from the intuitive notion of older ideas that entropy must somehow relate to a mechanical phase function or to some Hamiltonian variable. But this is wrong, and if one insists on understanding entropy in mechanical terms, entropy will never be understood. Entropy is a *statistical* concept, and has no meaning outside the context of a probability distribution. A probability measures our uncertainty of the occurrence of a single event. Conversely, entropy measures our uncertainty of the occurrence of a collection of events. There are, therefore, as many different entropies as there are probability distributions, and if the distributions describe different entities, the entropies will be unrelated to one another.

When we speak about the entropy of a system, what we mean by this is the entropy of an *observer's data* of that system. Some have wrongly held that this forces entropy to be subjective because it then becomes relative to the observer. This is also untrue. Entropy is not relative to the observer, but to the observer's data. It is, therefore, truly objective because it is the same for all observers with the same data.

However, this is not true for mechanical perceptions such as phase functions and phase points. These are subjective concepts because they cannot be measured in many body systems. As such, they are the metaphysical residue of an older time period.

The generalized entropy S(t) reduces to the familiar thermodynamic entropy at thermal equilibrium, and in general increases (although it need not be monotonic) as the system approaches equilibrium, i.e.,

$$S(t = 0) \leq S(t) \leq S(t \rightarrow \infty)$$

In addition, S(t) does not require thermodynamic variables but is valid for any macroscopic observable *and in nonequilibrium situations*, i.e.,

$$S(t = 0) < S(t \rightarrow \infty)$$

These last two relations consitute the New Generalized Second Law of Thermodynamics for closed systems.

Appendix 4.   Biological Reactions

Modern descriptions of chaotic forms of matter are based solely on quantum probabilistic considerations of mass and energy conservation, and our great success in this area indicates that the descriptions fully embrace the nature and content of these statistical ensembles. By way of contrast, however, the energy channels, directed growth, and the stable reproduction that attend living systems are attributes alien to the chaotic motion of matter. Even when external forces are applied, the physical distributions that result do *not* manifest the plurality of changing concentration gradients and diffusion processes so prevalent in living systems. Were we to ignore these facts and believe that life's traits somehow exist in the motion of matter, it would then imply the ludicrous proposition that physical distributions possess dynamic gradients that are both the effect and the cause of their existence.

The materialistic proposals are even less credible when we realize that the biological reactions necessary to life occur at the exact locations where they need to occur, and at the precise times. Moreover, they do so both within individual cells *and* throughout the organism taken as a whole. These reactions create biological harmonies that are foreordained by DNA which is transmitted in a self-sustaining cycle that preserves the information that regulates and conserves the system. This organizational miracle reeks of design—an attribute identified with intelligence, and *not* chaos.

Appendix 5.   Observations and Reality

Since the known reality of a physical object has no meaning outside of its description by an observer, and since the complexity of a physical object is measurable solely in terms of information contained in its description, it follows that the observer, the information, and the physical object exist in a relationship that assigns meaning to each only in terms of the other two. This inextricably interrelated interdependence stems from the fact that the substance of intellect (the observer or classical object), the thing observed (the physical or quantum object), and the meaning assigned (the informational or conjunctional object) constitute a mutually exclusive triunity.

For example, it is meaningless to talk about information without an observer, or to refer to an observer incapable of communicating information, or a physical object that can't be described. For this reason the information contained in an observer's description of a physical object *is as much a part of the physical object as it is a part of the observer's description of it.* The information obtained by an observer to quantify an object's complexity can be viewed as the ultimate reality of that object. The reason is that modern (quantum) scientific laws do not describe "things" that have an independent existence; they describe statistical relations among observations. Therefore, in the absence of an observer's description of that object, its physical existence cannot be logically defended.

Appendix 6.   Information Content

Information can be broken down into units commonly referred to as "bits." This should not be confused with "computer bits" whose nomenclature includes the radix. The number of informational bits increases logarithmically as the magnitude of the information grows, which means that large changes of information are measured by comparatively small numbers of bits. This is illustrated below. The number of bits of information corresponding to various library sizes is listed. The average book size is assumed to be 200 pages, and the letters K, M, B respectively denote thousand, million, billion. The 40 million books listed for the Library of Congress is an effective number corresponding to 24 million books, 19 million pamphlets, 3 million maps and 34 million miscellaneous items.

No. Books	Library	No. Bits
1	N/A	32
1K	Tiny	42
20K	Research Lab	46
100K	Public Library	48
4M	Large University	54
40M	Library of Congress	57
50B	All Human Knowledge	70

The information content of physical systems can be estimated several ways. For example, consider the universe. Its basic particle count is estimated to be of the order of 10^{80}. A blueprint specifying a distribution on a scale of this magnitude would contain on the order of 270 bits.

Another way to estimate an informational specification for the universe is to approximate the information content of a blueprint for planet earth, and then multiply by the appropriate number of planets. Since the earth's mass is about 2×10^{26} tons, and since the weighted mean of the atomic weight of all its elements is 24.3,* and if we assume that the average molecule is composed of at least three atoms, the

---

* In terms of percentages of the whole by weight, the earth consists of: 46.5 O, 28.0Si, 8.1A1, 5.1Fe, 3.5Ca, 2.8Na, 2.5K, 2.0Mg, 0.58Ti, 0.20C, 0.20H, 0.19C1, 0.11P, 0.10S plus 0.12 percent trace elements.[1]

maximum number of molecules that comprise the earth is of the order of 10^{54}. This gives a blueprint containing about 180 bits.

However, when employing this perspective, each molecule is envisioned within a space equal to one-half the quotient of earth's volume (2.6×10^{11} cubic miles) and the number of mean weighted molecules (1.6×10^{54}), i.e., a cube of the order of 2.7×10^{-10} inches on a side. This is over two orders of magnitude smaller than the minimum distance allowed by interatomic bond considerations (about 3.5×10^{-8} inches for triatomic molecules). If we use this more realistic constraint, the information content is lowered to about 160 bits. Golay independently calculated the information content of the earth from biological considerations and obtained a maximum of 150 bits.[2]

As regards the universe, the average number of stars in a galaxy is about 3×10^{11}; therefore allowing 2×10^{10} galaxies to exist out to the visible horizon, and further granting ten planets per star (an *extremely* generous assumption since *not one* has been established outside our solar system), estimates of the information content of the universe range from a low of 220 bits (Golay's number) to a high of 235 bits (earth's information extended through a 30 billion light-year diameter space).

The apparent discrepancy between these numbers and the earlier 270-bit estimate occurs because the latter ignores the information content of the stars. As a practical matter, they are primarily composed of hydrogen and their blueprint is informationally sterile when compared to earth. This, of course, includes our sun. However, if we choose to ignore this fact and artificially infuse the sun with substantive information, then its blueprint can be estimated as follows: The sun's mass is about 7×10^{28} tons giving a maximum of about 10^{58} hydrogen molecules and a blueprint of about 195 bits. Although unrealistically high, extending this to 300 thousand million stars per galaxy and 20 billion galaxies yields two bits short of 270 for the universe. If one wants to force the information content of the universe to a maximum, then a consideration of the number of photons (10^{88}) based upon the 3° Kelvin background temperature within its space yields 293 bits.

The reason that biological structures have considerably higher information content lies in the fact that unlike inorganic systems, the *sequence* of the building blocks is critical to the survival of the structure. Estimates of the information content of protein and bacteria[3] are given in the literature. Typical estimates for bacteria range from a low of 10^4 bits to a high of over 10^{12}. The spread is large because the calculations are based on widely differing interpretations of the biological structure.

However, a reasonable estimate can be made as follows: In the simplest of cells, such as a bacterium, a minimum of one hundred metabolic reactions must be performed by at least that many enzymes. In addition there must be ribosomes to synthesize these enzymes accompanied by RNA and regulatory molecules, as well as a long DNA double helix. The DNA of E. Coli has been well studied[4] and its one millimeter genome[5] is known to have about 2 million base pairs. Since each base pair triplet recruits enzymes[6] in accord with a uniform genetic code, they each define an amino acid residue.[7] Although the information content at each DNA site depends upon the number of synonymous residues as well as *which* ones are present,[8] we can reasonably estimate the order of magnitude of what we seek by approximating the information at three bits per residue.[9] This yields an information content for the genome of about 7×10^6 bits.

Interestingly, a reasonable estimate for the information content of the human body is possible by observing that each of its cells has a total of about 6×10^9 base pairs.[10] Since the genetic code is essentially universal,[11] we estimate the information content of a human cell to be about 2×10^{10} bits.* These results are summarized

---

* There is some evidence that the genetic code may not be universal.[12]

below. Some believe that all of the DNA may not be useful, and that certain segments may contain no information.[13] This, of course, means that we are presently unable to understand the function it performs. But even if the information existed along as little as 1 percent of the DNA, its magnitude would still be so vast that the conclusions remain unaltered. The actual estimate, however, is about 60 percent.

System	No. Bits
Earth	160
Solar System	170
Universe	235
Protein	1500
Simple Bacterium	7M
Human Cell	20B

Appendix 7.   The Real Message

An interesting parallel can be seen in the scout bee's message of food, and Christ's message of salvation. Both are a means of survival. If the hive is taken as the world, and the flowers the paradise to be reached after death, then accurate instructions on how to accomplish this are known only by the bee coming from the flowers. A message from any other bee will prove false and bring doom if followed, because he doesn't know where the flowers are. Likewise, the Bible warns of false Christs who, figuratively speaking, are in the hive with various messages, but don't know where the flowers are. Now picture an eagle flying over fields of flowers and choosing to become a bee so that he can enter the hive with the *true* message of how to reach the flowers, and you have the Christian parallel of Christ in the form of God choosing to incarnate himself into the man Jesus delivering the only message that can provide safe entrance into the world beyond this one.

Appendix 8.   Reprogramming Humanity

The Ten Commandments stand today as they were originally given, and they illuminate a standard of human behavior that would usher in Utopia itself were we willing and able to do what they say. Given that we have been unable to do this, the Bible explains that God incarnated himself in virgin-born flesh that was unaffected by Adam's fall, fulfilled his own law by living a sinless life in the person of Christ, and then satisfied divine justice by punishing Jesus for our misconduct. The result was the resurrection and departure of Jesus Christ from the earth and the coming of the Person of God's Spirit as an energizing transmitter for the purpose of reprogramming humanity.[1] Christian doctrine identifies this spiritual reprogramming as a "rebirth" that is essential for eternal life, but explains that it is accepted or rejected by each person individually.

This view likens human life to a computer composed of hardware (flesh) and software (spirit). The hardware can be pictured as millions of dots (microcircuits) in need of connection, and the software as millions of lines (wires) that define *how* they are connected. When Adam fell, defects entered both. The "spirit" of a computer can thus be viewed as the *way* it is internally organized—the lines connecting the dots; a rebirth alters this organization by connecting the dots in a new way. The result is a new spirit, but with dots (flesh) that retain the old defects because they are unchanged. Christian doctrine teaches that they are made new when a new resurrection body is received upon Christ's return to earth. But it also teaches that everyone will not be changed at this time because God will not entrust a supercomputer to a degenerate programmer.

Appendix 9.   The Moral Code

The biblical account of the origin of this code is interesting. The Old Testament records that it was part of a message initiated by a Supreme Intelligence, and entrusted to the nation of Israel. The partial fulfillment of its many prophecies is contained in the New Testament, which identifies this Intelligence with an eternally existing "Word" that entered the world in the flesh of Jesus Christ. The proof claimed for a divine presence on earth is the bodily resurrection of Christ three days after his public death. The Bible explains that the reason he came to earth was to give human beings a way to enter eternal life. This occurs when the Spirit of this Intelligence enters and reprograms whoever will personally commit himself to Christ's message and, therefore, to Christ. In so doing Christ becomes their Passport into eternity. Such hope is inaccessible to the animals and is available only to a life form capable of receiving and transmitting absolute truth through generations of its existence. *We* are this life form.

Christ testified that he came from a perfect world that existed beyond this one, and established his credibility by bodily returning from the grave. In view of the importance of his message we might think that its rejection would rest on logical inconsistencies or a fraudulent credential. But this is not the case. Honest inquiry has shown Christ's logic to be impeccable, and recent medical testimony has reaffirmed his death.[1] Furthermore, his bodily return from the grave has greater historical warrant than any other known event of the ancient world.[2] What's surprising is that whereas his credential is as secure as history can make it, we deny him the identity he claimed. Yet despite this we call him a great teacher. But is it sensible to accept teaching from someone whom we believe is self-deluded? And whom do we call great who doesn't know who he is? Yet in Christ's case, it's done all the time.

What's significant is that he wasn't killed for stealing bread or raping a woman or murdering someone. They killed him because *he claimed to be God.* Even the judge who condemned Jesus to death publicly stated that he could find nothing wrong with him. But if his message is logically consistent and his credential is historically established, why do most of us reject it? Is the reason for want of proof? Or that we will not have anything seem true that contradicts our passions and affections?

Appendix 10.   God's Proof to Mankind

The message is this: The person Jesus crucified two thousand years ago is the Incarnation of God, and, therefore, the Christ foretold as coming in Jewish Scriptures. The words and the deeds of Jesus thus become the words and the deeds of God, and identify Christ as the actual saving presence of God on earth.

This means that Jesus Christ is God's only provision for man to enter eternal life, and that his second coming for the Christian is the first glorious coming of Messiah for the Jew. The reason he is able to come a second time is that God bodily raised him from the dead. His resurrection is thus his sole identifying credential, and the "proof" God gave mankind to show that all other beliefs and claims are false (see Appendices 7, 8, 9).

Appendix 11.   The Rise of Humanism

Materialism emerged as a popular description of reality in the wake of the Renaissance. At that time, empirical observation and rational thinking became viewed as the *only* source of truth. The confusion was amplified by a failure to distinguish biblical truths from church traditions. This was followed by clerical disorientation, ecclesiastical intimidation, and theological capitulation. Disorientation occurred when rationalists forced the church to drink the wine of its traditions. Intimidation happened when technological signs strove with Christ to be an object of faith. Capitulation materialized when secular confusion attacked biblical truths using hidden presuppositions. All of this served to fan the flame of secular humanism—a religion that displaces deity with human reason and holds that progress is inevitable, science is invincible, and evolution is indomitable. It thrives because it teaches that man can decide what is evil without God; it is a doctrine that frees human conscience to indulge in fleshly appetites and that feeds human ego with the lie that man is king.

Notes

Chapter 1.   What Conflict Did Science Lose to Scripture?

1. Lubbock: ISD v. CLU, (1982) U.S. Supreme Court No. 82–805 Oct.
2. Bird W. Creation Science Defense to ACLU Tufts U. (1981) Jun 8.
3. Lewin R. *Science* (1982) 215:381 Jan 22. Keith W. CSLDF Release (1983) Shreveport, La. Jan 31 & Oct. 17.
4. Geisler N. *Eternity* (1982) :22 May.
5. Ruse M. *World Press Review* (1982) :32 Aug.
6. Shea J. *Jour. Geol. Ed.* (1984) 32(1):43 Jan.
7. McLean vs. Arkansas Bd. of Ed. Science (1982) 215:934 Feb 19.
8. Laszlo T. *Generalized Thermodynamics* (1978) MIT Press.
9. Newton J. & Teece P. *The Cambridge Deep-Sky Album* (1984) Press.
10. Trefil J. *Space Time Infinity* (1985) Pantheon/Smithsonian Bks.
11. Radmacher E. & Preus R. *Hermeneutics, Inerrancy & The Bible.* Papers from ICBI (1984) Academie Books.
12. Alpher R. *Proc. Am. Phil. Soc.* (1975) 119:325 Oct. Rees M. *New Scientist* (1981) :270 Jan 29.
13. Good I. *Physics Today* (1972) :15 Jul. Narlikar J. *New Scientist* (1981) :19 Jul 2.
14. Bondi H. & Gold T. (1948) *Mon. Not. R. Astron. Soc.* 108:252.
15. Kazanas D. & Schramm D. *Nature* (1978) 274:672 Aug 17.
16. Weinberg S. *The First Three Minutes* (1977) Basic Books. Harvard Univ. & Smithsonian Astrophysical Observ.
17. Penzias A. & Wilson R. *Astrophys. Jour.* (1965) 142:419. Wilson R. *Science* (1979) 205:866 Aug 31. Henry P. *Science* (1980) 207:939 Feb. 29.
18. Penzias A. & Wilson R. Nobel Prize (Physics) (1978) Dec 8.
19. Schramm D. *Tenth Texas Symposium On Relativistic Astrophysics Ann.* NY Acad. Sci. Ramaty R. & Jones F. ed. (1980) 375:54.
20. Silk J. *Tenth Texas Symposium* 375:188.
21. Trefil J. (1985) also Schramm D. (1980) ibid. Doroshkevich A. et. al. *Tenth Texas Symposium* 375:32. Sato H. Tenth Texas Symposium 375:43.

Chapter 2.   Has Our World Vanished and Reappeared?

1. Sandage A. *Astrophys. Jour.* (1961) 133:355.
2. Narlikar J. *New Scientist* (1981) :19 Jul 2.
3. Kumar N. *Prog. Theor. Phys.* (1969) 41(2):382 Feb.
4. Peebles P. *Tenth Texas Symposium* 375:157.
5. Wheeler J. *Gravitation* (1973) 44:1209 Freeman Misner C. et.al. Narlikar J. *New Scientist* (1965) 26(448):771. Tolman R. *Relativity, Thermodynamics & Cosmology* (1934) Clarendon Press (Oxford).
6. Henbest N. *Mysteries Of The Universe* (1981) Ch. 6 (Biography of the Stars) Van Nostrand Reinhold. Barrow J. *Nature* (1978) 272:211. Barrow J. & Matzner R. *Mo. Not. Roy. Astr. Soc.* (1977) 181:719.
7. Dicke R. & Peebles P. The Big Bang Cosmology—Enigmas & Nostrums in General Relativity—An Einstein Centenary Survey (1979) :504 Hawking S. & Israel W. ed. Cambridge Univ. Guth A. & Sher M. *Nature* (1983) 302:505.
8. Gorbatskii V. *Exploding Stars & Galaxies* (1967) Izdatel'stvo "Nauka" (Moskva).

9. Barrow J. & Turner M. *Nature* (1981) 291:469.

10. McCray R. *Tenth Texas Symposium* 375:391. Rowan-Robinson M. *Cosmic Landscape* (1979) Oxford Univ. P. Jugaki J. & Sargent W. *New Scientist* (1962) 269:96.

11. Buchdahl H. *The Concepts of Classical Thermodynamics* (1966) Cambridge University Press.

12. Lewis G. & Randall M. *Thermodynamics* (1961) McGraw-Hill.

13. Yourgrau W. et.al. *Treatise On Irreversible & Statistical Thermophysics* (1982) Dover.

Chapter 3.   Did a Supernatural Explosion Create the World?

1. Trefil J. *The Moment of Creation* (1983) Scribner's. Ne'eman Y. *Tenth Texas Symposium* 375:15.

2. Boynton P. et.al. *Phys. Rev. Let.* (1968) 21:462. Dicke R. & Peebles P. *Astrophys. Jour.* (1968) 154:891. Puzanov V. et.al. *Soviet Astron. Jour.* (1968) 11:905. Weinberg S. (1977) & Wilson R. (1979) ibid. Ch. 1.

3. Waldrop M. *Science* (1984) 5(1):44 Jan/Feb. North J. *The Measure of The Universe* (1965) Clarendon (Oxford).

4. Trefil J. *Space Time Infinity* :213. Kuhn T. *The Essential Tension* (1977) Univ. of Chicago. Mehra J. *The Physicist's Conception of Nature* (1973) Dordrecht. Gamba A. *Nuovo Cimento* (1955) 1:358. Misner C. et.al. *Gravitation* (1973) Freeman (20:460).

5. Rowe W. *The Cosmological Argument* (1975) Princeton Univ. Press.

6. Edwards P. & Pap A. ed. *Mod. Intro Philos.* (1965) Free Press.

7. Ne'eman Y. ibid. Stecker F. *Tenth Texas Symposium* 375:69. Kaufman W. ed. *Particles and Fields* (1980) Freeman. Kolb E. & Turner M. *Nature* (1981) 294:521.

8. Polkinghorne J. *The Particle Play* (1980) Freeman.

9. Trefil J. *From Atoms To Quarks* (1980) Scribner's.

10. Guth A. *Eleventh Texas Symposium on Relativistic Astrophysics Annal.* NY Acad. Sci. Evans D. ed. (1984) 422:1 Mar 23. Waldrop M. *Science* (1983) 219:375. Davies P. *The Sciences* (1983) 23(2):32 Mar/Apr.

11. Trefil J. Ibid. :221.

12. Atkatz D. & Pagels H. *Phys. Rev.* (1982) D25:2065.

13. Zeldovich Y. *Soviet Astronomy Let.* (1981) 7:579. Vilenkin A. *Physics Let.* (1982) B117:25.

14. Simpson C. *The Interpreter's Bible* (1952) 1:467 Abingdon. Harris R. et.al. *Theological Wordbook of Old Testament* (1980) Moody 1:127 (#278), Keil C. & Delitzsch F. *Commentary On the Old Testament* (1981) Eerdmans 1:46. Henry M. *Matthew Henry's Commentary* 1:2.

15. Harrison E. *Cosmology* (1981) Cambridge University Press. Brout R. et.al *Annals Of Physics* (1978) 115:78, Tryon E. *Nature* (1973) 246:396.

16. Harms R. et.al. *Tenth Texas Symposium* 375:178.

Chapter 4.   Has Science Discovered Something That Proves Karl Marx Wrong?

1. DeWitt B. *Physics Today* (1970) 23:30 Sep. Epstein P. *Amer. Jour. Phys.* (1945) 13:127. Einstein A. *Jour. Franklin Inst.* (1936) 221:349. Einstein A. et.al. *Phys. Rev.* (1935) 47:777. Bohr N. *Nature* (1935) 121:65. Bohr N. *Phys. Rev.* (1935) 48:696.

2. Stapp H. *Mind, Matter & Quantum Mechanics* (1981) LBL 12631 Lawrence Berkeley Laboratory. Popper K. & Eccles J. *The Self and Its Brain* (1977) Springer-Verlag. Zeh H. Fourth Int. Conf. on Unity of Sci. (1975) New York. Wigner E. *Proc. Amer. Phil. Soc.* (1969) 113:95. Good I. ed. *The Scientist Speculates* (1961) Heinemann/Basic B.

3. Kuhn H. & Waser J. *Biophysics* (1983) Hoppe W. et.al. ed. Springer-Verlag (17:830). Scott J. *New Scientist* (1981) :153 Jan 15. Prigogine I. *From Being To Becoming* (1980) Freeman. Sagan C. *Cosmos* (1980) Random House. Folsome C. *The Origin Of Life* (1979) Freeman.

4. Prigogine I. & Stengers I. *Order Out Of Chaos* (1984) Bantam Books (9:283).

5. Gott J. *Nature* (1982) 295:304.

6. Nicolis G. & Prigogine I. *Self-Organization In Nonequilibrium Systems* (1977) Wiley.

7. Davis B. *Science* (1980) 209:78 Jul 4.

8. Buchel W. *Nature* (1967) 213:319.

9. Trefil J. *Space Time Infinity* :233.

10. Montgomery J. *The Importance of a Materialistic Metaphysic to Marxist Thought and an Examination of Its Truth Value in the Shape of the Past* (1975) Bethany II.2:217. Berlin I. *Historical Materialism in Karl Marx* (1963) Time Reading Program Special Edition 6:101.

11. Trefil J. (1983) ibid. ch. 3.

12. Pugh G. *Zygon* (1976) 11:2.

13. Misner C. et.al. *Gravitation* (1973) Freeman 21.12:543.

14. Gombrich E. *Art and Illusion: A Study in the Psychology of Pictorial Representation* (1961) Princeton Univ.

15. Gregory R. *Mind In Science* (1981) Cambridge Univ. Press.

16. Montgomery J. ibid.

17. Popper K. ibid.

18. MacKay D. *The Clockwork Image* (1974) InterVarsity Press.

19. von Neumann J. *Quantum Theory and Measurement* (1983) Wheeler J. & Zurek W. ed. (V:549). Levine R. & Tribus M. ed. *The Maximum Entropy Formalism* (1979) MIT Conference (1978) May 2 MIT Press.

20. Wootters W. & Zurek W. *Quantum Theory and Measurement* (1983) Wheeler J. & Zurek W. ed. (III:443). Belinfante F. *Measurement and Time Reversal in Objective Quantum Theory* (1975) Pergamon.

21. Wigner E. *Mind-Body Question in Quantum Theory & Measurement*, Wheeler, J. & Zurek W. Ed. (1983) Princeton U. Press (I.12:180).

22. Wigner E. op.cit. (I.12:168). Wheeler J. *Quantum Mechanics a Half Century Later* (1977) Leite Lopes J. & Paty M. ed. Reidel Dordrecht (Holland).

23. Guth A. op.cit. ch.3.

24. Bohr N. *Atomic Physics and Human Knowledge* (1960) Wiley :92.

25. Wigner E. (1983) op.cit. (I.12:174).

Chapter 5.   Why Can't an Accident Design a Machine?

1. Eddington A. *The Nature of the Physical World* (1958) Michigan Univ. Press.

2. de Duve C. *A Guided Tour of the Living Cell* (1984) Scientific American Library (I.8:132).

3. Layzer D. *Constructing the Universe* (1984) Scientific American Library (7:244).

4. Greenleaf S. *Testimony of the Evangelists—Examined by the Rules of Evidence Administered in Courts of Justice* (1965) Baker Book H. (Reprint of 1847 ed.).

5. Schneider S. & Londer R. *The Coevolution of Climate & Life* (1984) Sierra Club Books.

6. Shannon C. & Weaver W. *The Mathematical Theory of Communication* (1949) Illinois Univ. (Urbana).

7. Whitfield P. ed. *Illustrated Animal Encyclopedia* (1984) Macmillan :220.

8. Kalmijn A. *Science* (1982) 218:916 Nov 26.

9. Kreithen M. Colloquium On Animal Navigation (1984) DSRC (Princeton) Jan 31.

10. Macbeth M. *Darwin Retried: An Appeal to Reason* (1971) Boston.

11. Brady R. Biol. *Jour. Linn. Soc.* (1982) 17(1):79; also: *Systematic Zoology* (1979) 28:600.

12. Schildknecht H. *Angewandte Chemie* (1961) (Germany) Jan 7.

13. Malins D. & Varanasi U. N.Ocea.Atm.Adm.NW.Ala.Fsh.Cnt Res.Prgm (1983) Spon: Seat.Univ. & Off.Nav.Res.

14. Norris K. & Mohl B. *American Naturalist* (1983) 122:85.

15. Alpher R. & Gamow G. *Proc. Nat. Acad. Sci.* (1968) 61:363.

16. Belinfante F. *Am. Jour. Phys.* (1978) 46:329.

17. Cohen R. et al. *The Fundamental Constants of Physics* (1957) Interscience (5:105).

18. Dirac P. *Nature* (1937) 139:323.

19. Wheeler J. *Quantum Theory and Measurement* (1983) Wheeler J. & Zurek W. ed. (I:182).

Chapter 6.   What Role Does Entropy Play in Destiny?

1. Popper K. *Brit. Jour. for Phil. Sci.* (1957) 8:151.

2. Levine R. & Tribus M. ed. *The Maximum Entropy Formalism* (1979) MIT Conference (May 2, 1978) MIT Press.

3. Prigogine I. & Stengers I. *Order Out of Chaos* (1984) Bantam B.

4. Zemansky M. & Dittman R. *Heat & Thermodyna.* (1981) McGraw Hill.

5. Jaynes E. *The Maximum Entropy Formalism* (1978 MIT Conf. May 2) Levine R. & Tribus M. ed. (1981) McGraw Hill.

6. Cardwell D. *From Watt to Clausius* (1971) Heinemann (London).

7. Clausius R. *Ann. Phys.* (1865) 125:353.

8. Boltzmann L. *Vorlesungen uber Gastheorie* (1896/1898) Brush S. (translator) (1964) Univ. Calif. Berkley.

9. Kitcher P. *Abusing Science* (1982) MIT Press (4:89).

10. Davydov B. *Jour. Phys.* Moscow (1947) 11:33.

11. Morris H. *The Biblical Basis For Modern Science* (1984) Baker (7:204); Futuyma D. *Science On Trial* (1983) Pantheon (10:183); Kitcher P. (1982) ibid. (4:91); Asimov I. *In the Beginning* (1981) Crown (1:17); Coppedge J. *Evolution: Possible or Impossible* (1973) Zondervan (14:238); and Gatlin L. *Information Theory and the Living System* (1972) Columbia Univ. Press (2:29).

12. Yourgrau W. et al. (1982) ibid. Ch. 2 (1:10).

13. Guggenheim E. *Research* (1949) 2:450.

14. McGlashan M. *Jour. Chem. Ed.* (1966) 43:226.

15. Schroedinger E. *What Is Life* (1955) Cambridge Univ. Press; Brillouin L. *Science and Information Theory* (1962) Academic P.

16. Schuster P. *Biophysics* (1983) Hoppe W. et al. ed. Springer-Verlag (8:346).

17. Dingle H. *Bull. Inst. Phys.* (1959) 10:218.

18. Yockey H. *Jour. Theor. Biol.* (1974) 46:369.

19. Khinchin A. *Math. Founda. of Information Theory* (1957) Dover.

20. Bernal J. *The Origin Of Life* (1967) World Publishing.

21. Yockey H. (1974) ibid.

22. Prigogine I. & Stengers I. (1984) ibid. Ch. 4. Asimov I. *Asimov's New Guide to Science* (1984) Basic Books (13:641); Futuyma D. (1983) ibid. (4:95); Kitcher P. (1982) ibid. (4:89); Eigen M. et al. *Scientific American* (1981) 244:88 Apr; Sagan C. (1980) ibid. Ch. 4 (2:31); Gatlin L. Sixth Berkley Symp. Proc. Math. Stat. (1972) Cal. U.; and Calvin M. *Chemical Evolution* (1969) Oxford Univ. Press.

23. Margenau H. *The Nature of Physical Reality* (1950) New York.

24. Hobson A. (1971) ibid. (5:142).

Chapter 7.   What Elusive New Law Governs All Living Systems?

1. Morris, H. *The Biblical Basis For Modern Science* (1984) Baker Book House Ch. 7. Williams E. "Entropy and the Solid State," in *Why Not Creation?* (1970) Lammerts W. ed. Presbyterian and Reformed Publishing Company.

2. Setlow R. & Pollard E. *Molecular Biophysics* (1962) Ch. 3 (7:63). Gatlin L. *Information Theory and the Living System* (1972) Columbian Univ. Press Ch. 8:189. Schuster P. and Sigmund K. *From Biological Macromolecules to Protocells—The Principle of Early Evolution* Ch.17 Sec. 2:874 in Biophysics Hoppe W. et.al. ed. (1983) Springer-Verlag, Berlin.

3. Slater, J. *Introduction To Chemical Physics* (1939) McGraw-Hill, NY. Hawkins, G. *Thermodynamics* (1946) Wiley & Sons, NY. Fowler, R. & Guggenheim, E. *Statistical Thermodynamics* (1939) Univ. Press Cambridge. Glasstone, S. *A Treatise On Physical Chemistry* (1942) Van Nostrand, NY. Page, L. *Introduction to Theoretical Physics* (1928) Van Nostrand, NY.

4. Hatsopoulos, G. & Kennan, J. *Principles of General Thermodynamics* (1965) Wiley & Sons, NY, Wilson, A. *Thermodynamics and Statistical Mechanics* (1957) Cambridge Univ. Press. Rossini, F. *Thermodynamics and Physics of Matter* (1955) Princeton Univ. Press. Groot, S. *Thermodynamics of Irreversible Processes* (1951) Interscience Publishers, NY. Reif, F. *Fundamentals of Statistical and Thermal Physics* McGraw-Hill, NY. Aston, J. and Fritz, J. *Thermodynamics and Statistical Thermodynamics* (1959) Wiley & Sons, NY.

5. Brillouin L. *Jour. of Appl. Physics* (1951) 22:334. Rothstein J. *Science* (1951) 114:171. Rothstein J. *Jour. Appl. Physics* (1952) 23:1281. Rothstein J. *Physics Rev.* (1952) 85:135. Raymond R. *Am. Jour. Physics* (1951) 19:109.

6. Katz A. *Principles of Statistical Mechanics: The Information Theory Approach* (1965) Freeman, San Francisco. Landsberg, P. *Thermodynamics* (1961) Interscience Publishers, NY. Tribus, M. *Thermostatics and Thermodynamics* (1961) Van Nostrand, Princeton. Jaynes, E. *Phys. Rev* (1957) 106:620; *Phys.Rev.* (1957) 108:171. Jaynes, E. *Statistical Physics* (1963) (1962 Brandeis Lectures) Ford K. ed., W. Benjamin, NY. Jaynes, E. *Am. Jour. Phys.* (1965) 33:391.

7. Hobson A. *Concepts In Statistical Mechanics* (1971) Gordon & Breach, NY.

8. Jaynes E. *Statistical Physics* op. cit. Robertson B. *Phys. Rev.* (1966) 144:151; (1967) 160:175. Schwegler, Z. *Naturforsch* (1965) 20a:1543. Zubarev D. *Doklady* (1962) 6:776. Scalapino D. *Irreversible Statistical Mechanics and the Principle of Maximum Entropy* (1961) Ph.D. Dissertation Stanford Univ. Kawasaki K. *Prog. Theor. Phys.* (1960) 23:754). Mori H. *Jour. Phys. Soc.* Japan (1956) 11:1029.

9. Shannon C. *Bell Sys. Tech. Jour.* (1948) 27:379; reprinted in *The Mathematical Theory of Communication* (1949) Illinois Univ. Press (Urbana).

10. Golay M. *Proc. IRE* (1961) :1378 Sep.

11. Setlow R. & Pollard E. *Molecular Biophysics* (1962) ch 3(10:71).

Chapter 8.   Did Intelligence Design the Earth?

1. Fraser R. *The Habitable Earth* (1964) Basic Books, NY.

2. Press F. & Siever R. *Earth* (1982) Freeman, San Francisco.

3. Hutchinson E. et.al. *The Biosphere* (Energy Cycles) *Sci. Am.* (1970) 223(3):45.

4. Davies M. & Murray B. *The View From Space* (1971) Columbia Univ. Press, NY.

5. Inbrie J. & Imbrie J. *Science* (1980) 207:943 Feb 29.

6. Friedman H. *Sun and Earth* (1986) ch.4:98 Freeman, NY.

7. Hammond A. *Science* (1975) 187:245 Jan. 24.

8. Namias J. & Cayan D. *Science* (1981) 214:869 Nov. 20.

9. Barron E. et.al. *Science* (1981) 212:501 May 1.

10. Friday A. & Ingram D. *Life Sciences* (1985) Cambridge Univ. Press Ch. 6:153.

11. Hughes T. *Science* (1970) 170:630 Nov. 6. Gaskell T. *Sci. Jour.* (1970) :31 Dec. Lliboutry L. *Sci. Jour.* (1969) :51 Mar.

12. Decker R. and Decker B. *Volcanos* (1981) Freeman, San Francisco.

13. Thews G. & Hutten H. *Biophysics of Respiratory Gas Transport* ch. 12 Sec 6:503 *Biophysics* Hoppe W. et.al. ed. (1983) Springer-Verlag, Berlin.

14. Cotterill R. *Cambridge Guide To The Material World* (1985) Ch.17:299 Cambridge Univ. Press.

15. Friday A. and Ingram D. *Cambridge Encyclopedia of Life Sciences* (1985) Ch. 5 Sec.3:136 Cambridge Univ. Press.

16. Stanley S. *Earth and Life Through Time* (1985) ch.10:288 Freeman, NY.

17. Karlin S. & Taylor H. *A First Course In Stochastic Processes* (1975) Ch.9 (6:489) Academic Press, NY. Loeve M. *On Almost Sure Convergence in Second Berkeley Symposium On Mathematical Statistics and Probability* (1951) II:279 Univ. Calif. Press.

Chapter 9.   How Did Life Originate?

1. Haldane J. *Rationalist Annual* (1928) 148:3. Oparin A. *The Origin of Life* (1957) Academic Press, NY. Calvin M. in: *Evolutionary Biology* Dobzhansky T. et. al. ed. (1967) V.1 Appleton Croft, NY.

2. Kaplan R. *Rad. Envir. Biophys.* (1974) 10:31.

3. Elsasser W. *The Physical Foundation of Biology: An Analytical Study* (1958) Pergamon, NY.

4. Thaxton C. et. al. *The Mystery of Life's Origin: Reassessing Current Theories* (1984) Philosophical Library, NY. Hoyle F. & Wickramasinghe C. *Evolution From Space* (1982) Enslow Publishing. Crick F. *Life Itself: Its Origin and Nature* (1981) Simon & Schuster.

5. Friday A. & Ingram D. *Life Sciences* (1985) ch. 5, Cambridge Univ. Press. Smith D. *Earth Sciences* (1981) ch. 25 Crown Publishers, NY. Friedman H. *Sun and Earth* (1986) ch. 4–6 Sci. Am. Lib., NY.

6. Davis B. *Science* (1980) 209:78 Jul 4.

7. Yockey H. *Jour. Theor. Biol.* (1977) 67:377.

8. Asimov I. *New Guide To Science* (1984) ch. 12:636 Basic Books, NY.

9. Kitcher P. *Abusing Science: The Case Against Creationism* (1982) ch. 2:37 MIT Press, Cambridge.

10. Gange R. Review: Abusing Science (1985) Genesis Found. Princeton.

11. Dancoff S. & Quastler H. in: *Information Theory In Biology* :263 (1953) Illinois Univ. Press, Urbana.

12. Shannon C. & Weaver W. *The Mathematical Theory of Communication* (1949) Illinois Univ. Press, Urbana.

13. Yockey H. ed. Symposium On Information Theory in Biology Gatlinburg, TN Oct. 29–31 (1956) Pergamon, NY.

Chapter 10.   Is Protein God's Fingerprint?

1. Thaxton C. et. al. *The Mystery of Life's Origin: Reassessing Current Theories* (1984) Philosophical Library, NY; Hoyle F. & Wickramasinghe C. *Evolution from Space* (1982) Enslow Publishing; and Crick F. *Life Itself: Its Origin and Nature* (1981) Simon & Schuster.

2. Yockey H. *Jour. Theor. Biol.* (1977) 67:345.

3. Renger G. "Biological Energy Conservation" in: Hoppe W. et. al. ed. *Biophysics* (1983) ch. 8(7.4c):358 Springer-Verlag.

4. Ruska E. *The Early Development of Electron Lenses and Electron Microscopy* (1980) Hirzel Verlag, Stuttgart.

5. Krause F. *Z. Phys.* (1936) 102:417.

6. von Ardenne M. Das Elektronen-Rastermikroskop, Theoretische Grundlagen, *Z. Phys.* (1938) 109:553; Praktische Ausfuhrung, *Z. Tech. Phys.* (1938) 19:407.

7. Zworykin V. et al. *Electron Optics and the Electron Microscope* (1945) Wiley, NY.

8. First International Congress Proceedings On Electron Microscopy (1953) Paris; Hillier J. "Electron Microscopy" in: Uber F. ed. *Biophysical Research Methods* (1950) :381; Cosslett V. *Practical Electron Microscopy* (1951) Academic Press, NY; Fischer R. *Applied Electron Microscopy* (1953) Bloomington Indiana Univ. Press; and Stroke G. & Falconer D. *Phys. Lett.* (1964) 13:306.

9. Warner J. et. al. *Electron Microscope Studies of Multiple Ribosome Units in Hemoglobin Synthesis* (1962) Preprint 135 Dept. of Biology, MIT, Cambridge; Selme P. *Biology: Le Microscope Electronique* (1963) Collection: "Que sais-je?" Presses Universitaires Francaises, Paris; Porter K. *An Introduction to the Fine Structure of Cells and Tissues* (1963) Lea & Febiger, Phil.

10. Shannon C. & Weaver W. *The Mathematical Theory of Communication* (1949) Illinois Univ. Press, Urbana.

11. Yockey H. *Jour. Theor. Biol.* (1977) 67:377.

12. Newton I. Assuming the planets had circular motions Newton declared in 1665 that their centrifugal forces must vary inversely as the squares of their distances from the sun in: *Philosophiae Naturalis Principia Mathematica* (1687).

13. Stacey F. & Tuck G. "Geophysical Evidence For Non-Newtonian Gravity" *Nature* (1981) 292:230 Jul 16.

Chapter 11.   Why Can't Nature Create Life?

1. Hartman H. et. al. eds. *Search for the Universal Ancestors* (1985) NASA, Washington, DC; Scott. J. *The Sciences* (1983) 23(6):38 Nov/Dec; Oparin A. *The Origin and Initial Development of Life* (1968) NASA, Washington, DC May; Bernal J. "Biochemical Evolution":11 in: Kasha M & Pullman B. eds. *Horizons in Biochemistry* (1962) Academic Press; Schmitt F. *Rev. Mod. Phys.* (1959) 31(1):5 Jan.

2. Gillispie C. *The Edge of Objectivity* (1960) Princeton U. Press; Taton R. *Reason and Chance in Scientific Discovery* (1957) Philosophical Library, NY; Baitsell G. ed. *Science in Progress* (1947) Sillman Lectures V.6; Mees C. *The Path of Science* (1946) Wiley, London.

3. Gros F. "Cell Machinery, Transfer of Genetic Information":34 (Part 3) in: Pullman B. & Weissbluth M. eds. *Molecular Biophysics* (1965) Academic Press, NY.

4. Yockey H. *Jour. Theor. Biol.* (1981) 91:13.

5. Rich A. *The Sciences* (1980) 20(8):10 Oct; Elias P. *Rev. Mod. Phys.* (1959) 31(1):221; Yockey H. ed. Symposium On Information Theory In Biology (1958) Pergamon Press at: Gatlinburg, TN Oct 29–31 (1956). Quastler H. ed. *Essays on the Use of Information Theory in Biology* (1953) Illinois Univ. Press, Urbana.

6. Wigner E. "Remarks On The Mind-Body Question" I(12):168 in: Wheeler J. & Zurek W. eds. *Quantum Theory and Measurement* (1983) Princeton Univ. Press.

7. Jaynes E. "Where Do We Stand On Maximum Entropy":96 in: Levine R. & Tribus M. eds. *The Maximum Entropy Formalism* (1981) MIT Press, Cambridge, MA MIT Conference May 2–4 (1978).

8. Yockey H. *Jour. Theor. Biol.* (1977) 67:377. Thaxton C. et. al. *The Mystery of Life's Origin: Reassessing Current Theories* (1984) Philosophical Library, NY.

9. Jurnak F. & McPherson A. *Biological Macromolecules and Assemblies* (1985) Wiley Interscience, NY.

10. Eigen M. et. al. *Sci. Am.* (1981) :88 Apr.

11. Scott J. *New Scientist* (1981) :153 Jan 15.

12. Gold M. *Science 85* (1985) 6(3):26 April.

13. Prigogine I. et. al. *Physics Today* (1972) 25:23.

14. Prigogine I. *From Being to Becoming* (1980) Freeman, NY.

15. Golay M. *Proc. IRE* (1961) :1378 Sep.

16. Shapiro R. *Origins: A Skeptic's Guide to the Creation of Life on Earth* (1985) Macmillan.

Chapter 12.   Why Do We Need Life to Create Life?

1. Green D. & Fleischer S. "On the Molecular Organization of Biology Transducing Systems in: Kasha M. & Pullman B. eds. *Horizons in Biochemistry* (1962) Academic Press, NY.

2. Yockey H. *Jour. Theor. Biology* (1977) 67:377.

3. Ohno S. *Nature* (1973) 244:259 London.

4. Yockey H. *Jour. Theor. Biol.* (1974) 46:369.

5. Cairns-Smith A. *Genetic Takeover and the Mineral Origins of Life* (1985) Macmillan, NY. Prigogine I. et. al. *Physics Today* (1972) 25:23. Eigen M. *Naturwissenschaften* (1971) 58:465. Bernal J. *The Origin of Life* (1967) World Publ., NY. Brillouin L. "Giant Molecules and Semiconductors" in: Kasha M. & Pullman B. eds. *Horizons in Biochemistry. Lawless H. & Morrison P. eds. Search for the Universal Ancestors* (1985) NASA Washington, DC. Scott J. *The Sciences* (1983) 23(6):38 Nov/Dec. Oparin A. ibid. Gatlin L. *Sixth Berkeley Symp. Proc. Math. Stat.* Univ. of Calif. Press, Berkeley.

6. Kitcher P. ibid.

7. Ochoa S. Enzymatic Mechanisms in "The Transmission of Genetic Information" Kasha M. & Pullman B. eds. *Horizons in Biochemistry.*

8. Smith A. *The Body* (1986) Macmillan, NY.

9. Brandt P. & Yancey P. *Fearfully and Wonderfully Made* (1980) Zondervan, Grand Rapids, Mich.

10. Ycas M. "The Protein Text" in: Yockey H. et. al. eds. Symposium on Information Theory In Biology (1958) Pergamon, NY II:70, Gatlinburg, TN (1956) Oct 29–31.

11. Capra F. *The Turning Point* (1982) Simon & Schuster.

12. Rich A. *Transfer RNA and the Origin of Protein Synthesis* (1981) Dept. of Biology, MIT Dec 12.

13. Jukes T. *Adv. in Enzymol.* (1978) 47:375.

14. Eigen M. et.al. "The Origin of Genetic Information" *Sci Am.* (1981) :88 Apr.

15. Orgel L. *Jour. Mol. Biol.* (1968) 38:381. Lohrmann R. et. al. *Science* (1980) 208:146.

16. Wolfgang Y. et. al. *Treatise on Irreversible and Statistical Thermophysics* (1982) ch. 1 (6:48) Dover Publ., NY.

17. Crick F. et. al. *Origin of Life* (1976) D. Reidel Publ. :389.

18. Hobson A. *Concepts in Statistical Mechanics* (1971) ch. 5 (4:137) Gordon & Breach.

Chapter 13.   Why Is Life a Miracle?

1. Atkins P. *The Second Law* (1984) ch. 9:190 Freeman, NY. Anshen R. Convergence :166 in Cavalieri L. *The Double-Edged Helix* (1985), Praeger, NY.

2. von Neumann J. *Lectures on Probabilistic Logics and the Synthesis of Reliable Organisms from Unreliable Components* (1952) Cal. Inst. Tech., Pasadena Jan 4–

15. *Theory of Self-Reproducing Automata* Burks A. ed. (1966) Univ. of Illinois Press, Urbana.

3. Maxwell J. Phil. Mag. for January and July (1860) 20(21) Read at the Meeting of the British Association Aberdeen (1859) Sep 21. *Theory of Heat* (1871) London: Longmans Green & Co. :328.

4. von Szilard L. *Uber die Entropie ver minderung in einem thermodynamischen System bei Eingriffen intelligenter Wesen* (1928) Mit 1 Abbildung (Eingegangen) am Jan 18. Reprinted in *Behavioral Science* (1964) 9(4) Oct.

5. Kolmogoroff A. *Inform. Trans.* (1965) 1:3.

Chapter 14.   Why Are Men and Apes Physically Similar?

1. Rensberger B. *Science 84* (1984) :29 Apr.
2. Cronin J. et. al. *Nature* (1981) 292:113 Jul 9.
3. Gardner M. *Fads & Fallacies in the Name of Science* (1957) Dover.
4. Cherfas J. *New Sci.* (1981) 91:518. Gribbin J. *New Sci.* (1981) 91:592.
5. Lewin R. *Science* (1984) 226:1179 Dec 7.
6. Morgan E. *The Aquatic Ape* (1982) Sourcebook Project, Glenarm, Md.
7. Sibley C. & Ahlquist J. *Jour. Mol. Evol.* (1984) 20:2.
8. Templeton A. *Evolution* (1983) 37:221.
9. Ciochon R. & Corruccini R. eds. *New Interpretations of Ape and Human History* (1983) Plenum Press, NY.
10. Parrinder G. *World Religions from Ancient History to the Present* (1983) Facts on File Publ., NY.

Chapter 15.   Why Does Physical Reality Terminate in Man?

1. Hawking S. & Rocek M. ed. *Superspace and Supergravity* (1979) Cambridge Univ. Press.
2. Robinson A. *Science* (1979) 205:777 Aug 24; (1981) 211:1028 Mar. 6. Schechter B. *Discover* (1981) :27 Jul.
3. Robinson A. *Science* (1980) 208:697 May 16. Reines F. Am. Physi. Soc. Meeting (1980) Washington, DC Jul; Univ. Calif. (Irvine). Boehm F. Am. Phys. Soc. Meeting (1983) Baltimore, MD. Jul; Calif. Inst. Tech.
4. Davies P. *The Sciences* (1982) :15 Jan.
5. Hoyle, F. *Evolution From Space* (1981) Enslow Publishers.
6. Crick F. *Life Itself* (1982) Simon & Schuster.
7. Schramm D. *Physics Today* (1983) :27 Apr.

Chapter 16.   Did Man Evolve from Apes?

1. Blinderman C. *Science 85* (1985) 6(5):47 Jun.
2. Announcement, *Science* (1927) Dec 16.
3. Weiner J. *Piltdown Forgery* (1981) Dover Press.
4. Macbeth N. *Am. Biol. Teach.* (1976) :495 Nov.
5. Bowden M. *Ape-Men: Fact or Fallacy* (1977) Sec. IV:78 Sovereign Publ. Bromley, Kent.
6. Templeton A. quoted in *Science* (1984) 226:1182 Dec 7.
7. Cronin J. et. al. ibid.
8. Holden C. *Science* (1981) 213 Aug 14.
9. Donahue P. *The Human Animal* (1985) Simon & Schuster.
10. *Astronomy* (1983) 11(10):66 Oct.
11. Johanson D. & Edey M. *Science* (1981) (45) April.
12. Pilbeam D. *Nature* (1982) Jan 21. Greenberg J. *Science News* (1982) 121:84 Feb 6.

13. Herbert W. *Science News* (1983) 123:88 Feb 5. Raeburn P. *Science* (1983) (40) Jun.

14. Sibley C. & Ahlquist J. *Curr. Ornithol.* (1983) 1:245. Sibley C. & Ahlquist J. *Auk* (1984) 101:230.

15. Cronin J. et. al. ibid.

16. Yunis J. & Miller J. *Science News* (1982) 121 Mar 20.

17. Yockey H. *J. Theor. Biol.* (1974) 46:369. Yockey H. ibid. 80:21.

Chapter 17.   What Do Animals and People Have in Common?

1. Hartnack J. *Language and Philosophy* (1972) Linguarum.

2. Marler P. & Peters S. *Science* (1981) 213 Aug 14.

3. Payne K. (NY Zoological Soc.) (1979) Meeting of AAAS.

4. Dyer F. & Gould J. *Science* (1981) 214:1041 Nov 27.

Chapter 18.   Does Man Reflect a Supernatural Image?

1. Heinrich B. *Science* (1981) 212:565 May 1.

2. Gladstone D. *American Naturalist* (1981) 117:779.

3. Gould S. *Natural History* (1979) 88(9):25 Nov.

4. Baker H. ed. *The Mystery of Migration* (1981).

5. Weisburd S. *Science News* (1984) 126:389.

6. Krebs J. *Nature* (1979) 282:14.

7. Stratton G. & Uetz G. *Science* (1981) 214:575 Oct 30. Lewis E. & Narins P. *Science* (1985) 227:187.

8. Howard R. et. al. *Science* (1980) 210:431.

9. Vogt R. & Riddiford L. *Nature* (1981) Sep 10.

10. Pollack G. & Hoy R. *Science* (1979) 204:429 Apr 27.

11. Shapley R. & Gordon J. *New Scientist* (1980) 88:366.

12. Sebeok T. ed. *Animal Communication* (1977) Bloomington.

13. Psalm 119:89 and John 17:17.

Chapter 19.   What Did "Clever Hans" Teach Man About Apes?

1. Cyrus G. *Orientalia* (1968) 37:75.

2. Thompson J. *Maya Hieroglyphic Writing* (1950) Washington.

3. Phillips P. *The Prehistory of Europe* (1980) London.

4. Corliss W. ed. *Ancient Man: A Handbook of Puzzling Artifacts* (1980) Sourcebook Project (Glen Arm, Md) references *NY Times* (1971 Jan 20) and reports: Marshack A. (Peabody Museum Of Archeology & Ethnology—Harvard) analyzed pit marks engraved in prehistoric bone and stone objects and concluded the inscriptions represent a lunar calendar; the notations were reportedly used in most of Europe from 34,000 to 10,000 years ago.

5. Hediger H. *Image Roche* (1974) 62:27. Fouts R. *Science* (1973) 180:978. Schrier A. & Stollnitz F. ed. *Behavior of Non-Human Primates* (1971) viz., V.4 Academic Press.

6. Woodruff G. & Premack D. *Nature* (1981) 293:568 Oct 15.

7. Gardner B. & Gardner R. *Science* (1969) 162:664. Gardner R. & Gardner B. *Jour. Exp. Psych. Gen.* (1975) 104:244.

8. Lilly J. *The Mind of the Dolphin–A Non-Human Intelligence* (1967) Doubleday.

9. Premack D. *Science* (1971) 172:808.

10. Rumbaugh D. et. al. *Science* (1973) 182:731.

11. Woodruff G. & Premack D. (1981) op. cit. Galdikas B. "Living with the Great Orange Apes" (1980) *Nat. Geo.* Jun. Patterson F. "Linguistic Capabilities of a Lowland Gorilla" (1979) Ph.D. Dissertation (Stanford Univ.). Fouts R. et. al. in *Understanding*

Language Through Sign Language Research (1978) Siple P. ed. Academic Press. Lilly J. *Communication Between Man and Dolphin*—The Possibilities of Talking with Other Species (1978) Crown Pub. Miles H. "Conversations with Apes: the Use of Sign Language by Two Chimpanzees" Ph.D. Dissertation (1978) Connecticut Univ. Patterson F. *Brain Lang.* (1978) 5:56. Premack D. et. al. *Science* (1978) 202:903 Nov 24. Rumbaugh D. ed. *Language Learning by a Chimpanzee: the Lana Project* (1977) Academic P. Premack D. *Intelligence in Ape and Man* (1976) Wiley.

12. Galdikas B. (1980) op. cit.

13. Rumbaugh D. et. al. (1973) op. cit.

14. Marx J. rp. *Science* (1980) 207:1330 Mar 21.

15. Premack D. (1971) op. cit.

16. Brines M. & Gould J. *Science* (1979) 206:571 Nov 2. von Frisch K. *Science* (1967) 168:1072. von Frisch K. *Dance Language and Orientation of Bees* (1967) Harvard U. Press.

17. Gould J. *Science* (1980) 207:545.

18. Sebeok T. (1977) ibid. ch. 25.

19. Bouissac P. "Behavior in Context: In What Sense Is A Circus Animal Performing?" in *Sebeok T Annals* Of The New York Academy Of Sciences (1981) Sebeok T. & Rosenthal R. ed. (364:18).

20. Gould J. *Science* (1975) 189:685 Aug 29.

21. Humphrey N. *Science* (1977) 196:755 May 13.

22. Sebeok T. & Rosenthal R. *The Clever Hans Phenomenon: Communication with Horses, Whales, Apes, and People* (1981) New York Academy Of Sciences V.364.

23. Woodruff G. & Premack D. (1981); Galdikas B. (1980); Patterson F. (1979); Fouts R. et. al. (1978); Lilly J. (1978); Miles H. (1978); Patterson F. (1978); Premack D. et. al. (1978) op. cit.

24. Savage-Rumbaugh S. et. al. *Science* (1980) 210:922.

25. Premack D. & Woodruff G. *Science* (1978) 202:532 Nov 3.

26. Menzel E. *Science* (1973) 182:943 Nov 30.

27. Premack D. et. al. (1978) op. cit.

28. Menzel E. & Halperin S. *Science* (1975) 189:652 Aug 22.

29. Gardner B. & Gardner B. *Science* (1975) 187:752 Feb 28.

30. Pepys S. in Marx J. (1980) op. cit.

31. Lubbock J. Note On The Intelligence Of The Dog (1885) Report to the British Assoc. for the Advanc. Sci.

32. Wolff G. *Die denkenden Tiere von Elberfield und Mannheim* :456 (1914) Suddeutsche Monatshefte, Berlin.

33. Mistler-Lachman J. & Lachman R. *Science* (1974) 185:871 Sep 6.

34. Epstein R. et. al. *Science* (1980) 207:543 Feb 1.

35. McConnell J. *New Scientist* (1961) 9:318.

36. Sedelow W. & Sedelow S. ed. *Current Trends In Computer Uses for Language Research* (1975) Mouton (The Hague).

37. Thompson C. & Church R. *Science* (1980) 208:313 Apr 18.

38. Pfungst O. *Das Pferd des Herrn von Osten* (Der kluge Hans) (1907) J. Ambrosius Barth (Leipzig) reprinted: Rosenthal R. ed. *Clever Hans: The Horse Of Mr. von Osten* (1965) Holt, Rinehart & Winston.

39. Koehler O. Die "zahlenden" Tauben und die "zahlsprechenden" Hunde Der Biologe (1937) 6:13.

40. Koehler O. ibid. :24

41. Sebeok T. & Umiker-Sebeok J. ed. *Speaking Of Apes: A Critical Anthology of Two-Way Communication with Man* (1980) Plenum Press.

42. Greenfield P. & Savage-Rumbaugh E. J. *Comp. Psy.* (1984) 98:201. De Luce

J. & Wilder H. ed. *Language in Primates* (1983) Springer-Verlag. Ristau C. & Robbins D. *Adv. Study Behav.* (1982) 12:141. Terrace H. "A Report To An Academy" in *Annals of the New York Academy of Sciences* (1981) Sebeok T. & Rosenthal R. ed. (364:94). Seidenberg M. & Petitto L. *Ape Signing: Problems of Method and Interpretation in Annals of the New York Academy of Sciences* (1981) Sebeok T. & Rosenthal R. ed. (364:115). Scheibe K. in *Annals of the New York Academy of Sciences* (364:160). Thompson C. & Church R. (1980) op. cit. Terrace H. et. al. *Science* (1979a) 206:891. Hill J. *Ann. Rev. Anthrop.* (1978) 7:89. Limber J. *Am. Psych.* (1977) 32:280. Seidenberg M. *There Is No Evidence for Linguistic Abilities in Signing Apes* (1976) Master's Thesis Columbia Univ.

43. Terrace H. et. al. (1979a) op. cit.

44. Terrace H. (1981) op. cit.

45. Terrace H. et. al. "On the Grammatical Capacity of Apes" in Nelson K. ed. *Children's Language* (1980) V.2 Gardner Press (NY). Terrace H. *J. Exp. Anal. Behav.* (1979b) 31:161. Terrace H. *Psych. Today* (1979c) 13:65.

46. American Sign Language (ASL) is a gestural means of communication common to North American deaf people; a good discussion in its use with apes is found in: Terrace H. et. al. (1980) op. cit.

47. Terrace H. (1980) op. cit. Terrace H. et. al. (1979a) op. cit.

48. Chevalier-Skolnikoff S. "The Clever Hans Phenomenon, Cuing, and Ape Signing: A Piagetian Analysis of Methods for Instructing Animals" in *Annals of the New York Academy Of Sciences* (364:60). (Note: Aspects of ape signing believed due by the writer to other then cuing and Hans's effects can be explained as statistical noise on the data).

49. Savage-Rumbaugh S. in *Annals of the New York Academy of Sciences* (1981) (364:36) indicates that an ape is separated from man by the absence in its natural state of the simultaneous array of representational and referential skills that emerge within humans. Terrace H. (1981) ibid. (364:112) indicates that a child's sophisticated (language) ability, against which language in ape experiments should be measured, stands as an important definition of the human species. Seidenberg M. & Petitto L. (1981) ibid. (364:127) indicate that there is nothing to warrant the conclusion that apes acquired linguistic skills in language experiments involving signs. Scheibe K. (1981) ibid. (364:166) indicates that there is no compelling argument or evidence to believe that apes possess true conversational capacity.

50. Gardner B. & Gardner R. "Comparing the Early Utterances of Child and Chimpanzee" in Pick A. ed. *Minn. Symp. On Child Psychology* (1974) Minn. Univ. (V.8). Register No. 16802–"Teaching Sign Language to the Chimpanzee Washoe" (1973) *Psych. Cinema Reg.* Univ. Park (PA). Gardner R. & Gardner B. "Communication With A Young Chimpanzee: Washoe's Vocabulary" in Chauvin R. ed. *Modeles Animaux du Comportement Humain* (1972) Centre National de la Recherche Scientifique (Paris).

51. Rumbaugh D. & Savage-Rumbaugh S. *Behav. Res. Method. Instrum.* (1978) 10:119.

52. Romski M. et. al. *Amer. J. Ment. Defic.* (1985) 89(4):441. Romski M. et. al. *Psychol. Rec.* (1984) 34:39.

53. Lilly J. (1961) op. cit.

54. Gish S. *Quantitative Analysis of Two-Way Communication Between Captive Dolphins* (1979) Ph.D. Diss. Cal. U. (Santa Cruz).

55. Lilly J. (1978) op. cit.

56. Fried I. et. al. *Science* (1981) 212:353 Apr 17.

57. Roberts S. BYTE (1981) 6(9):164.

58. Chomsky N. *Language and Mind* (1972) Harcourt Brace Jovanovich.
59. Romans 9:16.

Chapter 20.   Is There a Way to Live Forever?

1. 1 Cor. 2:14.
2. 2 Tim. 3:16.
3. Yockey H. *Jour. Theor. Biol.* (1977) 67:365.
4. Gen. 2:9.
5. Gen. 3:22.
6. 1 Thess. 5:23.
7. Rom. 7:14–25.
8. Gen. 1:31.
9. Rom. 5:12.
10. The brain is an organic computer, and the mind is the expression of the spirit through this "computer." Thus all mental disorders are due either to spiritual (programmer) or physical (hardware) disorders.
11. Rom. 7:23.
12. The biblical doctrine of God's foreknowledge (Jeremiah 1:5), foreordination (Romans 9:11), preparation (Romans 9:17) and utilization (Luke 22:22) of human personalities is therefore not a matter of preexisting spirits, but rather of organic space-time containers that configure the substance of "spirit."
13. Gen. 3:17.
14. Gen. 3:6.
15. Eccl. 7:20, 9:3; Rom. 3:10–12.
16. Psalm 51:5; Job 15:14–16.
17. Gen. 5:1–32, 9:19.
18. Rom. 12:2; Eph. 4:23, 24.
19. Gen. 3:3, 5:5.
20. Ezek. 28:13, 14; Isa. 14:13, 14.
21. Rom. 5:12, 17; 1 Cor. 15:21, 22.
22. Some say that man's fall was produced by the act of disobedience rather than the eating of "fruit." But why should disobeying God permanently alter human nature any more than eating "fruit"? A more serious objection to this idea is Genesis 3:7 which clearly assigns man's newly acquired shame to the "fruit" rather than any action on the part of God (which occurs later in Genesis 3:16–19).
23. Ezek. 31:2–9, 16–18.
24. Mark 7:18.
25. John 5:24; 1 John 5:11, 12.
26. John 5:21, 14:6.
27. John 6:28, 29; 8:23, 24.
28. Heb. 11:6.
29. John 1:12.
30. Heb. 7:25.
31. Rev. 3:20; John 4:14.
32. Matt. 7:13, 14.
33. Seventy-five percent of all human energy comes from only eight cereal species: wheat, rice, maize, barley, oats, sorghum, millet, and rye.
34. Hales D. *Science Digest* (1982) :28 Aug.
35. Reinisch J. *Science* (1981) 211:1171 Mar 13.
36. John 2:24, 25.

Appendix 1.   The New Inflationary Theory of the Universe

1. Bludman S. *Tenth Texas Symposium* 375:419.
2. Misner C. et. al. *Gravitation* (1973) Freeman (27:705/726).

Appendix 2.   Entropy and Disorder

1. Carathe'dory C. Sitz./Ber. Akad. Wiss. (1919) (Berlin) *Math./Phys. Kl.* :580.
2. Planck M. *The Theory of Heat Radiation* (1914) NY (tran.); idem. *Vorlesungen uber Thermodynamik* (1930) Leipzig.
3. Shannon C. (1949) op. cit. Ch. 5.
4. Jaynes E. *Phys. Rev.* (1957) 106:620; 108:171.
5. Hobson A. *Concepts in Statistical Mechanics* (1971) Gordon & Breach. Zubarev D. *Nonequilibrium Statistical Thermodynamics* (1974) Consultants Bureau (trans./ 1971 Russian original).
6. Zurek W. "Information Transfer in Quantum Measurements" (1983) in Meystre P. & Scully M. *Quantum Optics, Experimental Gravitation & Measurement Theory* Plenum (NY).
7. Wright P. *Contemp. Phys.* (1970) 11(6):581.
8. Brostow W. *Science* (1972) 178:123.
9. Bridgman P. *The Nature of Thermodynamics* (1941) Cambridge, MA.
10. Bekenstein J. *Phys. Rev. Lett.* (1981) 46:623.
11. Hobson A. (1971) ibid. (5:138).
12. Jaynes E. (1981) ibid. *Where Do We Stand on Maximum Entropy* :41.
13. Hobson A. (1971) op. cit.
14. Jaynes E. (1957) op. cit.
15. Hobson A. (1971) op. cit. also: Zubarev D. op. cit.
16. Jahn R. *The Role of Consciousness in the Physical World* (1981) Westview (Boulder); Stapp H. (1981) ibid. Ch. 4. d'Espagnat B. *Sci. Am.* (1979) 241:158 Nov. Wheeler J. (1977) ibid. Ch. 4.
17. Everett H. *Rev. Mod. Phys.* (1957) 29:454. Bell J. *Rev. Mod. Phys.* (1966) 38:447. and Wooters W. & Zurek W. (1979) *Phys. Rev.* D19:473.

Appendix 6.   Information Content

1. Cotterill R. *Cambridge Guide to the Material World* (1985) Ch. 7:100 Cambridge Univ. Press.
2. Golay M. *Anal. Chem.* (1961) 33:23A Jun.
3. Setlow R. & Pollard E. *Molecular Biophysics* (1962) Ch. 3(10):71 Addison-Wesley, Reading, MA.
4. Alfoldi L. "Origin of Amino Acid Sensitivity in Bacteria with RC rel Genotype" in: Monod J. & Borek E. ed. :150 *Of Microbes And Life* (1971) Columbia Univ. Press, NY.
5. Denhardt D. "The Transmission of the Genetic Message: DNA Structure and Replication" in: Florkin M. et al. ed. *Comprehensive Biochemistry* (1977) V.24 Ch. 1:2 Elsevier/North-Holland Biomedical Press, Amsterdam.
6. Neurath H. *Rev. Mod. Phys.* (1959) 31(1):185.
7. Lagerkvist U. *Am. Sci.* (1980) 68:192 Mar-Apr.
8. Yockey H. *Jour. Theor. Biol.* (1974) 46:369.
9. Yockey H. *Jour. Theor. Biol.* (1977) 67:365.
10. Davis B. *Science* (1980) 209:80 Jul 4.
11. Hinegardner R. & Engelberg J. *Science* (1963) 142:1063 Nov 22 *Science* (1964) 144:1030 May 22.
12. *Science News* (1985) 127(12):180.
13. Abelson J. *Ann. Rev. Biochem.* (1979) 48:1048. Pardue L. and David I. *Chromo-*

somal Locations of Two DNA Segments that Flank Ribosomal Insertion-like Sequences in Drosophila. Cambridge, Mass.: MIT Press, 1981. Lewin R. *Science* (1982) 218:1293 Dec 24. Douthart R. and Norris F. *Science* (1982) 217:729 Aug. 20.

Appendix 8.   Reprogramming Humanity

1. In sequence: John 16:7, Luke 23:46; 24:7; Acts 1:9; 2:32–33.

Appendix 9.   The Moral Code

1. Edwards W. et al. *On the Physical Death of Jesus Christ* JAMA (1986) 255(11):1455 Mar 21.

2. Morison F. *Who Moved the Stone?* (1971) InterVarsity Press, Downer's Grove, IL. McDowell J. *Evidence That Demands a Verdict* (1972) Here's Life Publ., San Bernardino, CA. Nichol R. *The Resurrection of Yeshua: Did It Really Happen?* (1981) Congregation B'nai Maccabim, Chicago and Ruach Israel, Boston (Pamphlet). Anderson J. *The Evidence for the Resurrection* (1966) InterVarsity Press, Downer's Grove, IL (pamphlet); see also full text—*Christianity: The Witness of History.* Greenleaf S. *An Examination of the Testimony of the Four Evangelists by the Rules of Evidence Administered in the Courts of Justice* (1847) rep. 1965 Baker Book House.

Bibliography

Alfoldi, L. "Origin of Amino Acid Sensitivity in Bacteria with RC Genotype," in *Of Microbes and Life*. New York: Columbia University Press, 1971.

Anderson, J. *Christianity: The Witness of History*. Downer's Grove, Ill.: InterVarsity Press, 1966.

Asimov, I. *New Guide to Science*. New York: Basic Books, 1984.

Aston, J. and Fritz, J. *Thermodynamics and Statistical Thermodynamics*. New York: Wiley & Sons, 1959.

Atkins, P. *The Second Law*. New York: Freeman, 1984.

Baker, H. *The Mystery of Migration*. Glen Arm, Md.: Sourcebook Project, 1981.

Belinfante, F. *Measurement and Time Reversal in Objective Quantum Theory*. New York: Pergamon, 1975.

Berlin, I. *Historical Materialism in Karl Marx*. Time Reading Program, Special Edition, 1963.

Bohr, N. *Atomic Physics and Human Knowledge*. London: Wiley, 1960.

Boltzmann, L. *Vorlesungen uber Gastheorie*. 1896/1898. Brush, S., trans. Berkeley: University of California Press, 1964.

Bouissac, P. *Behavior in Context: In What Sense is a Circus Animal Performing?* New York: Annals of the New York Academy of Sciences, 1981.

Bowden, M. *Ape-Men: Fact or Fallacy*. Bromley, Kent: Sovereign Publishers, 1977.

Brandt, P. and Yancey, P. *Fearfully and Wonderfully Made*. New York: Macmillan, 1980.

Bridgman, P. *The Nature of Thermodynamics*. Cambridge, Mass.: MIT Press, 1941.

Brillouin, L. *Science and Information Theory*. New York: Academic Press, 1962.

Buchdahl, H. *The Concepts of Classical Thermodynamics*. Cambridge: Cambridge University Press, 1966.

Calvin, M. *Evolutionary Biology*. Edited by T. Dobzhansky et al. New York: Appleton Croft, 1967.

Capra, F. *The Turning Point*. New York: Simon & Schuster, 1982.

Cardwell, D. *From Watt to Clausius*. London: Heinemann, 1971.

Chomsky, N. *Language and Mind*. New York: Harcourt, Brace, Jovanovich, 1972.

Ciochon, R. and Corruccini, R., eds. *New Interpretations of Ape and Human History*. New York: Plenum Press, 1983.

Cohen, R. et al. *The Fundamental Constants of Physics*. New York: Interscience, 1957.

Coppedge, J. *Evolution: Possible or Impossible*. Grand Rapids, Mich.: Zondervan, 1973.

Corliss, W., ed. *Ancient Man: A Handbook of Puzzling Artifacts*. Glen Arm, Md.: Sourcebook Project, 1980.

Cosslett, V. *Practical Electron Microscopy*. New York: Academic Press, 1951.

Cotterill, R. *Cambridge Guide to the Material World*. Cambridge: Cambridge University Press, 1985.

Crick, F. *Life Itself: Its Origin and Nature*. New York: Simon & Schuster, 1981.

Dancoff, S. and Quastler, H. *Information Theory in Biology*. Urbana: Illinois University Press, 1953.

Davies, M. and Murray, B. *The View from Space.* New York: Columbia University Press, 1971.

deDuve, C. *A Guided Tour of the Living Cell.* New York: Scientific American Books, 1984.

deLuce, J. and Wilder H. *Language in Primates.* New York: Springer-Verlag, 1983.

Decker, R. and Decker, B. *Volcanoes.* San Francisco: Freeman, 1981.

Denhardt, D. "The Transmission of the Genetic Message: DNA Structure and Replication." *Comprehensive Biochemistry,* 1977.

Dicke, R. and Peebles, P. *The Big Bang Cosmology: Enigmas and Nostrums in General Relativity: An Einstein Centenary Survey.* Edited by S. Hawking and W. Israel. Cambridge: Cambridge University Press, 1979.

Dillow, J. *The Waters Above.* Chicago, Ill.: Moody Press, 1982.

Eddington, A. *The Nature of the Physical World.* Ann Arbor: Michigan University Press, 1958.

Edwards, P. and Pap, A., eds. *Modern Introduction to Philosophy.* New York: Free Press, 1965.

Elsasser, W. *The Physical Foundation of Biology: An Analytical Study.* New York: Pergamon, 1958.

"First International Congress Proceedings on Electron Microscopy." Paris, 1953.

Fischer, R. *Applied Electron Microscopy.* Bloomington, Ind.: Indiana University Press, 1953.

Folsome, C. *The Origin of Life.* San Francisco: Freeman, 1979.

Fowler, R. and Guggenheim, E. *Statistical Thermodynamics.* Cambridge: Cambridge University Press, 1939.

Fraser, R. *The Habitable Earth.* New York: Basic Books, 1964.

Friday, A. and Ingram, D. *Cambridge Encyclopedia of Life Sciences.* Cambridge: Cambridge University Press, 1985.

Friedman, H. *Sun and Earth.* New York: Scientific American Library, 1986.

Futuyma, D. *Science on Trial.* New York: Pantheon, 1983.

Gange, R. *Review: Abusing Science.* Princeton: Genesis Foundation, 1985.

Gardner, M. *Fads and Fallacies in the Name of Science.* New York: Dover, 1957.

Gillispie, C. *The Edge of Objectivity.* Princeton: Princeton University Press, 1960.

Gish, D. *Evolution—The Fossils Say No.* San Diego: Creation-Life Publishers, 1978.

Gish, S. *Quantitative Analysis of Two-Way Communication Between Captive Dolphins.* Santa Cruz: University of California Press, 1979.

Glasstone, S. *A Treatise on Physical Chemistry.* New York: Van Nostrand, 1942.

Gombrich, E. *Art and Illusion: A Study in the Psychology of Pictorial Representation.* Princeton: Princeton University Press, 1961.

Good, I., ed. *The Scientist Speculates.* New York: Heinemann/Basic Books, 1961.

Gorbatskii, V. *Exploding Stars and Galaxies,* Moskva: Izdatel'stvo "Nauka," 1967.

Green, D. and Fleischer, S. "The Molecular Organization of Biology and Transducing Systems. *Horizons in Biochemistry,* 1962.

Greenleaf, S. *The Testimony of the Evangelists.* Grand Rapids: Baker, 1984 (reprint).

————. Examination by the Rules of Evidence Administered in Courts of Justice (1847). Grand Rapids: Baker, 1965 (reprint).

Gregory, R. *Mind in Science.* Cambridge: Cambridge University Press, 1981.

Groot, S. *Thermodynamics of Irreversible Processes.* New York: Interscience Publishers, 1951.

Gros, F. "Cell Machinery, Transfer of Genetic Information." *Molecular Biophysics,* 1965.

Harris, R. et al. *Theological Wordbook of Old Testament.* Chicago: Moody Press, 1980.

Harrison, E. *Cosmology.* Cambridge: Cambridge University Press, 1981.

Hartnack, J. *Language and Philosophy.* Hawthorne, N.Y.: Mouton, 1972.

Hatsopoulos, G. and Kenna, J. *Principles of General Thermodynamics.* New York: Wiley & Sons, 1965.

Hawking, S. and Rocek, M., eds. *Superspace and Supergravity.* Cambridge: Cambridge University Press, 1979.

Hawkins, G. *Thermodynamics.* New York: Wiley & Sons, 1946.

Henbest, N. *Mysteries of the Universe.* New York: Van Nostrand/Reinhold, 1981.

Henry, Matthew. *Matthew Henry's Commentary.* Old Tappan, N.J.: Fleming H. Revell.

Hitching, F. *The Neck of the Giraffe—Where Darwin Went Wrong.* New Haven, Conn.: Ticknor & Fields, 1982.

Hobson, A. *Concepts in Statistical Mechanics.* New York: Gordon & Breach, 1971.

Hoyle, F. and Wickramasinghe, C. *Evolution from Space.* Hillside, N.J.: Enslow Publishing, 1982.

Jahn, R. *The Role of Consciousness of the Physical World.* Boulder, Colo.: Westview, 1981.

Jaynes, E. *Statistical Physics.* Edited by K. Ford. New York: W. Benjamin, 1963.

Jurnik, F. and McPherson A. *Biological Macromolecules and Assemblies.* New York: Wiley Interscience, 1985.

Karlin, S. and Taylor, H. *A First Course in Stochastic Processes.* New York: Academic Press, 1975.

Katz, A. *Principles of Statistical Mechanics: The Information Theory Approach.* San Francisco: Freeman, 1965.

Kaufman, W., ed. *Particles and Fields.* San Francisco: Freeman, 1965.

Keil, C. and Delitzsch, F. *Commentary on the Old Testament.* Grand Rapids, Mich.: Eerdmans, 1981.

Kelly, D. and Matthews, P. *Decipherment of Mayan Hieroglyphics,* Toronto, Ont.: University of Toronto Press, 1978.

Khinchin, A. *Mathematical Foundation of Information Theory.* New York: Dover Press, 1957.

Kuhn, H. and Waser J. *Biophysics.* Edited by W. Hoppe et al. New York: Springer-Verlag, 1983.

Kuhn, R. *The Essential Tension.* Chicago, Ill.: University of Chicago Press, 1977.

Landsberg, P. *Thermodynamics.* New York: Interscience Publishers, 1961.

Laszlo, T. *Generalized Thermodynamics.* Cambridge, Mass.: MIT Press, 1978.

Layzer, D. *Constructing the Universe.* New York: Scientific American Library, 1984.

Levine, R. and Tribus, M., eds. *The Maximum Entropy Formalism.* Cambridge, Mass.: MIT Press, 1979.

Lewis, G. and Randall, M. *Thermodynamics.* New York: McGraw-Hill, 1961.

Loeve, M. *On Almost Sure Convergence in Second Berkeley Symposium on Mathematical Statistics and Probability.* Berkeley: University of California Press, 1951.

Macbeth, M. *Darwin Retried: An Appeal to Reason.* Boston, Mass.: Harvard Common Press, 1971.

MacKay, D. *The Clockwork Image.* Downer's Grove, Ill.: InterVarsity Press, 1974.

Margenau, H. *The Nature of Physical Reality.* New York: McGraw-Hill, 1950.

Maxwell, J. *Theory of Heat.* London: Longmans Green & Company, 1871.

McDowell, J. *Evidence that Demands a Verdict.* San Bernardino, Calif.: Here's Life, 1972.

Mehra, J. *The Physicist's Conception of Nature.* Hingham, Mass.: Kluwer Academic, 1973.

Misner, C. et al. *Gravitation.* San Francisco: Freeman, 1973.

Montgomery, J. *The Importance of a Materialistic Metaphysic to Marxist Thought and an Examination of its Truth Value in the Shape of the Past.* Minneapolis: Bethany Fellowship, 1975.

Morgan, E. *The Aquatic Ape.* Glen Arm, Md.: Sourcebook Project, 1982.

Morison, F. *Who Moved the Stone?* Downer's Grove, Ill.: InterVarsity Press, 1971.

Morris, H. *The Biblical Basis for Modern Science.* Grand Rapids, Mich.: Baker, 1984.

Newton, J. and Teece, P. *The Cambridge Deep-Sky Album,* Cambridge: Cambridge University Press, 1984.

Nichol, R. *The Resurrection of Yeshua: Did it Really Happen?* Chicago: Congregation B'nai Maccabim. Boston: Rauch Israel, 1981.

Nicolis, G. and Prigogine, I. *Self-Organization in Nonequilibrium Systems.* New York: Wiley & Sons, 1977.

North, J. *The Measure of the Universe.* Oxford: Clarendon Press, 1965.

Ochoa, S. "Enzymatic Mechanisms in the Transmission of Genetic Information." *Horizons in Biochemistry,* 1962.

Page, L. *Introduction to Theoretical Physics.* New York: Van Nostrand, 1928.

Pardue, L. and David I. *Chromosomal Locations of Two DNA Segments that Flank Ribosomal Insertion-like Sequences in Drosophila.* Cambridge, Mass.: MIT Press, 1981.

Parrinder, G. *World Religions from Ancient History to the Present.* New York: Facts-on-File Publishing Company, 1983.

Pfungst, O. *Clever Hans: The Horse of Mr. von Osten.* Edited by R. Rosenthal. New York: Holt, Rinehart & Winston, 1965.

———. *Das Pferd des Herrn von Osten (Der kluge Hans).* Leipzig: J. Ambrosius Barth, 1907.

Phillips, P. *The Prehistory of Europe.* Bloomington, Ind.: Indiana University Press, 1980.

Planck, M. *The Theory of Heat Radiation.* New York: Translation, 1914.

———. *Vorlesungen uber Thermodynamik.* Leipzig: J. Ambrosius Barth, 1930.

Polkinghorne, J. *The Particle Play.* San Francisco: Freeman, 1980.

Popper, K. and Eccles, J. *The Self and its Brain.* Paris: Springer-Verlag, 1977.

Porter, K. *An Introduction to the Fine Structure of Cells and Tissues.* Philadelphia: Lea & Febiger, 1963.

Press, F. and Siever, R. *Earth.* San Francisco: Freeman, 1982.

Prigogine, I. *From Being to Becoming.* San Francisco: Freeman, 1980.

Prigogine, I. and Stengers, I. *Order out of Chaos.* New York: Bantam Books, 1984.

Quastler, H., ed. *Essays on the Use of Information Theory in Biology.* Urbana: University of Illinois Press, 1953.

Radmacher, E. and Preus R. *Hermeneutics, Inerrancy and the Bible.* Papers from ICBI. Grand Rapids, Mich.: Academie Books, 1984.

Reif, F. *Fundamentals of Statistical and Thermal Physics*. New York: McGraw-Hill, 1965.

Rich, A. *Transfer RNA and the Origin of Protein Synthesis*. Cambridge, Mass.: MIT Press, 1981.

Rossini, R. *Thermodynamics and Physics of Matter*. Princeton: Princeton University Press, 1955.

Rowan-Robinson, M. *Cosmic Landscape*. Oxford: Oxford University Press, 1979.

Rowe, W. *The Cosmological Argument*. Princeton: Princeton University Press, 1975.

Ruska, E. *The Early Development of Electron Lenses and Electron Microscopy*. Stuttgart: Hirzel Verlag, 1980.

Scalapino, D. "Irreversible Statistical Mechanics and the Principle of Maximum Entropy." Stanford University, Ph.D. Thesis, 1961.

Schneider, S. and Londer, R. *The Coevolution of Climate and Life*. San Francisco: Sierra Club Books, 1984.

Schrier, A. and Stollnitz, F., eds. *Behavior of Non-Human Primates*. New York: Academic Press, 1971.

Schroedinger, E. *What is Life?* Cambridge: Cambridge University Press, 1955.

Schuster, P. and Sigmund, K., "From Biological Macromolecules to Protocells— The Principle of Early Evolution" in *Biophysics*. Edited by W. Hoppe et al. Berlin: Springer-Verlag, 1983.

Sebeok, T., ed. *Animal Communication*. Bloomington, Ind.: Indiana University Press, 1977.

————. *How Animals Communicate*, Ann Arbor, Mich.: Books Demand UMI, 1977.

Sebeok, T. and Rosenthal R. *The Clever Hans Phenomenon: Communication with Horses, Whales, Apes and People*. New York: New York Academy of Sciences, 1981.

Sebeok, T. and Umiker-Sebeok, J., eds. *Speaking of Apes: A Critical Anthology of Two-Way Communication with Man*. New York: Plenum Press, 1980.

Sedelow, W. and Sedelow S., eds. *Current Trends in Computer Uses for Language Research*. The Hague: Mouton, 1975.

Seidenberg, M. *There is No Evidence for Linguistic Abilities in Signing Apes*. New York: Columbia University Press, 1976.

Selme, P. *Collection: "Que Sais-je?"* Paris: Presses Universitaires Francaises, 1963.

Setlow, R. and Pollard, E. *Molecular Biophysics*. Reading, Mass.: Addison-Wesley, 1962.

Shannon, C. and Weaver, W. *The Mathematical Theory of Communication*. Urbana: University of Illinois Press, 1949.

Shapiro, R. *Origins—A Skeptic's Guide to the Creation of Life on Earth*. New York: Macmillan, 1985.

Slater, J. *Introduction to Chemical Physics*. New York: McGraw-Hill, 1939.

Smith, A. *The Body*. New York: Macmillan, 1986.

Smith, D. *Earth Sciences*. New York: Crown Publishers, 1981.

Stanley, S. *Earth and Life Through Time*. New York, Freeman, 1985.

Stapp, H. *Mind, Matter and Quantum Mechanics*. (LBL 12631) Berkley: Lawrence Berkley Laboratory, 1981.

Taton, R. *Reason and Chance in Scientific Discovery*. New York: Philosophical Library, 1957.

Terrace, H. et al. "On the Grammatical Capacity of Apes," in *Children's Language*. Edited by K. Nelson. New York: Gardner Press, 1980.

Thaxton, C. et al. *The Mystery of Life's Origin: Reassessing Current Theories*. New York: Philosophical Library, 1984.

Thompson, J. *Maya Hieroglyphic Writing.* Washington, D.C.: Carnegie Institution, 1950.

Tolman, R. *Relativity, Thermodynamics and Cosmology.* Oxford: Clarendon Press, 1934.

Trefil, J. *From Atoms to Quarks.* New York: Scribner, 1980.

——. *Space Time Infinity.* Washington, D.C.: Smithsonian Books, 1985.

——. *The Moment of Creation.* New York: Scribner, 1983.

Tribus, M. *Thermostatics and Thermodynamics.* Princeton: Van Nostrand, 1961.

von Frisch, K. *Dance Language and Orientation of Bees.* Cambridge, Mass.: Harvard University Press, 1967.

von Neumann, J. "Probabilistic Logics and the Synthesis of Reliable Organisms from Unreliable Components" (1952), in *Theory of Self-Reproducing Automata.* Edited by A. Burks. Urbana: University of Illinois Press, 1966.

——. *Quantum Theory and Measurement.* Edited by J. Wheeler and W. Zurek. Princeton: Princeton University Press, 1983.

Weinberg, S. *The First Three Minutes.* New York: Basic Books, 1977.

Weiner, J. *Piltdown Forgery,* New York: Dover, 1981.

Wheeler, J. *Gravitation.* San Francisco: Freeman, 1973.

——. *Quantum Mechanics a Half Century Later.* Edited by J. Lopes and M. Paty. Dordrecht, Holland: Reidel, 1977.

Whitfield, P., ed. *Illustrated Animal Encyclopedia.* New York: Macmillan, 1984.

Wiester, J. *The Genesis Connection.* Nashville: Thomas Nelson, 1983.

Williams, E. "Entropy and the Solid State," in *Why Not Creation?* Edited by W. Lammerts. Phillipsburg, N.J.: Presbyterian and Reformed Publishing Company, 1970.

Wilson, A. *Thermodynamics and Statistical Mechanics.* Cambridge: Cambridge University Press, 1957.

Wolff, G. *Die denkenden Tiere von Elberfield und Mannheim.* Berlin: Suddeutsche Monatshefte, 1914.

Wolfgang, Y. et al. *Treatise on Irreversible and Statistical Thermophysics.* New York: Dover, 1982.

Wootters, W. and Zurek, W. *Quantum Theory and Measurement.* Edited by J. Wheeler and W. Zurek. Princeton: Princeton University Press, 1983.

Yockey, H., ed. *Symposium on Information Theory in Biology.* New York: Pergamon, 1958.

Yourgrau, W. et al. *Treatise on Irreversible and Statistical Thermophysics.* New York: Dover, 1982.

Zeh, H. *Fourth International Conference on the Unity of Science.* New York: ICUS, 1975.

Zemansky, M. and Dittman, R. *Heat and Thermodynamics.* New York: McGraw-Hill, 1981.

Zubarev, D. *Nonequilibrium Statistical Thermodynamics.* New York: Plenum Publishers, 1974. (Translated from original 1971 Russian publication).

Zurek, W. "Information Transfer in Quantum Measurements," in *Quantum Optics, Experimental Gravitation and Measurement Theory.* Edited by P. Meystre and M. Scully. New York: Plenum, 1983.

Zworykin, V. et al. *Electron Optics and the Electron Microscope.* New York: Wiley, 1945.

Index